Reinforcement-Based Treatment for Substance Use Disorders

Reinforcement-Based Treatment for Substance Use Disorders

A Comprehensive Behavioral Approach

L. Michelle Tuten, Hendree E. Jones,
Cindy M. Schaeffer, and Maxine L. Stitzer

American Psychological Association • Washington, DC

Published by
American Psychological Association
750 First Street, NE
Washington, DC 20002
www.apa.org

To order
APA Order Department
P.O. Box 92984
Washington, DC 20090-2984
Tel: (800) 374-2721; Direct: (202) 336-5510
Fax: (202) 336-5502; TDD/TTY: (202) 336-6123
Online: www.apa.org/pubs/books
E-mail: order@apa.org

In the U.K., Europe, Africa, and the Middle East, copies may be ordered from
American Psychological Association
3 Henrietta Street
Covent Garden, London
WC2E 8LU England

Typeset in Goudy by Circle Graphics, Inc., Columbia, MD

Printer: United Book Press, Baltimore, MD
Cover Designer: Mercury Publishing Services, Rockville, MD

The opinions and statements published are the responsibility of the authors, and such opinions and statements do not necessarily represent the policies of the American Psychological Association.

Library of Congress Cataloging-in-Publication Data

Reinforcement-based treatment for substance use disorders : a comprehensive behavioral approach / by L. Michelle Tuten . . . [et al.]. — 1st ed.
     p. ; cm.
  Includes bibliographical references.
  ISBN-13: 978-1-4338-1024-4
  ISBN-10: 1-4338-1024-7
  1. Substance abuse—Treatment. 2. Reinforcement (Psychology) I. Tuten, L. Michelle.
II. American Psychological Association.
  [DNLM: 1. Substance-Related Disorders—therapy. 2. Behavior Therapy—methods.
3. Reinforcement (Psychology) 4. Social Environment. WM 270]

  RC563.R45 2012
  616.86'0651—dc22
                                    2011004929

British Library Cataloguing-in-Publication Data

A CIP record is available from the British Library.

Printed in the United States of America
First Edition

DOI: 10.1037/13088-000

CONTENTS

Reinforcement-Based Treatment for Substance Use Disorders

INTRODUCTION

Nothing is predestined: The obstacles of your past can become the gateways that lead to new beginnings.

—Ralph Blum

In the United States, abuse of alcohol and illicit drugs is a widespread problem that kills more than 100,000 individuals each year. Alcohol alone is the third leading cause of death, killing 85,000 individuals per year, and illicit drug use kills approximately 17,000 individuals per year (Mokdad et al., 2004). Although the mortality data underscore the severity of the public health problem, these fatalities represent only a small proportion of the men and women with substance use disorders. Furthermore, substance abuse has numerous related burdens, including work costs (e.g., absenteeism), chronic illness, crime, violence, and homelessness. Opioid users are at particularly high risk, with up to a 30 times higher risk of premature mortality than their non-drug-user counterparts. Because opioids like heroin are typically injected, and the behaviors many individuals have to engage in to obtain the drug are risky (e.g., prostitution), the health risks of contracting HIV, hepatitis, and sexually transmitted infections are high.

On the basis of these staggering individual and social costs, it would be expected that funding for the treatment of substance use disorders would be in proportion to the number of lives affected by these substances. Unfortunately, total spending on substance abuse treatment in the United States and the world

3

is only a fraction of what it needs to be. What largely drives this avoidance is ignorance about the illness of addiction and the effectiveness of its treatment, unrealistic expectations about the necessary duration of treatment, and the desire for a cure for this illness. For example, although the relapse rate for drug addiction is similar to those for asthma and hypertension (60%, 70%, and 55%, respectively), only substance use disorder treatments are held to an unrealistic expectation of 0% relapse. In part, this may be due to the undesirable behaviors associated with substance use disorders (e.g., stealing, prostitution, injecting) relative to the absence of these behaviors with other chronic illnesses such as asthma and hypertension.

Although some individuals from all levels of society have substance use disorders, the most impoverished and marginalized individuals receive the most negative reaction and bear the greatest stigma. The constant struggles against social, cultural, and economic subordination that individuals with substance use disorders face must be recognized, and the survival strategies that they have developed and implemented, which increase their sexual risk, HIV risk, homelessness, and violence, must be understood because these social problems exacerbate substance use disorders and, ultimately, make recovery more difficult to achieve and sustain.

THE NEED FOR POSITIVE, COMPREHENSIVE BEHAVIORAL TREATMENT

The varied and chronic nature of substance use disorders and their often devastating effects on multiple domains of people's lives have several implications for treatment. First, for treatment to be effective, it must be intensive and comprehensively address the full range of factors that initiate and maintain substance abuse. Substance dependence, related problems, and the risk factors that maintain both often take many years to develop and to become entrenched. Logically, creating a new, sustainable drug-free lifestyle also takes time, considerable effort, and extensive ongoing support. There is strong evidence in the empirical literature that multifaceted and intensive interventions of longer duration result in better outcomes following substance abuse treatment (Fiorentine, 2001; Moos & Moos, 2003; Ritsher, Moos, & Finney, 2002; TOPPS-II Interstate Study Group, 2003; U.S. Department of Health and Human Services [USDHHS], National Institute on Drug Abuse [NIDA], 2009).

A second implication is that for clients to regularly attend and remain engaged in intensive treatments that recommend difficult lifestyle changes, the treatment experience itself should be positive. Clients are unlikely to participate for long in programs that they do not experience as worthwhile and rewarding. Accordingly, clients should have individualized and personally meaningful treatment plans, experience only positive interactions with treatment staff, and receive rewards (both tangible and intangible) for meeting treatment goals. Historically, confrontational techniques such as challenging clients to "admit" that they have a problem were thought to be important for countering denial about the impact of their substance use and activating clients to take action. However, there is a growing consensus that traditional confrontational approaches elicit argumentative and resistant client behavior, threaten the therapeutic alliance, and impede treatment attendance and completion (Miller, Benefield, & Tonigan, 1993; Moos, 2005). In contrast, individualized incentive-based programs that avoid confrontation result in greater treatment retention, more treatment sessions attended, fewer drug-positive test results during treatment, and longer durations of documented continuous abstinence than traditional models (e.g., Petry et al., 2005; Stitzer & Petry, 2006).

A final implication for substance abuse treatment stems from the broader empirical literature about how people make behavioral changes, both naturally and in the context of therapy. A body of research from the fields of social, counseling, and clinical psychology suggests that ambivalence is a normal part of any change process. Clients struggling to stop their substance use are trapped in what Miller and Rollnick (2002) called a *double approach*–avoidance conflict, meaning that there are positive and negative aspects of maintaining and giving up substances. Thus, client ambivalence about giving up drugs and the lifestyle associated with them is to be expected. Accordingly, another implication for substance abuse treatment is that therapists should directly address client ambivalence about change through nonconfrontational therapeutic interventions.

Unfortunately, many clients seeking services for substance abuse do not experience treatment that is consistent with these ideas. For example, it is common for clients to receive medical detoxification and/or pharmacotherapy as stand-alone treatments. A wide-scale study found that only 25% of clients who complete a detoxification program receive any additional services (Ohio Department of Alcohol and Drug Addiction Services, 2006). Although it is critical to address any physical dependencies that contribute to substance abuse, detoxification alone can hardly be considered intensive or comprehensive. Indeed, research suggests that clinical outcomes for detoxification as a stand-alone treatment are poor. In a study of opiate-dependent individuals exiting medical detoxification, Chutuape, Jasinski, Fingerhood, and Stitzer (2001) found that 83% had relapsed within the first 30 days of discharge. As many as 25% of clients discharged from detoxification are readmitted within a year (Ohio Department of Alcohol and Drug Addiction Services, 2006). Similarly, pharmacotherapies such as methadone, buprenorphine, and naltrexone are extremely helpful for addressing withdrawal symptoms and cravings but are unlikely in and of themselves to alter entrenched drug use patterns. Research suggests that pharmacotherapies for substance dependence are far more effective when coupled with comprehensive behavioral treatments (Carroll, 2001; USDHHS, NIDA, 2009).

The extent to which clients experience substance abuse treatment as positive also is questionable. Nationally, substance abuse treatment completion rates are very low, ranging from about 20% for opiate replacement therapies (e.g., methadone, buprenorphine) to about 65% for detoxification or short-term residential hospital stays (USDHHS, Substance Abuse and Mental Health Services Administration [SAMHSA], Office of Applied Studies, 2006). Completion rates for outpatient therapy are only about 36% (USDHHS, SAMHSA, Office of Applied Studies, 2006). Although these low rates may in part be explained by health insurance limitations or other financial constraints, it seems likely that these numbers also reflect client dissatisfaction with treatment. A large-scale survey of clients recently discharged from publicly funded substance abuse treatment programs found that only 65% of clients reported feeling satisfied with the care they received (Zhang, Gerstein, & Friedmann, 2008). Those clients who report feeling satisfied with their substance abuse treatment have better posttreatment substance use outcomes, even after controlling for such factors as pretreatment characteristics or treatment duration (Carlson & Gabriel, 2001; Zhang et al., 2008).

Current substance abuse treatment programs also tend not to incorporate incentives for abstinence and/or not to use interventions that directly address the ambivalence many feel about stopping drug use. In a national survey of substance abuse treatment providers (USDHHS, SAMHSA, Office of Applied Studies, 2010), only 32% of programs reported providing incentives to clients for abstinence, and only 55% used a specified intervention (motivational interviewing [MI]; Miller & Rollnick, 2002) to address client ambivalence about change. Taken together, these findings suggest that unspecified treatments with a relatively narrow focus continue to dominate the field of substance abuse treatment and that there is much room for improvement in substance abuse service delivery.

REINFORCEMENT-BASED TREATMENT: A POSITIVE, COMPREHENSIVE TREATMENT APPROACH FOR MULTIPLE SUBSTANCE USE DISORDERS

We have developed an evidence-based, positive, comprehensive model for treating substance use disorders. Our model, called Reinforcement-Based Treatment (RBT), differs significantly from most existing treatment programs. First, it comprehensively addresses the multiple factors that maintain substance abuse, tailoring interventions to individual client needs. The treatment is intensive in both its service delivery structure and in the nature of the interventions themselves. With regard to service delivery, RBT was designed as an intensive outpatient treatment program; however, home-based models appear to be effective and are consistent with the comprehensive nature of the approach. Both modalities involve multiple client contact hours each week and low therapist-to-client ratios. With regard to the interventions themselves, RBT achieves intensity through well-monitored treatment plans that encourage clients to make continuous daily efforts in multiple domains to change lifestyle patterns. Second, in RBT, extensive efforts are made to ensure that treatment is a positive experience for clients, and this is done largely by creating an atmosphere in which clients consistently receive multiple forms of positive reinforcement (both tangible and intangible) for desired behaviors (e.g., attendance, abstinence, honesty about relapses). Third, RBT provides a full range of interventions to address client ambivalence about stopping substance use, using techniques from the MI approach (Miller & Rollnick, 2002).

RBT integrates interventions from extant substance abuse treatment models that have strong empirical support for their efficacy, unifying them within a single conceptual framework. RBT incorporates aspects of the Community Reinforcement Approach Plus Vouchers (CRA-V) model (Budney & Higgins, 1998), relapse prevention (Irvin, Bowers, Dunn, & Wang, 1999; Marlatt & Gordon, 1985), and MI (Miller & Rollnick, 2002). In addition, RBT provides extensive case management services to clients, a component that has been shown to improve treatment retention and sustained abstinence following treatment (Vanderplasschen, Wolf, Rapp, & Broekaert, 2007). RBT also is fully compatible with medically oriented adjunctive treatments such as detoxification and pharmacotherapy. Since the original clinical trials of RBT with opiate-dependent individuals exiting detoxification facilities (Gruber, Chutuape, & Stitzer, 2000; Jones, Wong, Tuten, & Stitzer, 2005; Katz, Gruber, Chutuape, & Stitzer, 2001), the model has been adapted for the treatment of substance use disorders other than opiate dependence (e.g., cocaine and alcohol dependence) and for both relapse prevention (i.e., postdetoxification services) and abstinence initiation (i.e., when RBT is provided as a stand-alone intervention). Currently, the RBT model is being implemented successfully in a real-world community substance abuse treatment agency and as part of comprehensive treatment for parents involved in the child welfare system as a result of substance-related child maltreatment. By *real-world*, we mean a fee-for-service community practice setting absent grant funding. This translation of RBT from science (i.e., large-scale research studies) to real-world community practice makes RBT very well suited to address the needs of clients across the full range of substance use disorders.

PURPOSE OF THIS BOOK AND INTENDED AUDIENCE

This book serves as the treatment manual for RBT and is the elaboration of several unpublished manuals used in clinical trials testing the efficacy of RBT. This text provides complete clinical information and tools for how to administer all RBT components as well as guidelines for how to implement the model administratively and to supervise clinicians using this approach. The techniques, tools, and clinical examples described herein are based on our many years of experience developing, refining, adapting, disseminating, and clinically delivering RBT in both research and standard practice settings. When used in conjunction with several other texts recommended throughout this book (e.g., the MI clinical manual; Miller & Rollnick, 2002), clinicians wishing to provide RBT should be able to administer it to clients who have a variety of substance use disorders.

The primary intended audience for this book is clinicians working in substance abuse treatment programs and program administrators who have the authority to select and implement treatment models for their agencies. For clinicians, this manual can serve as a practical guide for how to incorporate more behavioral and motivational techniques into their own practice with substance-abusing clients. For administrators, this volume can serve as the foundation for how to implement a full RBT program involving all treatment components within an outpatient or home-based treatment setting. This book also is intended for graduate students in counseling, social work, psychology, and related fields to learn more about one of the most comprehensive and effective behavioral treatment packages available for substance abuse. This book provides a strong foundation in the latest behavioral and motivational interventions for substance use disorders, how they are delivered in real-world practice settings, and their application to specialized client populations.

As indicated in subsequent chapters, fully implementing RBT requires full-scale adoption of the model at the level of the clinic or agency. Several components of RBT, such as drug testing, the use of vouchers to reinforce abstinence, and program-sponsored recreational activities, require administrative buy-in, investment, and support. Clinicians who wish to provide RBT are encouraged to implement as many parts of the model as are feasible within their work context.

In the remainder of this chapter, we review the development of RBT and the clinical outcome studies that support its efficacy; we follow this with a brief overview of the RBT intervention model itself and the core program features that are required to successfully implement RBT, topics that receive additional attention in subsequent chapters. The chapter concludes with a definition of key terms and concepts used in RBT and an outline of the structure of the rest of the volume.

DEVELOPMENT OF REINFORCEMENT-BASED TREATMENT AND EFFICACY RESEARCH

RBT was originally developed for an underserved population, opiate (heroin) abusers in Baltimore, Maryland, and was designed to address a critical gap in the substance abuse service delivery system: the need for community-based support and aftercare treatment following brief inpatient medical detoxification. Currently, the RBT model is being implemented successfully in Baltimore by a community substance abuse treatment agency and in Connecticut (as part of comprehensive treatment for parents involved in the child welfare system as a result of substance-related child maltreatment) by a government agency. Thus, RBT is a rare example of an evidence-based intervention that has progressed from Stage 1 (feasibility) to Stage 2 (efficacy) testing, made possible through funding from the NIDA, to real-world community practice.

Conceptual Framework and Background for Reinforcement-Based Treatment

The conceptual foundation of RBT is derived from the fundamental principles of operant conditioning. The primary tenets of this approach are that behaviors are learned and maintained as the result of interactions with environmental consequences and are thus amenable to change by altering these consequences. The principles of operant learning rely on the ability of reinforcers to exert a powerful modulating influence on behavior. Consequences that increase the likelihood of behavior occurring under similar circumstances in the future are considered reinforcing; those that decrease the likelihood of behavior occurring in the future are considered punishing. Within this conceptual framework, reinforcement-based interventions for treating substance use disorders have the overarching goal of systematically weakening the influence of reinforcement derived from drug use and the related lifestyle while increasing the frequency and magnitude of reinforcement derived from healthier alternative activities, especially those that are incompatible with drug use.

The original applications of operant conditioning to the treatment of drug abuse dates back to the late 1960s and into the early 1980s. At that time, small sample demonstration projects were conducted showing that individuals with alcohol use disorders could modulate and limit their usual excessive alcohol consumption if appropriate contingencies were placed on their drinking behavior (Cohen, Liebson, & Faillace, 1972). Furthermore, drug users enrolled in methadone maintenance could be motivated to stop their use of both opiates (Stitzer, Bigelow, & Liebson, 1980) and benzodiazepines (Stitzer, Bigelow, Liebson, & Hawthorne, 1982) during treatment when offered monetary rewards or clinic privileges as a consequence of abstaining from use of these target drugs.

Subsequently, the principle of competing reinforcement was incorporated by Higgins and colleagues into an elegant multicomponent therapy package, CRA-V, designed for the treatment of cocaine users in outpatient psychosocial counseling (Budney & Higgins, 1998; Higgins et al., 1993; Higgins et al., 1994). The voucher reinforcement procedure was designed to directly counter potent drug reinforcement and promote sustained abstinence. Vouchers of monetary value were earned for submission of cocaine-free urines. Vouchers could be used to purchase tangible goods selected by clients and purchased by research staff. Thus, the opportunity to earn immediate tangible consumer goods was available as an incentive to refrain from drug reinforcement. An individual CRA-V counseling program was implemented concurrently with the abstinence incentives with the intent of building sources of naturalistic reinforcement into the client's lifestyle that could provide alternative nondrug reinforcement after therapy ended.

CRA-V is a comprehensive, proactive behavioral treatment designed to systematically facilitate changes in the client's daily environment that will reduce drug abuse and promote a healthier lifestyle. This is accomplished by increasing the number of alternative reinforcers that can effectively compete with drug use. Specifically, CRA-V attempts to increase the density of alternative reinforcers in the drug abuser's natural environment, including reinforcement from productive activity (work) and from social interactions and recreational activities. To accomplish this goal, CRA-V therapy includes a strong emphasis on job counseling and employment seeking, on recreational therapy to instill new leisure time activities, and on relationship and communication therapy to engender more rewarding interpersonal relationships. There is an active outreach feature to CRA-V that encourages counselors to seek clients in the community when they miss sessions and to accompany them on employment-seeking and recreational activities to provide support and ensure that these activities actually occur. RBT incorporates several key features of CRA-V, including a focus on implementing alternative, competing environmental reinforcers, the use of incentives when target behaviors are emitted, the provision of vocational counseling, an emphasis on client participation in recreational activities, and a proactive approach to engaging and retaining clients in treatment. Although the two approaches are guided by the same behavioral principles and share some key features, they differ in terms of how these features are implemented (e.g., types of incentives delivered, frequency of administration of reinforcers, reinforcers that are program sponsored vs. naturally occurring) as well as the populations with whom the interventions have been used (e.g., type of drug use targeted, demographic characteristics).

RBT also differs from CRA-V in several key respects, including (a) an emphasis on the treatment atmosphere as a reinforcer for retention and abstinence (see Chapter 1, this volume), (b) the incorporation of MI techniques to facilitate behavior change (Chapter 3), (c) attention to the role of housing in the individual's treatment and recovery from substance use disorders (Chapter 7), (d) inclusion of program-sponsored recreational activities (Chapter 4), and (e) program benefits that are contingent on abstinence (Chapter 6). Each of these unique features is discussed in the aforementioned chapters and throughout the book.

Reinforcement-Based Treatment Efficacy Research

The context in which RBT was developed provided the opportunity for rigorous research to evaluate its efficacy. Although there was a high volume of patients served by the medication-assisted taper units in Baltimore, many of these patients faced considerable barriers when attempting to access treatment aftercare. Initial studies compared abstinence rates for those who received aftercare in the form of RBT versus those who received referrals to community providers (usual care). The first outcome evaluation study (Gruber et al., 2000) enrolled participants in 1997–1998, shortly after the RBT program was implemented. RBT was offered daily for 1 month with 3 times per week counseling available for an additional 2 months. Incentives for housing, transportation, bill payment, and recreational activities were provided during the first month of treatment contingent on clinic attendance and drug abstinence. One month after detoxification, 61% of heroin users randomly assigned to RBT ($n = 28$) versus 17% of those referred to community treatment resources ($n = 24$) were enrolled in outpatient treatment ($p > .01$). Further, 50% of RBT versus 21% of controls reported 30 days of postdetoxification drug abstinence with confirmatory urinalysis ($p < .05$). By 3 months, most of the clients in both groups were no longer in treatment, and drug use outcomes were not significantly different across the groups. This study yielded promising results for during-treatment outcomes and suggested that longer term enrollment in the intensive RBT would be beneficial.

A second randomized outcome study using a similar design was conducted in 2000–2001, after the RBT program had been well established (Jones et al., 2005). This study enrolled 130 clients drawn from one of two short-term inpatient detoxification units. Study participants were 58% male and 71%

African American, with a mean age of 38 years. They had 11.3 years of education on average and were predominantly (92%) unemployed. All were opioid dependent, and 68% submitted a cocaine-positive sample at intake to the detoxification unit. Participants were randomized to receive RBT, which included abstinent-contingent recovery housing as well as program-sponsored recreational activities and transportation for a 3-month period ($n = 66$), or usual care, which including referrals to community treatment programs ($n = 64$). Abstinence-contingent treatment elements were based on being negative for both opiates and cocaine. Figure 1 shows that the groups differed significantly on the percentage of urines testing simultaneously negative for opiates and cocaine. This difference was significant at 1- and 3-month follow-ups. Group differences missed significance at 6 months primarily because of a small increase in abstinence rate for the usual care group. The groups were clearly not significantly different at 12 months, when there was both a decrease in abstinence for the RBT group between 6 and 12 months and a further increase in abstinence for the control group.

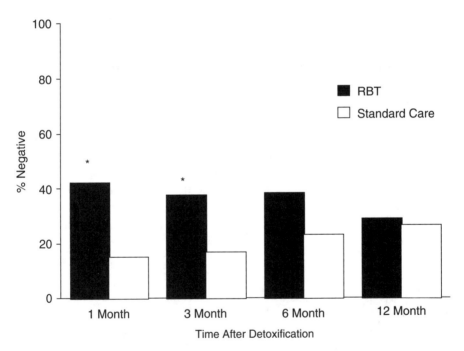

Figure 1. Percentage of participants reporting no drug use in the past 30 days and submitting a confirmatory urine sample that tested negative for both opiates and cocaine, by time point. Data are shown for participants randomly assigned to a 6-month treatment with Reinforcement-Based Therapy (RBT; $n = 62$) or to standard care referral ($n = 69$) following a brief residential detoxification.

TABLE 1
Process and Outcome Measures From a Reinforcement-Based Treatment (RBT) Clinical Trial

Measure and group	Follow-up (in months)			
	1	3	6	12
In treatment (%)				
RBT	64	49	39	15
Control	12	12	21	32
In recovery housing (%)				
RBT	29	18	17	8
Control	8	6	5	3
Mean days worked (+ *SD*)				
RBT	6 (9.1)	11 (10.6)	11 (10.3)	10 (10.4)
Control	5 (7.7)	5 (8.1)	6 (8.3)	5 (9.1)

Note. Data for this table are from a study by Jones, Wong, Tuten, and Stitzer (2005).

Table 1 shows two process indicators and one outcome indicator from the Jones et al. (2005) trial. Consistent with the intervention protocol, significant between-groups differences were seen throughout on percentage enrolled in any treatment program. Interestingly, however, the pattern reversed for the two groups at 12 months when control clients were more likely than RBT clients to be enrolled in any treatment. Also consistent with the protocol, RBT participants were significantly more likely than controls to be living in a recovery house at 1, 3, and 6 months. Between-groups differences in employment (mean days worked) were significant throughout, indicating that the job-seeking skills training and support provided by the RBT was an effective treatment component.

Tuten, Defulio, Jones, and Stitzer (2011) sought to replicate the Jones et al. (2005) study and to examine the role of recovery housing in the treatment outcomes for opioid dependent individuals. Opioid-dependent participants ($N=243$) exiting medication assisted taper programs were randomly assigned to receive RBT plus recovery housing (RBT + RH, $n=81$), recovery housing alone (RH, $n=81$), or usual care (UC, $n=81$).Outcomes were assessed at 1, 3, and 6 months post-treatment enrollment. The primary outcome measure was opioid and cocaine abstinence at each assessment period as measured by a negative urine test and no self-reported drug use during the preceding 30 days. Results showed a graded response among the treatment conditions; that is, participants in the RBT + RH condition were more likely to be opioid and cocaine abstinent at all three assessment points compared to UC. RH participants were more likely to be opioid and cocaine abstinent at 1 and 3 months compared to UC but not at 6 months. Differences also existed between the two

experimental conditions. RBT + RH participants were more likely to be abstinent at 1 and 3 months compared to RH alone; however, the two groups no
longer differed at 6 months. Participants in the RBT + RH remained in recovery housing longer than those in the RH condition (49.5 and 32.2 mean days,
respectively, $p = 0.0014$). A mediation analysis indicated that retention in
recovery housing for greater than 60 days was associated with improved treatment outcomes. Notably, those assigned to the RBT + RH condition also
were more likely to remain in recovery housing for 60 + days compared to the
RH condition (54% of RBT + RH versus 31% of RH retained more than
60 days ($\chi^2(2) = 10.15$, $p = 0.006$). On the measure of employment, the RH
condition had higher rates of money earned compared to UC at the 3 month
assessment; the RBT + RH condition had higher rates of money earned from
employment at both the 3 and 6 month assessment compared to UC. Overall, these findings suggest that both the RBT + RH and RH conditions con-
fer benefits beyond those seen in UC. However, the most intensive services,
which include behavioral counseling and recovery housing (RBT + RH) appear
to provide the largest contribution to improved treatment outcomes in a
population of inner-city opioid dependent individuals.

RBT is beneficial for reducing and controlling drug use during a critical
postdetoxification time period. For many clients, the intervention also con-
fers benefits in other important life areas, including employment and associated legal earnings and recreation. Further research is needed to explore
other potential psychological benefits of RBT.

Current Status of Reinforcement-Based Treatment

Since the completion of the original clinical trials, RBT has been implemented successfully in two real-world community contexts. In Baltimore,
the Cornerstone Clinic provides RBT to clients with various substance use
disorders, using an intensive outpatient day treatment program model of
service delivery. The clinic serves clients referred for substance abuse treatment through various public sources (e.g., probation departments, homeless
shelters) and private sources (e.g., word-of-mouth from former clients, detoxification facilities). Cornerstone uses a fee-for-service model for its funding,
involving both public (i.e., Medicaid) and private insurance reimbursement.

RBT has also been successfully disseminated and implemented within
the child welfare system in Connecticut. Several projects have successfully
adapted RBT for use with parents whose substance abuse treatment needs
have come to the attention of child protective services officials in the context of a child maltreatment investigation. Parents are offered RBT as part of
a comprehensive treatment package (involving, e.g., mental health treatment

for parents and children and parent training interventions) designed to address both parental substance abuse and other factors related to the risk of ongoing child abuse (e.g., poor parenting skills, family conflict), with the ultimate goal of preventing child removal from the home. Interestingly, RBT provided in this context uses an in-home model of service delivery to reduce treatment access barriers often faced by families in the child welfare system. To date, RBT provided within the child welfare system has been publicly funded by the Connecticut Department of Children and Families. In Chapter 12, we discuss factors to consider in the treatment of substance abuse problems with parents who have maltreated their children as well as specific modifications made to RBT for this population and mode of service delivery.

STRUCTURE AND ADMINISTRATION OF REINFORCEMENT-BASED TREATMENT

In the following sections, we discuss how RBT has been structured and administered to date.

Mode of Service Delivery

RBT has been administered in two forms: (a) as the clinicwide mode of treatment within an intensive outpatient treatment (i.e., day treatment) program for substance use disorders at the Cornerstone Clinic in Baltimore and (b) as part of a comprehensive set of home-based services (e.g., mental health treatment, parent training, family therapy) for parents involved in the child welfare system throughout Connecticut. Both of these service delivery models allow for the treatment to be provided with sufficient intensity (i.e., sessions occurring multiple times and for several hours each week) to effectively alter the use patterns of clients with severe and chronic histories of substance abuse.

Populations Served

RBT has been used with individuals experiencing a variety of substance use disorders, primarily opiates, alcohol, cocaine, and marijuana, and polydrug use. As noted, RBT was originally designed as a relapse prevention model for opioid-dependent individuals who had completed a detoxification. Since the original clinical trials, RBT has been applied with populations of cocaine and marijuana users first to initiate abstinence and then to prevent relapse. Detoxification remains a precursor to RBT treatment for substances such as alcohol, opiates, and benzodiazepines, given the need for medical stabilization and oversight. Ideally, RBT begins immediately after detoxification is completed (i.e., same day or next day).

Treatment Duration

RBT has been implemented for varying lengths of time. Given the challenges of effecting change with substance use disorders, we generally recommend a treatment length of 6 months to give the intervention sufficient time to alter environmental contingencies and for behavior changes (e.g., abstinence, stable employment, relationships with nonusing peers) to be maintained outside of the treatment environment.

Treatment Intensity

Drug use disorders are maintained by a wide number of environmental variables and classical conditioning patterns associated with chronic drug use. Often, clients have a long history of conditioning when it comes to drug use; therefore, small doses of treatment are not likely to adequately compete with the operant and responding factors that maintain drug use behavior. Treatment intensity should be sufficient to replace much of the time the individual spends procuring and using substances. This is especially true early in treatment, when the individual is most vulnerable to relapse. In outpatient treatment, a typical RBT schedule includes no fewer than 4 days of therapy weekly for the first month or two of treatment, followed by a titrated scheduled based on the client's progress. This titration should allow for sufficient weaning from treatment (i.e., should not involve stark drops in treatment intensity even when the client is doing well). Clients need time to internalize and practice the newly acquired skills and behaviors, so sudden drops in treatment may precipitate a relapse. In other words, short-term abstinence should not result in an immediate decrease in treatment goals; rather, abstinence should indicate that treatment at the current level is working for the client, so decreases should only occur after it is clear that the client is stabilized and sustaining new behaviors.

The general recommendation for intensity, then, is that treatment begin quite intensively and gradually become less intensive according to the client's response. We recognize, however, that this schedule may not be feasible in fee-for-service environments where insurance companies dictate the frequency and length of treatment. We experience these difficulties in our own fee-for-service program, Cornerstone, so we appreciate that ideal conditions are not the same as real-world conditions. In such circumstances, we are forced to shorten the duration of treatment and/or spread out the sessions that are reimbursable so that the client gets as much treatment as possible over a reasonable period of time. Of course, advocating with insurance providers on behalf of clients also is important to ensure the client receives as much service as possible.

Treatment Referrals

The treatment process begins at referral to the program, which may be through a phone call or through a walk-in to the clinic. This initial contact provides the client with a first impression of the program—whether staff is helpful, friendly, available—as such, much emphasis is placed on this initial contact (for more information, see Chapter 1).

A couple of broad program techniques are worth mentioning here. *In reach* can be an effective way of reaching out to potential clients and maximizing the likelihood of engagement with the program. When possible, a program staff member engages with the client at the source of the referral. For example, if a client is leaving detoxification to come to the RBT aftercare program, a staff member meets him or her at the detoxification unit to introduce the program and to help facilitate transition to aftercare. When possible, transportation also is provided to avoid "detours" when transitioning from one program to another. Although in reach is not always feasible in person, a phone call conversation with the client on the day of discharge to welcome him or her to treatment and to convey that staff is looking forward to seeing the client requires little effort and can start the engagement process before he or she comes to the program.

Barrier Removal

There are considerable barriers to accessing drug and/or alcohol treatment. Some barriers are structural, such as lack of child care, lack of transportation (or cumbersome transportation, e.g., bus rides that take more than 1 hr), lack of funds for food during the treatment day, and more. To the extent possible, the program should help to eliminate as many structural barriers as feasible so that clients are more likely to access and benefit from treatment. Transportation (bus tokens), lunch during the treatment day, and assistance with procuring day-care vouchers (or direct provision of day care if possible) are a few program incentives that assist with barrier removal.

Other barriers are motivational (i.e., the client is not ready yet or is ambivalent about treatment), psychological (i.e., feeling guilty or bad about oneself for needing treatment, mood or other psychological disorder) or cultural (i.e., stigmatization associated with seeking treatment) in nature. These barriers can be addressed in part by focusing much care and attention to customer service (for more information, see Chapter 1), which involves conveying a distinct message that the program is friendly and respectful and that the services delivered are of high quality. When psychiatric needs are evident, the program should inform the client early in treatment that it will do everything it can to address this domain. This type of message conveys that staff cares about all of the client's needs and helps to instill hope that changes can occur. Ideally, a program should provide multiple services on-site so that clients can get the treatment they need in different life arenas (i.e., medical, psychiatric, psychosocial, day care, etc.). However, most programs do not have the financial resources to support such a breadth of services. In such cases, strong collaborations with community programs can enable the client to receive multiple services simultaneously, services that, although occurring in different locations, are better coordinated than they would be otherwise. For example, the RBT therapist can help the client to locate psychiatric services that are available in the same neighborhood as drug treatment and that will work with the client to provide appointments after the treatment day has commenced (alternatively, the client's treatment schedule can be modified on days he or she has psychiatric appointments).

Individual Treatment Sessions

RBT is a highly individualized treatment. As such, the majority of the therapeutic work occurs during one-on-one sessions. Such sessions focus on goals stemming directly from a functional assessment (FA) of drug use for each client (see Chapter 2, this volume). Although there are common themes that contribute to drug use across clients, each client has a unique history of conditioning that must be addressed and a repertoire of positive behaviors to build on to effectively compete with drug use. Other formats for therapy, such as group therapy, are unlikely to achieve the degree of individualization necessary for changes to occur.

CORE CLINICAL FEATURES: THE 10 ESSENTIAL ELEMENTS OF REINFORCEMENT-BASED TREATMENT

RBT is a flexible model, designed to address a range of substance use disorders within various treatment settings and reimbursement structures. This flexibility makes it potentially more appealing to implement than other behavioral treatments, and one explicit goal of this book is to facilitate the wider dissemination of RBT to more real-world settings. However, to achieve outcomes similar to those obtained in the clinical trials of RBT and in pilot research conducted on child welfare system adaptations (see Chapter 12), it is necessary to maintain several key features of the approach. In this section, we introduce the 10 essential elements involved in delivering RBT with fidelity, and these elements are expanded on in subsequent chapters.

In All Facets of Reinforcement-Based Treatment Interventions, an Atmosphere of Reinforcement Is Maintained

A fundamental principle of RBT is that the treatment program should be a reinforcing place to be. The model places equal emphasis on the tone of treatment delivery and the mechanics of the techniques used. Treatment itself is delivered in a nonjudgmental, nonconfrontational, and strengths-based manner. More broadly, RBT conceptualizes this positive tone as striving to create an atmosphere of reinforcement that completely surrounds the client during all contacts with the program. All program staff are expected to be friendly, courteous, and helpful to clients. This includes the client's contacts with receptionists, maintenance staff, therapists and supervisors, or any professional who interacts with the client in any way, no matter how incidental.

The guiding notion for RBT is that consumers of drug abuse treatment should be treated similarly to clients seeking any private or for-profit service, such as the experience one might have when seeking services at a day spa or beauty salon. Good consumer service is emphasized from the point of contact (referral) through the entire treatment process. Although good consumer service may seem a basic feature of client care, it is an often overlooked or undervalued consideration in substance abuse treatment. If clients have a good experience in the treatment program, they are more likely to return. If clients feel that they will be helped (not scolded) when they relapse, they are more likely to present to treatment when they need help the most. The efficacy of the other techniques described (e.g., client feedback, behavior graphing) is affected by the quality of customer service delivered to the client early on and throughout treatment. We expand on this element in Chapter 1.

A Functional Assessment Is Conducted for Each Client so That Treatment Can Be Matched to the Needs of the Individual

The FA is the primary assessment tool for determining (a) the conditions under which drug use is most likely to occur and (b) the behaviors most likely to initiate or maintain drug abstinence. All of the intake assessment tools contribute to treatment planning for the individual. However, the FA provides information about the specific conditions of drug use and allows for immediate and concrete intervention in a manner that is truly individualized. In essence, the FA provides very specific information on the people, places, and things associated with the client's drug use. Every individual has his or her unique history with drug use; the treatment plan should address the unique patterns of drug use for each client. We expand on this element in Chapter 2.

Efforts Should Be Made to Remove or Reduce the Effects of Environmental Cues for Substance Use

Certain cues can very quickly trigger drug use. The people, places, or things that are associated with drug use (often referred to as *triggers*) should be reduced or eliminated to assist the client in initiating (and sustaining) drug abstinence. In the same way that an individual who wants to quit smoking is advised to throw out cigarettes and ash trays and to avoid situations that have been paired with smoking (e.g., a morning coffee ritual, bars), the triggers for substance use should also be identified and discussed with the client. This is a common topic in drug abuse treatment. We intensify this component in our treatment by discussing the individual's specific triggers for drug use and getting a commitment from the client to discard drug paraphernalia, to avoid contact with the specific people with whom he or she has used drugs (learned from the FA session), and to not engage in behaviors associated with drug use (e.g., prostitution, dealing, hacking).

We also evaluate the individual's living situation and how it sustains drug use. Optimal housing is a place where the substance-abusing client has never used drugs (given the specific stimuli and cues for this particular client) and where there is not easy access to drugs. However, meeting one or both of these goals is a formidable task of treatment. Many clients have unstable and unsafe housing arrangements, and we work with them to secure the safest housing possible. We use as many public-, community-, and family-provided resources as we can to assist with stabilizing the individual's housing (public housing, housing vouchers, recovery houses, extended family members, shelters). Our intensive vocational assistance also has aided clients in gaining employment, which has allowed many individuals to secure safer housing. Therapists must develop creative and individualized plans for linking clients to housing that first meets the client's basic needs and second supports the goals of abstinence. We expand on this element in Chapters 2, 4, 5, 7, and 8.

The Client Should Be Given Feedback Regarding His or Her Drug Use and Abstinence Patterns

Client feedback, a technique used in MI (Miller & Rollnick, 2002), has been shown to foster engagement and retention in treatment. Thus, we use this technique within 1 week of each client's admission to the program (when dropout risk is high). Client feedback is a semistructured session using MI techniques (e.g., open-ended questions, reflective listening) and principles (e.g., expressing empathy, developing discrepancy). The session serves to summarize the client's health behaviors, history of drug use, history of success with drug abstinence, and risk behaviors. During the feedback session, the therapist also gains valuable information about what the client values and how he or she sees drug use fitting into the goals he or she has for him- or herself or his or her family. We expand on this element in Chapter 3.

Every Client Has an Employment or Education Goal and Receives Extensive Assistance From the Therapist in Meeting That Goal

The goal is to have 100% employment among RBT clients (with the exception of those who are disabled or otherwise unable to work, e.g., caregivers for children). The program provides group vocational training and assistance (Job Club), and every client completes a series of job-seeking activities supplemented by direct therapist assistance (including barrier removal). We expand on this element in Chapter 4.

Every Client Has Recreational Goals and Engages in Recreational Activities Both Inside and Outside of Therapeutic Encounters

Non-drug-using activities within and outside of the program should be a focus of interventions. The decision to stop using drugs is an important personal choice, with many individual, social, familial, and public health benefits. However, the function that drug use has served for the individual leaves a void that must be replaced with reinforcing activities that do not involve the use of drugs. Within RBT, much effort is placed on helping the client to identify and engage in pleasurable and meaningful activities, particularly those that occur in the natural environment. We expand on this element in Chapter 4.

Clients Receive Social Reinforcement for Their Accomplishments and Social Feedback on Challenges

Another essential element of RBT is participation in a program-sponsored intervention called Social Club, designed to provide clients with social reinforcement for meeting their goals. Social Club is a weekly group during which goals and activities for the weekend are reviewed and each client is presented with a certificate indicating the number of days he or she has been attending the clinic. The presentation of the attendance record is a formal process that naturally results in peer encouragement and reinforcement. Social Club is an important time during which clients receive reinforcement not just from the clinical staff but also from their peers. This peer social reinforcement is distinct from the reinforcement provided to clients by program staff. It also provides an opportunity to practice skills for interacting socially with peers in an abstinent context. We expand on this element in Chapter 4.

Client Progress Is Graphed and Reviewed With the Client

Graphs are a clinical tool designed to emphasize the connection between target behaviors (treatment attendance, drug-free recreation, job seeking) and success in treatment (drug abstinence). Alternatively, graphs can depict a lack of progress on treatment goals and identify risks for relapse. Graphs emphasize to the client that drug abstinence does not just happen but is the result of real, concrete behavioral changes. Using graphs in therapeutic sessions also allows the therapist to praise the client on his or her progress and to revise treatment goals that are not working. In other words, graphs are a mechanism for both the client and the therapist to understand what works and what does not. The graphs are presented as periodic summaries of the client's progress in treatment, with emphasis on successes as well as advice about what additional changes will facilitate ongoing drug abstinence. We expand on this element in Chapter 5.

Motivational Incentives Are Used to Acknowledge Client Accomplishments

Clients should receive reinforcers that serve to emphasize important accomplishments and to encourage additional abstinence behaviors. Tangible reinforcers include such items as stickers, certificates, hand-written notes, congratulation slips, prizes, and vouchers. Commonly reinforced behaviors include attendance to the program, drug abstinence, employment acquisition (or meeting goal targets for job seeking), and changing recreational pursuits. Both tangible and intangible (e.g., praise) reinforcers should be used to reward goal attainment. We expand on this element in Chapter 6.

The Therapist Should Make Every Effort to Engage and Reengage (if Necessary) Clients During the Course of Treatment

If a client misses a treatment session, every effort is made to contact the individual that day. Immediate outreach following a break in attendance provides the client with an opportunity to hear a message of concern and compassion from the therapist. Numerous clients have told us that this has been beneficial in preventing a relapse or minimizing its severity. The sooner the outreach occurs, the more likely it is that the client will return to treatment before a relapse happens, before needing detoxification for a relapse, and/or before getting reacquainted with drug use patterns and their reinforcing properties. Therapists use many forms of outreach, including visits to the home, phone calls, letters, and contact with the client's social network. We expand on this element in Chapters 7 and 8.

STRUCTURE OF THIS BOOK

The chapters that follow expand on the essential elements of RBT outlined in the preceding sections, using a sequence that roughly adheres to the timeline of a client progressing through RBT. For example, the atmosphere of reinforcement (Chapter 1) is the first treatment component that clients encounter, occurring as early as the initial phone call to set up services. The FA of drug use (Chapter 2) is a critical component of the intake process, and a feedback session (Chapter 3) occurs within the first week of treatment. Setting and revising treatment goals (Chapter 4), using graphs to monitor and reinforce goal attainment (Chapter 5), providing motivational incentives contingently (Chapter 6), and engaging in case management interventions (Chapter 7) are essential model components that are implemented as early as possible and occur continuously throughout treatment. Involving significant others and other family members in the client's treatment (Chapter 8), though not an essential element of RBT per se, is encouraged whenever possible to enhance treatment outcomes. Taken together, Chapters 1 through 8 constitute the core treatment manual portion of this book.

We consider Chapters 9 and 10 to be supplemental to the core clinical chapters; they provide guidance from the RBT perspective about training and supervision (see Chapter 9) and common challenges faced within substance abuse treatment programs, such as missed sessions and clients with multiple relapses (Chapter 10). Two additional chapters provide information regarding how RBT has been used with two special populations: pregnant and child-rearing women (Chapter 11), and substance-abusing parents involved in the child welfare system as a result of child maltreatment (Chapter 12). The use of RBT as described in Chapter 12 is considered an adaptation of the model because core features of the model have been modified to fit within the home-based setting and within the context and demands of the child welfare system. Such adaptations fit well with a behavioral model because the focus is on tailoring treatment to need of the individual, which includes the context in which the individual is seeking care.

The majority of the chapters in this book present the essential elements of the RBT model. It is noteworthy that each of these elements has considerable merit on its own. As such, it is our hope that practitioners will use one or more of the efficacious treatment elements presented here as a way of improving on existing services. Combined, the treatment elements more adequately cover the range of services and interventions needed to effectively compete with substance use.

I

CORE PROGRAM FEATURES

1

THE ATMOSPHERE
OF TREATMENT DELIVERY

Research has consistently shown that retention in substance abuse treatment is a significant predictor of positive treatment outcomes (e.g., Hubbard, Craddock, & Anderson, 2003; Simpson, Joe, & Rowan-Szal, 1997). Research on the specific factors associated with substance abuse treatment retention has largely focused on client characteristics, with little research focused on how quality of services or perceived satisfaction with services may impact client outcomes. Fortunately, this area of inquiry appears to be growing. Hser, Evans, Huang, and Anglin (2004), in a sample of 35 substance abuse treatment programs, found that satisfaction with treatment was associated with greater client retention and treatment completion. Zhang, Gerstein, and Friedmann (2008), in a sample of 3,255 clients across 62 drug treatment programs, found that global satisfaction with substance abuse treatment was associated with improvements in drug use outcomes 1 year post treatment discharge.

Therapist qualities also have been associated with differential treatment outcomes. In fact, some researchers have suggested that therapist characteristics may account for more variance in treatment outcomes than client characteristics (e.g., Miller, Benefield, & Tonigan, 1993). More specifically, perceived therapist empathy has been associated with improved client outcomes in substance abuse treatment (Miller, Taylor, & West, 1980; Ritter et al., 2002). Najavits and Weiss (1994), in an empirical review of therapist effectiveness, found that the establishment of a helping alliance and therapist interpersonal skills were predictive of treatment efficacy (whereas therapist experience and training were not). Further research is needed to explore the program- and therapist-level qualities—particularly as perceived by the client—associated with treatment outcomes rather than focusing solely on pretreatment client qualities. These qualities may be conceptualized under the umbrella of "customer service" in substance abuse treatment.

Clearly, a primary challenge encountered by providers is how to engage and retain clients in treatment. Often, the onus is placed on the client to access and to take advantage of treatment, regardless of the quality of the service provided. In short, the prevailing attitude seems to be that if clients want treatment, they will attend it. Likewise, absence from treatment is an indication that the client is unmotivated or not ready for treatment. Thus, little attention has focused on the aspects of treatment that actually encourage clients to be engaged participants in the treatment process. One must wonder how the perceptions and even outcomes of substance abuse treatment might change if practitioners took responsibility for creating an atmosphere that clients perceive as helpful and engaging.

In the business world, there is much emphasis on the provision of good customer service. Business leaders recognize that organizational behaviors that ensure client satisfaction are likely to be rewarded by repeat customers and word-of-mouth referrals (which draw new customers). The motto "The customer is always right" is well suited for a behavioral approach to substance abuse treatment. If a client is not doing well or is not happy with treatment, the first line of thinking should be: What can practitioners do better so that they can succeed with this client? Simply put, clients are affected by the services they receive. If they receive good service, they are more likely to make the most of that service; if they receive poor service, the implications are enormous: They may not access the service again or may generalize to other providers (e.g., "I will never do outpatient again—I tried that once, and they made me feel horrible"). Consumers of substance abuse treatment should expect to receive quality treatment delivered in a respectful manner. However, there appears to be very little focus placed on the importance of customer service in the drug treatment setting. Some questions to ponder are: What if providers treated clients who were seeking drug and/or alcohol treatment in the same fashion as customers at a day spa? What can providers do to create an atmosphere that encourages clients to remain in treatment and to be successful at the treatment episode? It may be that simply being nice and creating a culture of respect goes a long way toward this all-important goal.

From a behavioral perspective, a focus on customer service just makes sense. Consistent with operant conditioning, as discussed in the Introduction to this volume, the client's experience in the treatment setting will influence whether he or she returns. How then can providers make treatment desirable? What can providers offer clients so that they see the benefits of their services?

In this chapter, we discuss the all-important goal of making treatment a reinforcing place for clients to work on the difficult task of rebuilding their lives. An underlying assumption of the Reinforcement-Based Treatment approach—perhaps most evident in this chapter on the atmosphere generated by treatment—is that clients seeking substance abuse treatment deserve to receive high-quality services delivered in a nonjudgmental and friendly manner. In this chapter, we review methods for improving treatment delivery on the basis of our collective expertise and experience in the field. The techniques and activities are offered mostly at no or low cost.

SEE CLIENTS AS INDIVIDUALS WHO ARE AMBIVALENT RATHER THAN PATHOLOGICAL

Historically, many providers in the helping professions have been reluctant to treat substance use disorders, and few practitioners make substance abuse their primary area of clinical focus. This may be, in part, because of the high caseloads that exist in many agencies. It is also likely that the prevailing notions of "drug addicts" as manipulative criminals, liars, and the like do not entice practitioners to work with this population. Although individuals with substance use disorders often enter treatment with a wide range of needs and challenges, they are not unlike others seeking assistance for a range of psychological disorders or other forms of addiction.

According to Miller and Rollnick (2002), ambivalence is a normal part of behavior change. If practitioners see clients as individuals struggling with a powerful dependence on substances yet striving to make changes, they are more honest to the experience of substance use disorders. More important, practitioners see clients as complex individuals who are struggling with drug dependence, rather than drug addicts who only think of using drugs. This perspective will go a long way toward improving customer service because the spirit embodied by the perspective is consistent with each of the elements covered in this chapter. Although it seems grossly unethical that a lower quality of care would be offered to clients in drug treatment (as opposed to other forms of treatment or other services), biases and prejudices about drug users may diminish the quality of care these vulnerable clients receive. If practitioners see clients as individuals with strengths, opinions, and values, they are more likely to provide clients with the quality of care practitioners themselves would expect.

BE KIND

Being kind is a way of describing the positive attitudes and behaviors exhibited by program staff that foster a respectful, enriched environment for clients. More concretely, being kind means to engage with clients in a respectful manner, which includes using a respectful tone in communication, paying attention to clients when they speak (undivided attention), making adequate time for clients (i.e., not rushing sessions), engaging in outreach activities for clients who have missed appointments, smiling (and other demonstrations of positive attitude and regard for clients), reinforcing client successes, and generally using nonconfrontational approaches that convey a respect for the client as an individual. The mantra "Be kind" is a good reminder that sometimes the most basic of behaviors can have important effects.

MAKE A GOOD FIRST IMPRESSION

Clients receive their first impression of a program when they call to schedule an intake session. This is often a time during which the client is also very vulnerable (e.g., in need of treatment, unsure if he or she will be accepted into the program, in withdrawal). The extra care and attention a practitioner provides during this time can affect how the client feels about accessing treatment (whether it is worth the effort) and certainly can affect whether he or she shows up for the program. It makes sense that a client who is greeted by someone who is warm and helpful will associate that behavior with the type of program he or she is planning to attend. If the potential client's initial contact with the program leaves the impression that the staff are too busy, or even rude, it is not likely that the client will follow up (except under circumstances in which he or she feels that he or she desperately needs treatment anyway), and the client may well not be very hopeful that such a program can really help him or her. Because practitioners are in the business of helping individuals, it behooves them to give the impression that they are willing to and capable of doing so.

MAKE A GOOD SECOND IMPRESSION

When clients come to treatment, they often first encounter an intake coordinator or other personnel in the waiting area. This person provides new clients with the first in-person impression of the program. It is certainly a success to get potential clients to show up to treatment, as there are many detours between the initial call and actually showing up. It is important to convey to clients that providers are glad that they are in treatment. Additionally, it is important to convey that the staff at the program is helpful and the client can expect staff to be nice. It is certainly easier for the client to show up for treatment when he or she can expect to be treated with such respect. For example, consider the following welcome:

> Hello. Are you Mr. Smith? Good to see you here. I am Sara. I am the one who scheduled your intake appointment. I thought that must be you because I have you down here for a 1 p.m. appointment. Welcome to XX. You took a really important step by coming to treatment today, and we are here to help you. Let me just take a few minutes to gather some forms for you to get you started.

Welcome certificates (see Appendix A) are a particularly nice way to welcome new clients and reinforce their decision to begin treatment.

GREET THE CLIENT BY NAME AND BE FAMILIAR WITH THE CLIENT

People like to be recognized as unique individuals; this can be especially true for clients who have experienced a one-size-fits-all approach to treatment. By being familiar with clients, particularly when they are greeted on entering treatment, practitioners are conveying the notion that clients matter to them as individuals. If there are multiple staff roles within an organization (intake coordinator, program director, billing person, counseling staff, students), it is especially valuable that all of these individuals are familiar with the clients. Although not everyone will know the same detailed information as would a counselor, it is helpful to have all staff familiar with some basics about clients so that exchanges with staff can feel warm. For example, if a client is meeting with a student volunteer, that student can also follow up with the client ("I understand that you had a job interview on Friday. How did that go?" "I heard you were speaking in group this Friday about your experience. That is going to be really beneficial to the group").

OFFER EXTRAS

Consumers are likely to remember a provider if that provider does something extra to draw attention to his or her service or culture. This can mean offering coffee, water and sodas, or inexpensive snacks in the mornings or afternoons. If offering these on a regular basis is cost prohibitive, it can be done once a week or less as an unexpected gift to the clients.

CREATE AN ENVIRONMENT THAT SPEAKS TO WHAT THE PROVIDER IS TRYING TO ACCOMPLISH

Although designer furniture and oil paintings are out of the question for most providers, keeping a clean, well-organized, and professional-looking environment should be within reach for every program. A cluttered environment conveys the message that services will be unorganized and chaotic, so such an environment should be avoided. An office environment that contains multiple signs with messages about rules conveys an expectation that clients will not behave, and such messages are often written in confrontational language (remember that capitalization can be similar to yelling). An example of such a sign is, "Do Not Walk to the Back Unless You Have Left a Urine Sample. No Exceptions! No Excuses!!!" This sort of message is best given verbally and consistently to clients at intake and on several occasions during treatment until the behavior becomes normative. In the rare instances when clients do not follow this rule, the issue can be discussed with the client individually. Signs can be useful but should be kept to a minimum and used only in cases in which verbal reminders have proved insufficient. A good rule of thumb is to communicate through signs in the same professional fashion that one would communicate verbally, for example, "Please be sure to leave a urine sample before proceeding to group. Thank you."

If the goal of the program is to convey an image of high quality and high professionalism, it might be useful to display certificates of achievement or awards given to the program in the waiting area. Additionally, a framed mission statement in the waiting room is useful so that clients (and visitors) can read about the provider's goals and values, which will also convey what clients can expect to get from treatment. A mission statement is also a reminder to staff about what the program intends to convey.

- Artwork or inspirational pictures can also convey the attitude, culture, and expectations the provider has for program staff and clients.
- Information about community programs (pamphlets) and a neat, organized community information board are also useful in educating clients and conveying the importance that the program places on helping the client with multiple needs.
- Decorations for different events (e.g., football playoffs) and seasons can also help set the tone that the program and its clients are worth the effort and are something to celebrate. Clients can help with the decorations, too, which may not be an activity that they engage in at home. For clients who live particularly chaotic lives, the act of investing in something may be especially meaningful.

ELIMINATE UNCOMFORTABLE
OR EMBARRASSING SITUATIONS

Entering treatment can be an intimidating experience for many clients. If the client is unclear about program procedures or directions on where to go, the stage is set for her or him to feel unsettled or even embarrassed about the treatment process. To the extent possible, program staff should eliminate unclear situations.

Lack of clarity can be present even before the client arrives at the provider's program. The client may lack a clear idea how to get to the program (i.e., directions), whom to ask for, what forms to bring, and how long he or she will be staying; the situation is ripe for misunderstandings and embarrassment. Thus, it is important that the intake coordinator provide detailed information about what the client should bring and what to expect from treatment on day 1. Not only does this help to avoid embarrassment but it may also give the client a little more patience with the expectations on day 1 (e.g., forms to complete) simply because he or she is aware of the expectations and therefore can be prepared for them. Information necessary for day 1 can also be mailed to the client if there is sufficient time between the intake call and the admission to the program.

The call and the follow-up letter, if applicable, should minimally include the following:

- statement that the program looks forward to seeing the client;
- date and time of appointment;
- directions to the program, including a map of the campus (if applicable), bus routes, or other relevant information to the specific client;
- information about any transportation assistance that will be provided (e.g., "You will be provided with bus tokens for your return home from the program.");
- expectations for the intake process and treatment on day 1 (e.g., "Your appointment with us is on 01/15/10 at 1:00 p.m. Please bring your insurance card and identification with you to your appointment. You can expect to leave the program at around 4:30 p.m. after the last group of the day. When you arrive, we will complete some intake forms, and then you will meet a counselor at the program. If time allows, you also will participate in group. Please make arrangements to stay at the program until the end of the day on 01/15/10.");
- directions for canceling or rescheduling the appointment; and
- phone number and person to call if there are any questions.

Once the client has arrived for her or his appointment, there remain a number of procedures routinely conducted by the clinic that may be unclear to the client. Providers should not expect clients to understand the clinic's routines. For example, most programs request a urine sample at the time of admission to the program. Although many clients have experience with drug treatment and this expectation, the purpose of the sample and the directions for leaving it should be very clear because the procedure can be particularly embarrassing otherwise. Programs have different procedures for collecting samples, and some clients do not have experience with the process at all. Here is a sample script:

> Tony, I am going to ask you to leave a urine sample before I walk you back to meet your counselor. Let me show you how we do this here. This is the men's bathroom. It is vacant now, so I can show you the procedure [male staff member walks into restroom with the client]. You just open this silver door here, and there is a cup in there labeled with your name on it. On the other side is a window from the lab, where I can observe the sample. We observe all samples here, and we conduct temperature testing to ensure that we are getting a sample from the client and that it is a good sample. A male observes male clients, and a female observes female clients, and it is all done in a professional manner. You will leave a sample in this cup, and then put the lid on it and place it back in this window. Then you are set to go. Just let me know that you have left the sample, and I will then walk you to the back. Do you have any questions about our procedures?

If there is a misunderstanding about the urine sample process, staff should handle such situations with professionalism and sensitivity. For example, if a client walks out of the restroom with the sample in hand, this is not a comical situation but a basic misunderstanding. The staff member should respond in a delicate way: "Oh, you are finished. Can I get you to just leave the sample in the silver window in the bathroom? I will then get it in a minute and take it into the lab. Thanks." Such a response clarifies the directions for leaving the sample and avoids unnecessarily embarrassing the client.

Clients should be given clear instructions for completion of all forms, and any reading disabilities should be accommodated to ensure that the program is getting accurate information. For self-report assessments, the client should be instructed to ask any questions about any items that are unclear.

PROVIDE THE CLIENT WITH CLINICAL CONTACT ON THE INTAKE DAY, IF AT ALL POSSIBLE

Often, the day of admission is reserved exclusively for the completion of intake forms. Clients may come in simply to complete paperwork and then return later (sometimes with a rather long delay between the intake paperwork and the actual start of therapeutic services). Although the length of time required for paperwork and staffing issues may make therapeutic contact with the client difficult, it is important that programs structure these processes so that clients get some level of therapeutic exposure on day 1. Otherwise, programs miss a valuable opportunity to give the client a dose of hope for change, and the impression of the program is of one that is administrative rather than therapeutic (e.g., the program cares more about asking me a thousand questions than helping me).

Programs should streamline intake paperwork to avoid redundancy in questions. Divide the paperwork across multiple days (complete only the paperwork necessary for the admission on day 1 and then follow up with other paperwork on day two). Schedule the appointment early enough so that the client has time to meet with a counselor at the program, if only for a few minutes.

Optimally, the client should have contact with his or her own counselor on the day of intake. If the client's counselor is not available, the client can meet with another clinician. The purpose of this meeting is twofold: (a) to signal to the client that he or she will be receiving help for his or her substance use disorder (the program does not continue to focus on paperwork) and (b) to allow the clinician to reinforce the client for his or her decision to enter treatment and offer a positive message about the program's efficacy and the client's hope for change.

Providers should think about the difference between coming to an intake appointment at which the client only completes paperwork (1½ hr of sensitive questions) and then is told to return the next day versus an intake session at which the counselor meets with the client to convey a message about what the program has to offer. A script of this message might be something like the following:

> First, I want to congratulate you on your decision to come to treatment. We are glad that you are here. Today is your intake day, so we needed to get information from you so that we can determine how best we can help you. I also wanted to meet with you to tell you just a little bit more about the program. You have come to the right place to get help with your cocaine dependence. We have XX years of experience in treating cocaine dependence, and we have been successful with treating a lot of different people with many of the same issues that you are struggling with. There is a good reason for you to feel like we will be able to help you. Of course, you are the person who will do most of the work on your recovery, but we are going to work hard for you, too. Let me explain to you some more about what we have to offer you [explain details of schedule].

We focus a lot of attention on good customer service. We respect our clients, and we feel that we get that respect back from them. We provide a treatment that has been shown scientifically to work so you can feel more confident that we know what we are doing. We offer vocational counseling, which not only helps with recovery but can help you obtain a goal that is important to you and your family. We give you individual attention. We recognize that no two clients are alike, so your treatment plan will be based on what works for you. If we find that that something does not work for you, we will revise what we are doing to better meet your needs. So, tomorrow, when you come back, your day will be different from today. You will join the group in the morning, go to lunch with the other clients here on our campus, and then we will meet to talk further about how we can help you. I have given you a folder that has all of the information we just discussed. Do you have any questions for me? OK. I am going to have you join the group discussion now. You can sort of sit back and take everything in if you want, or you can participate right away—whichever you are comfortable with doing. I will introduce you to the group first.

PROVIDE MOTIVATIONAL INCENTIVES EARLY AND THROUGHOUT TREATMENT

Motivational incentives are typically thought of as tangible items that can serve to reinforce desired behaviors. The topic of incentives is discussed in detail in Chapter 6. Some incentives, however, are not tangible. Instead, they are based on interactions that serve to either increase or decrease a client's desire to return to treatment. All of the previously discussed examples, if implemented effectively, can make the clinic a more welcoming environment and thus a place where the client is more likely to return.

IN STAFF INTERACTIONS, CONVEY THE TYPE OF PROFESSIONALISM THAT IS EXPECTED OF CLIENTS

All people have had the experience of being a consumer and noting interactions among staff members in an office setting, restaurant, or other business. These interactions provide a sort of window into how the business really operates. If one notes interactions that are negative (e.g., a supervisor berating an employee or two employees arguing about schedules), one's impression of the service as a whole may well be diminished. On the other hand, if employees treat each other with respect and are kind to one another, the impression is that this is truly how the employees feel about each other and their jobs. Few things are more off-putting to customers than staff who visibly show their frustration with their employment. Such visible signs of frustration (e.g., scowling, rubbing the forehead) send the message that the employee (counselor, intake worker) is frustrated with the client (or other clients who are placing unwanted demands on them). The message is "Leave me alone," because it is quite normal to want to avoid frustrating someone further. It is a good idea to keep in check frustration levels and to be mindful of how these may be projected to clients, either through nonverbal body language or through the tone and manner of communications.

CONDUCT ROUTINE CLIENT SATISFACTION SURVEYS

A good way of knowing the quality of a provider's service is to ask customers about their level of satisfaction with it. A well-constructed satisfaction survey can tell providers the areas in which they are performing well and the areas in need of further attention. Surveys should be anonymous because clients often fear getting a counselor or other staff member in "trouble" and thus may not be completely forthright in their reporting. Additionally, survey items should assess specific behaviors (length of wait times, whether certain information was provided to the client) and other more global concepts (the staff here made me feel like they cared about me). Although it is good to assess for larger feelings, there need to be objective markers that represent these concepts, when possible. Multiple questions that assess the particular domain "cared for" might be useful for assessing what behaviors the program actually emits that constitute that concept:

- The staff here is familiar with my background and my current activities.
- The staff here understands my unique qualities.
- The staff here understands where I am coming from.
- The staff here has done extra things to make me feel comfortable.
- The staff here rewards me for my successes.
- The staff here listens to me.

LIMIT WAIT TIMES

Given the large caseloads in many substance abuse treatment agencies, it is not unusual for clients to occasionally wait for long periods to meet with an intake worker or counselor. Although wait times are not always avoidable, efforts should always be made to reduce the frequency of long waits and the length of time the client waits to be seen. When possible, the client should be engaged in a clinical activity while waiting to be seen (e.g., join a group session before finishing day 2 of intake paperwork). If a client must wait to see a counselor or other program staff, he or she should be offered a drink and/or snacks and reading material about the program or magazines. Another idea is to provide each client with a program workbook of recovery-related activities or assignments (e.g., journal writing) so that he or she is making productive use of the time.

REMOVE REDUNDANCY

Redundancy is a common feature in substance abuse treatment, most notably in the paperwork that is required by reporting authorities, insurance companies, and the program. Where possible, duplicate questions and assessments should be avoided. The reduction of redundancy is beneficial to program staff because it reduces workload; it is also beneficial to clients, who may become frustrated by having to repeat information on multiple occasions. Although program staff may have an understanding of why certain questions are asked on multiple occasions, it certainly does not make sense to clients why information asked on one occasion is not sufficient.

Another source of redundancy is group topics. It is often challenging to accommodate the basic education and psychotherapeutic needs of incoming as well as ongoing clients. Thus, group topics are often repeated so that new clients receive requisite information (e.g., drug education, HIV curriculum, relapse prevention); however, clients who have cycled through a series of group topics may hear the same information to the point where it loses its value and clients may wonder why they even need to be present in group. The following are ideas for reducing redundancy and maintaining client interest while ensuring that newcomers receive core group information.

- Develop "variations on a theme" for major group topics. For example, if the umbrella topic is drug education, program staff can develop multiple modules, with each covering similar material but sufficiently different to interest those who have completed the topic on several occasions. In one module, a game (e.g., "Drug Jeopardy") can be used to illustrate and reinforce the material. In another module, several clients teach a portion of the material to the group; in another, a video is used to supplement material. The basic idea is to have well-developed modules that give consideration to the redundancy experienced by clients who have attended the same group topic multiple times.

- Invite guest speakers to all or a portion of the group. Guest speakers can range from former successful clients, experts in a particular topic, staff at social service agencies, or others.
- Use different forms of technology in group (e.g., computers, PowerPoint presentations, YouTube, Internet resources, music, videos, crafts, games).

DO THE UNEXPECTED

This notion follows the ideas presented in the Remove Redundancy section. The notion here, though, is to provide a treatment experience that is unlike what the client has experienced previously. The provision of high-quality customer service alone may enable a program to stand out above others. Other unexpected activities include use of the following:

- various technologies in group, such as slide presentations, computer assignments and interactive software, the Internet (e.g., employment searches conducted online);
- guest speakers, including those in recovery and/or experts in various topics (e.g., mood disorders, anger management);
- creative methods for illustrating therapeutic material, such as art therapy; and
- interesting group topics, such as relaxation techniques, acupressure, self-massage, and how to access needed resources in the community.

TAKE THE APPROACH THAT THE CUSTOMER IS ALWAYS RIGHT

The slogan "The customer is always right" illustrates how important customer perception of quality is to a business's bottom line. The idea behind this slogan is that whatever a customer believes is necessarily correct because that perception (right or wrong) will affect future behavior (e.g., whether he or she returns to treatment). Customer service in substance abuse treatment can be thought of in the same fashion. If a client perceives that he or she is not treated with respect, for example, he or she is not likely to return to the program. If a provider is fortunate enough to know that a client does not feel that he or she has received good-quality treatment (e.g., through satisfaction surveys), the provider can take steps to improve the quality of services or to correct any misperceptions that exist.

TAKE RESPONSIBILITY FOR A JOB POORLY DONE, AND TAKE CREDIT FOR A JOB WELL DONE

In service businesses, such as restaurants, employees are encouraged to take responsibility for poor customer satisfaction ratings or decreases in revenue and, conversely, to take credit when customer satisfaction and revenue expectations have been exceeded. The underlying assumption in this scenario is that employees are at least partly responsible for the success or failure of a business and its endeavors. Although clients in drug treatment are certainly responsible for their efforts in treatment, practitioners also play a critical role in client success or failure. Practitioner education, skill, and, perhaps most importantly, engagement and empathy contribute to client outcomes. As such, practitioners should take some level of responsibility and/or credit for these outcomes.

SET REALISTIC EXPECTATIONS

In a desire to assist clients with rapid behavior change (especially when the stakes are high), providers may expect that clients are able to make changes as soon as beginning treatment. A frustrating dynamic can develop when clients fail to meet the unrealistic goals set by counselors early in the treatment process. For example, counselors may not have patience for early client relapses or missed appointments (either inside or outside of treatment). Counselors may express this frustration to clients who, in turn, feel defeated and disappointed in their own lack of progress and may also feel that they have disappointed their counselor. Much of this frustration can be minimized when practitioners are equipped with a good understanding of the chronic nature of substance dependence and the long-standing history of conditioning that clients bring with them to treatment. When seen in this light, small gains in treatment should be noticed and reinforced so that larger behavioral goals can be met. Clients often have engaged in drug use behavior for such a long period of time that breaking the cycle of use and the stimuli associated with it is a monumental task.

REMOVE BARRIERS TO TREATMENT

Clients often face considerable barriers to accessing treatment, including stigmatization, lack of transportation or inconvenient modes of transportation (e.g., a bus ride that takes 1½ hr), unfriendly systems of care, paperwork requirements for social services (e.g., a need for birth certificates,

Social Security cards), insufficient money for food while at the treatment program, and a general lack of reinforcement for treatment. To the extent possible, programs should help to remove the barriers faced by clients when attempting to access or attend treatment. Transportation assistance, help with navigating social services, lunch vouchers or on-site meals, and friendly staff go a long way toward helping the client to access and attend treatment and to meet broader psychosocial needs.

CONCLUSION

The concept of customer service in the area of substance abuse treatment is nearly nonexistent. Attention (both research and clinical) should be given to how program and therapist qualities are related to successful client outcomes. Some factors, such as therapeutic alliance, empathy, and satisfaction with services, have been associated with improved outcomes. Such findings are intuitive and deserve greater attention and a higher degree of implementation, particularly with populations who are so often stigmatized. In this chapter, we have conceptualized the atmosphere of reinforcement as a constellation of behaviors and attitudes that make it more likely that the client will be satisfied and therefore retained in treatment.

2

CONDUCTING A FUNCTIONAL
ASSESSMENT OF SUBSTANCE USE

The *functional assessment* (FA) is the primary tool used in Reinforcement-Based Treatment (RBT) for the purposes of tailoring treatment to the individual. Horner and Carr (1997) defined the FA as "a method for identifying the variables that reliably predict and maintain problem behavior" (p. 84). The use of the FA for drug and alcohol interventions involves determining the following information:

- details of the client's longest period of abstinence,
- what precedes (antecedents) and follows (consequences) drug use,
- which drugs (including alcohol and prescription drugs) are being used and in what order (if multiple drugs are used) and quantity,
- when drugs are being used (how many times a day, at what times),
- with whom substance use occurs,
- where substance use occurs (i.e., on the street, in a crack house, at home), and
- what motivated the client to seek treatment.

Appendix B details the questions that the therapist should ask during the FA. Detailed information gathered in each of the areas listed in the preceding paragraph enables the RBT therapist to determine treatment goals that best compete with the function(s) or purpose(s) that the drug use serves. Once the therapist has a clear understanding of the conditions under which drug use is maintained, he or she is equipped to intervene. That is, the therapist puts together a constellation of goals that best competes with the conditions of the drug use. For example, an individual may plan to use alcohol because she finds the effects of this drug desirable, particularly for temporarily lifting her mood and relieving boredom. She begins her evening with the plan to use alcohol only, although she has a history of polysubstance use, including crack cocaine. Despite her intentions, once she tires from drinking, she immediately desires cocaine to pep her up by offsetting the sedative effects of alcohol (and also because crack cocaine has been paired with alcohol use for a long period of time). Thus, she begins by using alcohol and then relapses to cocaine. She uses cocaine in a crack house because it is where the drugs are readily available in her neighborhood and because she is able to exchange sex for drugs in this location. Clearly, alcohol and crack cocaine use serve important functions for this individual, and the drugs differ in the functions they serve. Also, behaviors associated with drug use (using in a crack house, sex work) serve to maintain the problematic behavior of drug and alcohol use.

Research has demonstrated that use of FAs increases the effectiveness of interventions for reducing problematic behaviors compared with non–function-based interventions (e.g., Carter & Horner, 2009; Ellingson, Miltenberger, Stricker, Galensky, & Garlinghouse, 2000; Ingram, Lewis-Palmer, & Sugai, 2005). FA has been used in a variety of settings and with both child and adult populations; however, most of the research summarizes single-subject design interventions with children. Although the underlying principles supporting FA support its use across a range of populations, FA-based interventions for individuals with substance use disorders are rare. Notably, Budney and Higgins (1998) were pioneers in the translation of the FA for treating substance use disorders in their evidence-based intervention, the Community Reinforcement Approach.

In this chapter, we review the FA process and how it relates to treatment planning for individuals with substance use disorders. The chapter includes a detailed description of important information to be obtained from the FA, the structure of the FA interview session, and how to conceptualize the functions of behavior. Additionally, in this chapter, we review the ways in which treatment planning is informed by the FA. Last, we provide a case example for illustrative purposes.

INFORMATION TO BE DETERMINED
BY THE FUNCTIONAL ASSESSMENT

In the sections that follow, we describe the information that the therapist ascertains in the FA and how this information is useful for treatment planning and intervention.

What Precedes and Follows Drug Use

The most important information to assess is what precedes and follows drug use, that is, antecedents and consequences, respectively.

Antecedents

By identifying the antecedents to drug use behavior, the therapist and client are able to specify the people, places, and situations that serve as stimuli or *triggers* for drug use. Frequently, clients enter treatment without a clear understanding of how the behaviors that precede drug use influence the likelihood of drug use. Clients often report, for example, that they use anywhere and with anyone. In fact, drug use is typically relegated to relatively few settings or locations and with a fairly consistent group of individuals. The questions contained in the FA are not about where the individual *would* use if given the opportunity but where the individual *does* use typically. The latter question should elicit information on the typical conditions of drug use that have been practiced and repeated over the course of time such that they have conditioned a pattern of drug use for this individual. By identifying the specific features of the individual's unique pattern of drug use, the RBT therapist can design a treatment plan that will avoid exposure to these settings and situations.

Consequences

Although the settings that precede behavior influence the conditions for drug use, the consequences of drug use serve to reinforce or increase the likelihood of future drug use behavior. Some of the consequences of heroin use, for example, include both positive and negative reinforcement: Positive reinforcement includes a feeling of euphoria, a feeling of well-being, and increased confidence; negative reinforcement includes relief from withdrawal, relief from anxiety, and removal of unwanted thoughts or feelings.

Once the consequences of drug and alcohol use are understood, alternative reinforcers or rewards can be implemented that have a good probability of competing with the positive consequences of drug use. These replacement behaviors are called *competing reinforcers*. A very important component of the FA is an assessment of the individual's longest period of abstinence. This component identifies what has worked for the person in the past (essentially it is an FA of non-drug-using behaviors). Very often, clients have a history of one or more sustained periods of abstinence. This window in time offers valuable information about the kinds of behaviors and environments that have sustained abstinence for the individual in the past. It is critical that clinicians understand and implement interventions that have worked for clients previously. In the same way that a psychiatrist would prescribe an antidepressant that has worked well for a patient in relieving depression (and not prescribe one that did not work), the RBT clinician uses what has previously worked for the client to avoid treatment failures. The identification of activities that the person was engaged in during periods of abstinence assists the RBT therapist in designing a plan that has the highest likelihood of working (i.e., there is "proof" that these activities promote abstinence for this individual). For example, if an individual reports that she remained abstinent for 6 months when she was going to church, attending Narcotics Anonymous (NA), and working, then all of these previously effective behaviors should be translated into current treatment goals.

Which Drugs Are Being Used, in What Order, and in What Quantity

A goal for abstinence will be set for all drugs and alcohol, not just the client's current drug of choice. Although setting a goal of abstinence from all drugs may seem like common sense, it is important that the therapist and client continuously monitor all drug use because therapists may unknowingly focus attention on the primary drug of choice and fail to inquire about other drugs specifically. The FA provides detailed information on each drug (including alcohol and prescription drugs) the client is using because the function(s) served by these drugs often differ considerably. For example, the client might report that he only uses alcohol when he is using large quantities of cocaine and needs to come "down." This information is critical because alcohol and cocaine have been paired for this individual over time, thus strengthening the relationship between these drugs. The two drugs also have pharmacological effects that offset the undesirable effects of the other substance, making the use of both even more desirable for the client. This conditioning means that the therapist must be vigilant about the use of either substance and inquire about both on a regular basis. The therapist also should educate the client that use of alcohol, for example, is not only an issue for his or her recovery but also makes it much more likely that a relapse will include cocaine.

When Drugs Are Being Used

Information on when drugs are being used and when they are not being used is extremely valuable for implementing alternative behavioral goals. The therapist should assess how many times per day and at what times the client uses drugs. An example of when drug use occurs, as determined by an FA, follows:

- use between 8 a.m. and 10 a.m., after children leave for school;
- use again between 11 a.m. and 2 p.m. (usually between 12 p.m. and 1 p.m.);
- stop using by 2 p.m. to "recover" before children come home from school;
- do not use again until around 8 p.m. (sometimes put kids to bed by 7:30 p.m. in order to go out early); and
- use one time in the evening around 8 p.m., except on a rare occasion when might use again at about 10 p.m. or 11 p.m.).

This detailed information about when drug use occurs will aid the therapist in determining what time frames are most critical for implementing alternative or new behaviors. The pattern described in the preceding list is helpful because the individual already sets limits on her drug use when the children are awake. It is critical to assist this client with new behaviors for the daytime hours when her children are at school and also later in the evening when they are asleep. These periods of downtime serve to trigger drug use for the individual, and the time must be replaced with behaviors that decrease the desire to use. The most promising treatment goal in this scenario is employment because it offers structure for the time that the individual is currently spending using drugs (or in pursuit of drugs).

With Whom Substance Use Occurs

The therapist's goal is to gather very specific information on the conditions of drug use, including the people with whom the individual uses substances. The number of individuals with whom a client uses tends to be rather limited, except in circumstances in which the person uses in an abandoned house where multiple individuals come and go. The therapist asks for the names (or nicknames) of the persons with whom the client uses so that treatment goals can be set for avoiding contact with these individuals. The client is educated (or reminded) that people are triggers for drug use in the same way that places trigger cravings for drug use.

Where Substance Use Occurs

Information on where substance use occurs (e.g., on the street, in a crack house, at home) tells the therapist what locations should be avoided. Again, the locations of drug use tend to be limited. To the extent possible, these areas should be avoided. It is often useful to provide a map of the area where drug use occurs and outline the area that is now off limits to the client. Alternative bus routes can be identified to further assist the client to avoid these high-risk areas. When the general area cannot be avoided (i.e., it is where the client lives), specific corners or areas where drugs are obtained must be avoided. Although it is optimal that clients avoid drug use areas altogether, this is often not feasible for financial reasons. Thus, the therapist should work with the client on avoiding high-risk areas to the extent possible while the longer term goal of obtaining new housing is implemented.

What Motivated the Client to Seek Treatment

The FA also inquires about the reason the individual has chosen to enter treatment. This information informs the therapist about the potential factors that may also assist with initiating or maintaining abstinence for the individual. The reasons are variable but often include being tired of using, fear of losing a significant other or child (or fear of being a bad parent), guilt, depression, or external factors such as being court mandated. The factors that have led the person to take the important step of entering treatment can be used to encourage ongoing treatment engagement and success and can specifically be used in treatment planning to compete with drug use. For example, children are often powerful motivating forces for individuals. Treatment planning that focuses on positive time spent with children and encourages development as an efficacious parent (reinforcing the client for making the choice to spend valuable time with his or her children) can, along with other treatment goals, serve to compete with the powerful reinforcement the person previously received from drug use.

THE STRUCTURED INTERVIEW

The structured interview to conduct the FA, or the FA *session*, should be held with the client during a treatment session. The FA session takes about 45 to 60 min to complete. During this session the therapist should avoid talking about other topics and maintain a focus on the client's history of substance use and periods of abstinence. For the client, the session should feel like a structured experience in which there is a specific agenda to be accomplished. Other assessment material, such as standardized assessments completed at intake (e.g., the Addiction Severity Index), contain data that can be used to supplement the information gathered during the FA.

The FA is introduced in a manner that encourages detailed information and establishes a clear reason why personal information is needed to improve treatment planning. The therapist might begin as follows:

You answered some questions for us about your history of drug (or alcohol) use. In this session I need to ask about more specific information that will help us to understand the conditions that surround your drug use—the people, places, and things associated with your drug use. We call this a functional assessment interview, and we follow this form together to get the best information possible. At times I will ask you for additional information or to clarify to make sure we have good information that will help us to develop a treatment plan that will work best for you. The information you tell me is completely confidential except in the circumstances where you report you want to harm yourself or someone else or if you report information about child abuse. Once we have completed the functional assessment, I'll spend some time summarizing it for you to make sure I have the right information. The goal of this session is to find out more about your drug and alcohol use so that we can tailor treatment to your individual needs so that you have the best shot at remaining abstinent. Do you have any questions before we start?

The therapist proceeds to ask about the factors listed previously in this chapter as guided by the FA (see Appendix B).

TREATMENT PLANNING

Once an initial FA has been completed, the therapist, in collaboration with the client, chooses treatment goals that will most approximate the function that drug use serves for the individual. The FA process involves identification of the problem behaviors (a separate FA is completed for each drug used) and an exploration of the antecedents and consequences of drug use. On the basis of this information, an informed guess is made as to the likely functions of the drug use; next, alternative behaviors that are likely to serve similar functions are identified and implemented. Figure 2.1 illustrates this process.

As mentioned previously, the treatment goals should include behaviors and activities that have worked for the individual in the past. Several goals will be implemented to compete with drug use for the individual because drug use has served important functions for the individual and is unlikely to remit without intensive intervention on multiple levels.

Common treatment goals include abstinence from drugs and alcohol (with the drugs specifically listed), procurement of housing that removes the individual from the drug cues, recreational and social activities to eliminate boredom (i.e., competing reinforcers), an agreement to avoid all locations in which the client used drugs (i.e., no time spent in the neighborhood or at the crack house), and no time spent with individuals with whom she has used drugs and no time engaged in behaviors associated with drug use (i.e., drug dealing, prostitution).

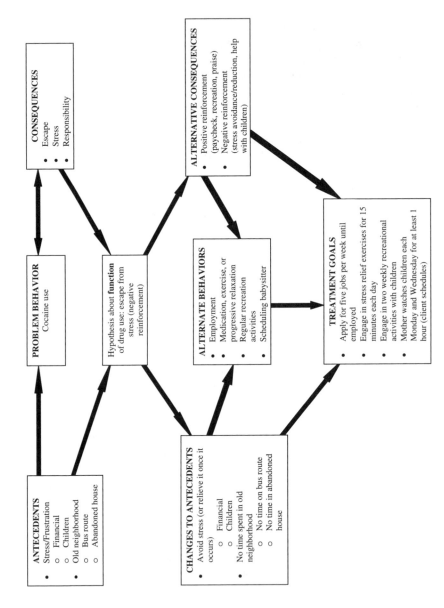

Figure 2.1. The antecedents and consequences of drug use are identified during the functional assessment session. Based on the functional assessment, the therapist and client plan and implement alternative behaviors that are likely to serve a similar function as drug use.

CASE EXAMPLE

Tanya is a 29-year-old African American woman. Tanya got pregnant with her first child at age 19 and was referred to child protective services (CPS) after testing positive for crack cocaine at delivery. She reports that her son never saw her use drugs and that she was a good mother, but CPS took her son from her anyway. She has two other kids who are with her currently but are being raised primarily by their maternal grandmother. All of Tanya's friends are drug users. Tanya has been in outpatient treatment on five occasions. Her longest period of abstinence was 18 months. She attended outpatient drug treatment for 6 months, was working in retail, had a non-drug-using boyfriend, was attending NA, had an NA sponsor, and attended church weekly. However, Tanya relapsed when "the pressure got to be too much."

Tanya reports that she feels so depressed at times that she cannot even get out of bed. She hates being addicted to crack but cannot see any way out of the situation because she feels she has to have it. She knows that she is a disappointment to her family because she "used to be a smart kid." She says that her family has tried to support her but just cannot believe her anymore. Tanya reports that she has burned too many bridges and that her family will never trust her, no matter what she does. She feels she has lost everything important in her life, especially since she lost custody of her son.

Tanya would like to be a better mother to her kids and for her family to trust her. She is angry with her family because her mother accused her of stealing $40 from her dresser, and Tanya denies that she would steal from her mother. Tanya says that she has to pay her bills and the only way to do that is prostitution or to do what she has to do to take care of her kids. She has two kids at home, and she is not going to lose them like she did the last one. She wants the therapist to tell CPS that she is doing well in treatment.

An FA of Tanya's drug use is provided here.

> *Therapist:* I want to start by asking you about a time after you started using when you were abstinent from drugs completely. Can you tell me about your longest period of abstinence?
>
> *Client:* I was clean for a long time from about 2002 to 2004—almost 2 years straight. I think it was like 18 to 19 months.
>
> *Therapist:* That is quite a long period of abstinence. I think we can learn a lot from it. I'd like to get some details regarding what you were doing and basically what worked for you then.
>
> *Client:* I was living in Baltimore with my mom at the time. We used to be real close.
>
> *Therapist:* What else was going on with you? What other things were you doing that helped you to be successful?

Client: I was doing a lot of things. I was working and going to church back then, and I was seeing this guy who was really religious, and I just turned my life around. I was going to NA just about every day, and I had a sponsor. I was also in a pool league back then. I used to be pretty good.

Therapist: Your boyfriend at the time—was he in recovery?

Client: No, he wasn't into drugs at all.

Therapist: So, you mentioned that you were working. What kind of work were you doing?

Client: I had a job at this toy store in the mall. It was a retail job. I loved it. I was really good at the cash register and talking to the customers.

Therapist: So, let me summarize what you have told me about your longest period of abstinence. It was for about 18 to 19 months. You had completed outpatient treatment, and you were really involved with NA. You were living with your mom, working, going to church, seeing someone who was not using drugs, and you were also involved in pool league. What did I leave out?

Client: That's about it.

Therapist: Now, I want to talk about the people, places, and things associated with your crack use. I am going to ask you the conditions surrounding your drug use generally. Who are you typically with when you use crack?

Client: Too many people to tell you—a bunch of people. I use in a crack house. Tom and Erika are the people I talk to there, but there are lots of people coming and going. I guess I would say Tom and Erika are the ones I use with, really.

Therapist: What do you like about using crack with Tom and Erika (as opposed to other people)?

Client: I guess they remind me of the old days. I don't know—I don't really like using with them most of the time, but sometimes we joke around and have fun. I like being with people when I use in case something happens. They are really the only friends I have.

Therapist: Who else do you use with—even occasionally?

Client: I don't really use with anyone else. It is with them, or I just find a space by myself and use alone.

Therapist: Who do you know well that you would never use with or around?

Client:	I would never use with my kids. Is that what you mean?
Therapist:	OK, yes. Anyone else besides your kids?
Client:	I would never use around my mom. I don't really know anyone else anymore who doesn't use.
Therapist:	Who do you think you might have a relationship with if you were not using crack?
Client:	Lots of people. I am a people person. If I wasn't using, I would have lots of friends. I would like to find out what is going on with my old boyfriend. I might talk to him. I would talk to my sponsor again.
Therapist:	Besides yourself, who cares most about you getting assistance with your drug use?
Client:	I would say my mom. Maybe my old sponsor, but I haven't talked to her in a long time.
Therapist:	You mentioned that you typically use at a crack house. Where is it located?
Client:	On Park Street.
Therapist:	What do you like about using crack in the abandoned house (as opposed to another location)?
Client:	I don't like it, but I don't want to use at my house where my kids might find something. I guess I like that there is a place to go even though it is pretty unsafe. Also—to be honest—that is where people will pay for sex.
Therapist:	Where do you go or visit where you don't use drugs?
Client:	I don't use at my mom's house. And I don't use at church [laughs], but I haven't been there in a while.
Therapist:	What about places where you would go if you were not using?
Client:	I would go to lots of places. The movies, anywhere—if I weren't using I would go anywhere I wanted and not have to feel like I was making a fool of myself.
Therapist:	How do you usually use crack (what route)?
Client:	Smoking.
Therapist:	What do you like about using crack this way?
Client:	It's a rush. I won't use IV.
Therapist:	Why is it that you won't use IV?
Client:	I don't want to risk catching HIV or some other disease.

Therapist: That is something you have decided you just won't do because of the risks. Good for you.

Therapist: And how much—dollar amount—do you typically use?

Client: Usually $40 to $50 a day but sometimes up to $250 a day when I'm binging. Sometimes more than that. I use pretty much every day.

Therapist: How would you describe your mood or what you are feeling typically before you use crack?

Client: I am usually feeling excited about it, thinking about how good it is going to feel but also about where I'm going to get my next fix when what I have wears off. Sometimes I think about my kids, especially the one CPS took away from me. I get really angry and depressed about it.

Therapist: What about what you are feeling after you use crack?

Client: I feel nothing really. I feel better. I don't feel depressed. Sometimes I feel guilty when I'm high, which ruins it for me.

Therapist: Can you think of any pleasant feelings or thoughts you have after you use?

Client: I just feel good. I think about the things I can accomplish. I feel like things will get better.

Therapist: What are you usually feeling physically right before you use crack?

Client: I get butterflies in my stomach. I start to feel better physically even before I use. I don't know what that is about.

Therapist: What are you usually feeling physically after you use crack?

Client: I don't know, really. I don't think, I just know I don't hurt. If I feel sick before I use or I'm sore or have a backache, I don't feel anything like that when I'm high. Now I feel like a million times worse when it wears off, but when I'm high I don't feel any pains like that. But mainly I don't feel depressed.

Therapist: Can you walk me through a day of your crack use, including the time of day for each use?

Client: Start using at 6 p.m. or 7 p.m. after kids go to my mom's. Then use again at like 9 p.m. or 10 p.m. and maybe at 12 a.m. or 1 a.m. and then I crash. I might eat in there somewhere but sometimes not. I don't use when my kids are home from school—like if they are sick or off from school. And sometimes my mom won't watch them for me 'cause she gets tired so I will get them, and I don't use when I have my kids. When I'm binging I use nonstop until 1 a.m. or 2 a.m. I might stop for a half hour between uses, but that is all.

Therapist: What would you say is your motivation for treatment? Why did you come to treatment now?

Client: My kids. They are everything to me.

On the basis of this interview, the therapist can determine that the potential functions of Tanya's behavior are (a) to relieve symptoms of depression, (b) to experience the drug's effects (feels good/automatic reinforcement), and (c) to cope with guilt feelings over loss of her son and guilt over not parenting her children as effectively as she wants (and leaving them with her mother).

Tanya's longest period of abstinence will provide necessary and valuable information on the conditions under which she was abstinent. The therapist knows that several combined behaviors were effective in maintaining abstinence for Tanya, including being around non-drug-using individuals, employment, attending church, involvement with NA (with sponsor) and recreating in a pool league.

Tanya's primary goal, as with all clients in RBT, is abstinence. The following treatment goals will support her abstinence:

1. daily NA attendance and procurement of a sponsor,
2. employment,
3. mental health treatment,
4. social and recreational activities with adult non-substance-users (e.g., pool league should be first option) and with her children, and
5. church attendance.

The use of the FA underscores the highly individualized nature of RBT. Treatment planning should be derived from the FA, and RBT therapists should be able to cogently argue how an individual's treatment goals directly stem from the results of the FA. In fact, treatment success is largely associated with the therapist's ability to adequately assess the functions of drug use for his or her clients and to determine appropriate treatment goals.

RELAPSES

An FA also is used when relapses occur because relapse provides an opportunity to identify the very specific and recent conditions of drug use (see Appendix C for a list of questions that the therapist should ask during a relapse). Although the intake FA assesses typical patterns of drug use, the relapse FA inquires about the exact circumstances of the relapse. Thus, information on the when, where, and why of drug use is much more specific to the individual because the relapse has just occurred. As we discuss in Chapter 10, relapses are approached as an opportunity to assist the client with the issue that he or she has entered treatment for, and thus the client is commended on sharing the relapse information with the therapist and for remaining engaged in treatment.

It is critical that the assessment is thorough and that vague responses are probed so that specific information is gathered. For example, when asked where and with whom they typically use drugs, clients may answer "anywhere" or with "anyone." However, clients do not routinely use drugs just anywhere—with adequate probing it becomes clear that clients only use drugs in a few designated places that are generally close to where they live. The RBT therapist will need to remind the client throughout the interview about the need for specific information that will help the program to gain an understanding of that individual's unique drug use patterns (i.e., each person's drug use history is unlike another's).

CONCLUSION

The FA is an important tool for identifying the conditions that have served to maintain drug use. Information gathered from the detailed FA provides a foundation of information that assists the RBT therapist with making an informed guess as to the function that drug use currently serves for the individual. Once the conditions maintaining drug use behavior are identified, the therapist can identify and implement alternative behaviors for the client's treatment plan. These alternative behaviors are then translated into measurable goals that are monitored and reinforced using behavioral graphing (discussed in Chapter 5, this volume).

3

THE FEEDBACK SESSION: AN ADAPTATION OF MOTIVATIONAL INTERVIEWING

Motivational interviewing (MI; Miller & Rollnick, 2002) is an important component of Reinforcement-Based Treatment (RBT) because the approach is person centered and nonjudgmental and sets the conditions for behavior change. Miller and Rollnick (2009) defined MI as "a collaborative, person-centered form of guiding to elicit and strengthen motivation for change" (p. 137). MI is defined as much by the spirit of the approach as by the specific elements it uses. MI is collaborative in nature, in that a key role for the therapist is to elicit the client's perspectives and ideas regarding behavior change. The approach also emphasizes client autonomy such that clients are ultimately responsible for their own behavior change. The specific principles that are applied throughout MI are as follows:

- Expressing empathy: This element has to do with the therapist's role in understanding events and experiences from the client's perspective and expressing that understanding to the client.
- Developing discrepancy: This is one of the more directive elements of the approach; the therapist develops discrepancy by highlighting differences in client goals and values and current behavior (i.e., desire to be a good mother vs. continued drug use).

- Rolling with resistance: In MI, the therapist avoids the role of arguing with the client because such behaviors are seen as ineffective. Alternatively, the therapist avoids argumentation by deflecting resistance—typically by expressing empathy for the client and reframing the resistance. For example, if a client argues that getting to treatment is too difficult because of transportation issues, the therapist might respond by saying, "It is really inconvenient to take two buses to treatment each day. I commend you on your efforts to get here, despite how difficult it has been for you."
- Supporting self-efficacy: Through this element, the therapist supports the client's belief that change is possible on the basis of the client's abilities, desires, and/or past history of success.

In this chapter, we describe a meta-analysis of research on adaptations of MI (AMIs) and explain how client feedback—an AMI—is used for bolstering client commitment for change. The logistics of implementing the feedback session are reviewed, including the MI techniques that are incorporated into the feedback session. For a full review of MI techniques and principles, see Miller and Rollnick (2002).

RESEARCH SUPPORT FOR MOTIVATIONAL INTERVIEWING

Burke, Arkowitz, and Menchola (2003) conducted a meta-analysis of 30 clinical trials using MI for treating a range of problems (e.g., drug use or alcohol use, smoking, diet and exercise, HIV risk behaviors, treatment adherence, eating disorders). The most common format for MI in the research literature involves the use of client feedback in which the client receives personalized and objective information regarding the identified problem behavior (Burke et al., 2003). Such interventions are considered AMIs because they involve the use of techniques that are not exclusively defined as MI (though they are intended to use the spirit of the approach and to use MI elements and techniques). Such adaptations are common in research because they allow for interventions to be studied in a prescribed manner (i.e., it is easier to describe, implement, and measure two MI sessions in which the practitioner uses specified techniques than to implement MI in its pure sense). Overall, Burke et al. (2003) found that the efficacy of AMIs for drug, alcohol, and diet and exercise programs was within the moderate range (ds approximately .50) and that the effects persisted for up to 4 years following treatment. Individuals who received AMIs were more likely to improve in the specified problem area (51% showed improvement) than those who did not receive AMIs (37% showed improvement).

CLIENT FEEDBACK AS AN ADAPTATION
OF MOTIVATIONAL INTERVIEWING

As described in the Introduction, MI techniques are used in RBT to supplement and enhance the treatment environment, to promote client engagement, and to assist the client with resolving ambivalence. All RBT therapists are trained in MI techniques (for a description, see Chapter 9, this volume) which are used throughout the treatment process as a supplement to the behavioral therapy. Although the style of MI is less directive and concrete than many of the techniques used in RBT, MI is consistent with the behavioral approach. We find that the focus on engagement and "meeting the client where he or she is," is essential for client engagement and that facilitating the client's thinking about change is a precursor to many of the observable behavior changes the RBT approach seeks to elicit.

Client feedback refers to an individualized summary (i.e., feedback) of the client's history of drug and alcohol use based on information gathered from standardized assessments. Because client feedback can have an impact on client engagement and retention in treatment, it should be used as early in treatment as possible, ideally within the first week. Feedback uses the supportive style of MI and has often been used in studies of MI (most notably Project MATCH Research Group, 1997). Client feedback is most accurately considered an AMI because the intervention emphasizes the use of the feedback session rather than the broader use of MI (Burke, Arkowitz, & Dunn, 2002). Several studies support the efficacy of client feedback, particularly for the treatment of alcohol use disorders, either as a prelude to treatment (Bien, Miller, & Boroughs, 1993; J. M. Brown & Miller, 1993) or as a stand-alone treatment (e.g., Borsari & Cari, 2000; Heather, Rollnick, Bell, & Richmond, 1996; Marlatt et al., 1998; Miller, Benefield, & Tonigan, 1993). There is a need for further study of the nature, format, and efficacy of client feedback across substance use disorders; however, this AMI appears promising as a brief intervention for promoting initiation of treatment or as a stand-alone intervention.

Feedback is both a verbal discussion (a structured therapeutic session) and a report (a tangible description of the client's drug and/or alcohol use). In the verbal discussion, the therapist should avoid trying to prove anything to the client or use the feedback session as a scare tactic. Rather, although the session material may elicit strong, negative feelings in the client, the session itself and the therapist's tone should feel supportive to the client.

The report can be brief or longer, depending on type of assessment data available and the time constraints for conducting the feedback session. Two example feedback reports are included in this volume: (a) a report that can be formatted on regular 8.5 × 11-in. paper (see Appendix D) and (b) a feedback pamphlet, which uses a folded format, with the report on one panel of the pamphlet along with a description of the results contained within the pamphlet (see Appendix E).

ESSENTIAL CONDITIONS OF CLIENT FEEDBACK

Three conditions are essential for client feedback: (a) The information describing the client's drug or alcohol use (or related factors) must be objective, (b) the use of information must be consistent with the supportive style of MI, and (c) assessment results must be translated in a way that is useful and understandable to the client.

Objective Information

Objective results are available from standardized assessments and from client self-report and can be categorized into the following main areas of client feedback: drug and alcohol use, risk factors, and motivation for behavior change. Examples of objective data for drug and alcohol use include urinalysis or breath alcohol test results and results of standardized assessments, for example, the Addiction Severity Index (McLellan et al., 1992); the Alcohol Use Disorders Test (Saunders, Aasland, Babor, de la Fuente, & Grant, 1993); the Drinker Inventory of Consequences (Miller, Tonigan, & Longabaugh, 1995); the Cut Down, Annoyed, Guilty, Eye-Opener—Adapted to Include Drugs (R. L. Brown & Rounds, 1995); and the Drug Abuse Screening Test (Gavin, Ross, & Skinner, 1989).

A potent component of the client feedback is the presentation of normative data on the prevalence of alcohol and substance use by age category in the United States. The *National Survey on Drug Use & Health* (U.S. Department of Health and Human Services, Substance Abuse and Mental Health Services Administration, Office of Applied Studies, 2009) provides up-to-date information for this purpose, which allows for comparisons between the client's drug use and drug use among others in his or her age group. Other forms of objective information include observable behaviors on the part of the client or self-reported information, such as that contained in the functional behavior assessment (i.e., when, where, and why drugs are used). Observable behaviors that can be summarized in the report include entry to treatment, attendance in treatment, living in recovery housing, attendance at Narcotics Anonymous (NA) or Alcoholics Anonymous meetings (signed slips can confirm attendance), and more. These factors are objective indicators of a client's behavior, and as such, they are useful for including in the feedback session. Objective indicators of treatment progress are particularly useful when relayed in the Healthy Behaviors section of the report, along with the Behaviors to Consider section, both of which are described in the discussion that follows.

Information regarding the client's risk factors related to substance use can be derived from the aforementioned assessments or from self-reported client information (e.g., living with another drug user can be specified as a risk factor for continued drug use). This information can be gathered from the Addiction Severity Index or simply from client self-report. Risk factors for problems related to substance use (transmission of communicable diseases) can be gathered from other sources, such as the Risk Assessment Battery (Metzger et al., 1993).

Motivation for behavior change can be gathered through standardized instruments, such as the University of Rhode Island Change Assessment (McConnaughy, Prochaska, & Velicer, 1983) or the Stages of Change Readiness and Treatment Eagerness Scale (Miller, 1992), or from the client's self-reported reasons for entering treatment (as summarized in Chapter 2, this volume).

Supportive Style of Motivational Interviewing

This key condition is relevant to the choice of assessment results that are described in the report. For example, there are standardized assessments that determine substance abuse or dependence. However, it would not be consistent with the supportive style of MI to include an assessment result that indicated that the client is an alcoholic or drug addict. In our interpretation, the deemphasis on labeling in MI would preclude the use of this type of result. The value of such information is compromised by the effect it may have on the client (Why change if there is nothing I can do about it?). Rather, a result that indicates "problematic use" is less stigmatizing and thus more easily digestible by the client.

Translatable Assessment Results

This condition relates to the utility of the feedback language to the client. Practitioners should not expect that clinical jargon will be understood by clients or that such terms have any relevance to their functioning. The language used in the feedback report should be easily understood by the client. For example, rather than list "taking prescribed psychiatric medication" as a healthy behavior, a better description would be "taking Zoloft." Instead of "results of urinalyses," a better description might be "urine testing results." As described previously, labels are typically avoided in MI; many of these labels also are difficult for clients to interpret (i.e., our tests show that you are *abusing* cocaine, but you are *dependent* on alcohol). These terms often have little relevance to the client's treatment.

LOGISTICS OF CLIENT FEEDBACK

The feedback session is designed to organize a variety of information about the client's substance use, including current healthy (prorecovery) behaviors, descriptions of aspects of the client's drug and alcohol use history, risk factors, self-reported need for treatment, and results of the functional behavioral assessment. Objective data are used to provide a realistic picture of the client's drug and/or alcohol use, and the session is designed to promote behavior change.

The results of the client feedback are discussed with the client, and the client's thoughts about the material are solicited. Clients should leave the feedback session with accurate information about key aspects of their substance use and with suggestions for lifestyle changes that could be valuable for them to undertake to improve their chances of initiating or maintaining abstinence. The session typically takes about 45 to 60 min to complete (depending on the length of the report).

INTRODUCING THE FEEDBACK SESSION TO THE CLIENT

The therapist should provide the client with a context for understanding the feedback session before beginning. It is helpful to point out that the client can use the information in any way that he or she wishes:

> Over the past week you've been giving us some good information about yourself and your substance use. Now I want to spend some time giving this information back to you in a way that I hope you will find helpful. The feedback that I will give you is totally unique to you—it is sort of like a doctor's office visit at which the doctor might tell you what your cholesterol level is or whether or not your baby's weight is on target for her age. You may use this information in any way that you wish. In working with other clients we have found that the information I am about to give you is really helpful in organizing our work together and helping us decide what our next steps should be.

CONDUCTING THE FEEDBACK SESSION

The therapist should provide the client with a copy of the feedback report and let the client know that the therapist will review each section and ask questions or elicit input along the way. The therapist also should inform the client that if anything on the form does not look accurate, he or she should let the therapist know so that it can be discussed and updated. The therapist starts at the beginning of the report and reads through the data in each section, pausing to explain or clarify any pieces of information that might be confusing to the client.

As shown in Appendices D and E, the feedback report and pamphlet begin with the Healthy Behaviors section. Thus, the feedback session should always start by relaying this positive information. The therapist might say something like the following:

> You'll see that this report is divided into different sections; these double bars separate each section. First, I want to start by going over with you the healthy things that I see you doing that are really likely to help you in your recovery. The most obvious things that you're doing to address your drug use are that you've been meeting with me and the other team members regularly and that you've stayed abstinent for about 6 days now.

The therapist should proceed through each section in a similar fashion, introducing each section, reminding the client where the information in the section comes from (if unclear), confirming the accuracy of the information on the report, and pausing to ask some open-ended questions about how the client is feeling about the information in each section (or on specific items) before moving on to the next section. The therapist should also attempt to elicit self-motivational statements from clients by asking the client about his or her feelings regarding the feedback at the end of each section of the report. Ideally, if the client is receptive to the feedback provided, he or she will make statements such as, "It looks like I really do have a problem" or "I need to do something about this."

When providing the client normative information regarding his or her drug use or scores on tests, the therapist should provide additional information about where the norms come from. For example, the therapist can explain that the percentages of Americans in the client's age group who have used _____ (fill in name of drug) in the past year come from a national survey of all Americans throughout the country that the government conducts and posts on the Internet. Similarly, the therapist can explain that the estimated dollar amounts were based on calculations made from the information that the client provided (i.e., therapists should make sure that clients understand the math behind those estimates).

Clients are often quite stunned to hear the information provided in the Your Drug Use: A Description section. It may be the first time that they have ever stopped to think about the financial impact of their use or to consider that unlike their own peer group, the vast majority of people in the United States do not use drugs.

Clients will need some assistance in understanding what constitutes a *risk factor* for drug use. The therapist can explain that risk factors are things that make drug use more likely or abstinence less likely. The therapist might say something like the following:

> We know from research that if a person lives with people who use drugs or spends time with friends who use drugs, that person is more likely to use herself. It makes sense; the drugs are just more available, and people use together to be social. So, in your case, you told me that your boyfriend uses cocaine and that some guys in your neighborhood deal drugs out of their cars outside your building, so those are risk factors that are likely to make it harder for you to stop using. However, you do not have a history of someone in your family having a drug or alcohol problem, so that is a good sign for you.

The Thinking About Change section of the report comes from the University of Rhode Island Change Assessment measure filled out during the intake process. This section is a reflection of the client's stage of change, or where he or she is in terms of motivation to change. Stages of change is a concept derived from the transtheoretical model of health behavior change, which describes the processes by which behavior change occurs (e.g., Prochaska & DiClemente, 1983; Prochaska, DiClemente, & Norcross, 1992; Prochaska & Velicer, 1997).

The therapist should explain to the client what each stage means, beginning with the precontemplation stage, and explain the rating that the therapist gave and why he or she gave it. Here is a script of how the therapist might present the stages in general and how the therapist can explain to the client his or her own stage:

> This wheel describes the stages that people tend to go through as they give up substances. This first stage is called *precontemplation*. Basically, precontemplation means that the person is not really thinking about stopping drug use yet; the person might occasionally have what he calls *moments of clarity*, but generally, he continues to use drugs, does not really see it as a problem, and is not thinking about stopping.

This next stage is called *contemplation*. In this stage, a person is kind of going back and forth about whether he should give up using. He is starting to think about it but has not stopped using yet.

People who are in the *determination* stage have decided to stop using and are starting to take action to stop their drug use, but they are not really sure what to do to make sure that they stop. People in this stage are often still gathering information, finding out about detox programs or checking out an NA meeting, for example.

People who are in the *action* stage have stopped using and are doing all sorts of things to keep themselves from using again, like attending NA meetings regularly or participating in therapy. They are also making lifestyle changes to help ensure that they do not use again.

Finally, *maintenance* is a stage for those people who have been in recovery for a long time and have a long streak of not using. The lifestyle changes that they have made have really taken hold and now come pretty naturally to them. One important thing to notice about this wheel is that people tend to cycle around these stages; sometimes people in action or maintenance have a relapse and are in a different stage again, and lots of time people move from thinking about not using to actually not using.

Now, you fit into the contemplation stage of change. That is the stage at which you are thinking about giving up use but are not entirely convinced that you want to do that or that you can do that. Does that sound like an accurate summary of where your thinking is regarding your drug use?

Open-Ended Probes to Use During the Feedback Session

To encourage a dialogue during the feedback session, therapists should use a variety of open-ended questions, such as the following:

- How does that feel to you?
- How does that compare with your experiences?
- Do you remember what that was in reference to—when we talked about that?
- What else would you like to add here?
- Why do you think it's important to understand this section?
- What else could you have done with that money?
- It seemed like there were a few things in that section that surprised you. What surprised you?
- What do you make of all this?

Remember that clients' reactions to a feedback session vary. Some people will want to discuss the information at length with the therapist; others will want to reflect on the information privately. Pausing between sections or at other critical points in the report may allow the client time to reflect and digest the information and perhaps respond. Therapists should not annoy or offend clients by insisting that they discuss the material.

Maintaining a Motivational Stance During a Feedback Session

A *motivational stance* consists of three crucial therapist behaviors: affirming the client, pointing out and developing awareness of discrepancies in the client's current situation, and accurately summarizing the client's situation and feelings about it. Simple affirmative statements, such as the following, help to reinforce recovery-oriented thoughts and behaviors.

- You are insightful about the information we are discussing today.
- I know that hearing this information can be uncomfortable. I appreciate your participation.
- I appreciate the ideas you have for what you can do to be successful.

Therapists should avoid statements and behaviors that are demotivational or promote defensiveness on the part of the client. Therapist behaviors to avoid include the following:

- arguing with the client (remember, the client is always right),
- scare tactics (i.e., if you do not stop using, this or that will happen to you or your family),
- challenging,
- criticizing,
- persuasion with logic or evidence (the therapist should only provide a straightforward statement of the facts, not draw conclusions from those facts; the client should draw the conclusions),
- confronting with authority,
- using sarcasm,
- disagreeing,
- moving too quickly through the report, and
- labeling the client's behaviors even if the client asks the therapist directly (e.g., "Does that mean that I am an alcoholic?").

Labels are not helpful for clients in changing their behavior; in fact, many labels connote finality and suggest hopelessness. If clients ask about a label, the therapist can respond with something like the following:

Your information is consistent with the responses of people who have sought treatment for problems with alcohol. I am not so concerned with giving you a label that may not be helpful to you. What I am wondering, though, is if you have concerns about your alcohol use.

Clients who experience these behaviors from therapists often become more resistant to change, not less so. They may feel backed into a corner and/or feel bad or guilty about their behavior and wind up feeling hopeless and overwhelmed as to whether change is possible. The point of the feedback session is not to prove to the client how "bad off" he or she is but rather to have the client consider his or her current (or recent) behavior in a realistic context.

Reflective Listening During the Feedback Session

The therapist should listen to the client's statements and nonverbal cues and communicate that he or she understands the client's reactions or concerns. Strong emotional responses to the feedback session are not uncommon, and the therapist should be prepared to deal with them. Here are some examples of reflective listening statements that communicate support and concern:

- This really surprises you. It's not what you expected.
- It looks like this is difficult for you to hear.
- I imagine this is scary for you.
- You are beginning to think, "What can I do about all of this?"
- This information is causing you some concern or confusion.
- It must be hard for you to hear this, but some of it also makes sense to you.
- There are some things that you are doing that are helping you.

Paying Attention to and Discussing Nonverbal Behaviors

Therapists should question and discuss any nonverbal responses that the client might have during a feedback session. Nonverbal responses may indicate that the information is inaccurate, that the information is difficult for the client to hear, or that the client is disengaged from the process. Some common examples of nonverbal responses include

- shaking the head,
- scowling or frowning,
- sighing,
- whistling,
- raised eyebrows, and
- tears.

Reinforcing Productive Client Statements and Behaviors and Deemphasizing Unproductive Ones

As the client discusses his or her reactions, the therapist should be listening for statements of strength and should reinforce such statements verbally. For example, in response to the probe "How are you feeling about all of this," a client might say, "It is a lot to take in, but I know I can beat this thing. I am determined to really make the change this time." This is an example of a self-motivational statement, and the therapist should respond positively. The therapist might respond by saying, "Absolutely, I am confident that you can beat this thing too, and I think it's really great that you see it that way." In contrast, a therapist may choose to ignore (i.e., not reinforce) a statement of weakness or resistance expressed by the client, such as, "There is no way I am going to stop—you can tell me as much bad stuff as you want," or respond neutrally to such a statement by saying something like, "OK. This information is for you to use any way that you choose to. My only goal is that you have accurate information to base your decisions on." Statements of hopelessness, for example, "There is no way I am going to be able to stop," should be responded to with reflective statements, such as the following: "That statement sounds to me like you want to be able to stop but that you are worried that it will be really hard to do it."

Concluding the Feedback Session

The therapist should conclude the session by summarizing the general pieces of information discussed and assessing the client's thoughts about change after hearing everything. The therapist should assume a stance of "gentle nudging" to get the client to discuss his or her personal interpretations of the report and respect the fact that some clients will need time to reflect on the material. The following is a brief example of how a therapist might conclude a feedback session:

> This report says to me that you have done well on some things, such as (provide examples), and that there are still other things that you can do even better, like (provide examples). What do you think would need to happen for you to change that?

CONCLUSION

Research on MI has been conducted exclusively on adaptations of this approach, primarily through the use of client feedback (Burke et al., 2003). The feedback session provides objective information regarding the client's history of drug and alcohol use (and life areas impacted by this behavior) and allows for a framework to use various MI principles and techniques in a structured manner. Client feedback serves to organize the arguments for change, to highlight discrepancies in the client's behavior and goals, and to motivate initial or continued behavior change.

4

ESSENTIAL GOALS FOR
COMPETING WITH DRUG USE

Removing cues that trigger drug use and cravings, and substituting new behaviors to meet the functions previously met by drug use, are likely to be insufficient to sustain abstinence in the long run. Clients must also find alternative ways to fill the time previously spent in drug activity and experience positive reinforcement for remaining drug free.

Although a century of behavioral research indicates that positive reinforcement is the most effective way to change behavior, this basic concept is often underemphasized in traditional substance abuse treatment models. In Reinforcement-Based Treatment (RBT), ensuring that abstinence becomes increasingly reinforcing to a client is critical for a successful treatment outcome. Providing immediate microlevel motivational incentives, such as monetary vouchers and certificates for negative drug testing results, is one way clients experience reinforcement for abstinence from the RBT program itself; these treatment components are discussed in Chapters 5 and 6 of this volume.

In this chapter, we discuss how to help clients set and meet goals for broader lifestyle changes that will reinforce abstinence more comprehensively in their day-to-day lives outside of the treatment context and will "compete" with drug use patterns. We devote most of this chapter to the two lifestyle changes that have the most empirical support for their effectiveness in reducing drug use and preventing relapses: (a) engaging in recreational activities that do not involve drugs or alcohol and (b) obtaining and sustaining a job. First, we review the empirical literature that establishes a link between engaging in these activities and maintaining abstinence. Second, we discuss clinical techniques for eliciting client agreement to pursue these activities as part of their treatment plan. Next, we provide additional details regarding how to tailor recreational and vocational goals to individual client's needs and how to strike a balance between program-sponsored and independently initiated recreational and vocational activities. Finally, we address other behaviors and lifestyle changes that help to maintain abstinence for many clients, namely, attending abstinence-oriented support groups and attending to physical and mental health needs.

RATIONALE AND EMPIRICAL SUPPORT FOR RECREATION AND EMPLOYMENT

In the sections that follow, we discuss the lifestyle changes that are most effective for preventing relapses, and we also discuss recreational activities and employment.

Rationale for Competing Behaviors as Treatment Goals

Having explicit treatment goals to increase drug-free recreation and employment is critical for at least two reasons. First and most simply, these behaviors require abstinence, are time-consuming, and can be done on an ongoing basis. Accordingly, they are excellent substitution behaviors to fill the hours previously spent by the client acquiring and using drugs. Second, each of these activities has the potential to be highly reinforcing, and their benefits are generally available only to those who are drug free. As such, they effectively compete with the benefits provided by drug use.

Alternative Use of Free Time

For many clients, drug acquisition and drug use has been an organizing principle of their lives for many years. For example, a client may experience hangover or withdrawal symptoms on waking and engage in behaviors to feel better, such as sleeping in late or taking a maintenance dose of a drug. Several daytime hours may be spent acquiring drugs and planning activities with drug-using peers, and many evening hours may be reserved for actual drug use. In this example, stopping drug use will result in many unfilled hours in a single day. To sustain abstinence, appropriate substitution behaviors will be necessary at every point in the day previously associated with drug use, not just at times of actual use. There must be alternative, appealing activities that will compete for the client's time.

The idea that clients must find new drug-free ways to fill their time is so basic that it is easily overlooked or underemphasized in treatment. Clients and therapists both tend to underestimate just how challenging it can be to identify ways to spend time and to actually engage in new behaviors that may be unfamiliar or that the client feels he or she is not good at. The importance of planning how free time will be spent is further obscured by the structure that treatment itself provides. Spending time attending treatment sessions (especially if sessions occur at times of the day previously spent using drugs) is itself a substitution behavior that, when a client's attendance is regular, may be largely responsible for the client's abstinence during the course of treatment. (This fact is particularly true for residential treatment programs.) In our experience, finding ways to fill time previously spent in drug activities is so challenging to so many clients that it warrants an explicit focus in treatment (i.e., weekly goals for specific behaviors) and a considerable portion of session time each week.

Alternative Means of Positive Reinforcement

Clients seeking treatment for substance abuse want to stop using drugs and often have experienced negative consequences from their use. However, it is also true that substance use "works" quite well for the client given his or her current context. Substance use fills various functions for the individual and takes up considerable time. There may be few things in the client's life, other than drug use, that are rewarding at all. Frequently, drug use has become so encompassing that many aspects of the client's life are connected to use in some way (e.g., peer groups, places where they spend their time). Stopping use and avoiding people and settings that are cues for use are likely to leave a tremendous void in the client's life. Even if clients no longer desire drugs or enjoy their effects, the boredom and social isolation associated with abstinence may lead them to feel that quitting is not worth the effort and may lead to relapses. Clients may come to feel they have nothing to lose if they resume use, and much to gain.

The concept of choices that alter the cost–benefit ratio for maintaining a maladaptive behavior is a central tenet of behavioral economics and behavior choice theories (Bickel & Vuchinich, 2000). To make quitting worthwhile, clients must experience multiple benefits to a drug-free lifestyle. Abstinence potentially provides many perks that are not available to those who use, including pleasurable experiences that do not involve guilt or shame, a sense of efficacy from engaging in meaningful work, and the respect of family members. These benefits, if experienced consistently, can compete with those that drug use has to offer. They provide answers to the questions Why bother quitting? and What have I got to lose if I relapse?

Empirical Support for Behaviors That Compete With Drug Use

The positive effects of competing activities in reducing substance use are described in both the basic research and treatment outcome literatures. Basic research studies of the natural course of drug use and spontaneous remission (i.e., stopping use without a formal course of treatment) indicate that engagement in rewarding activities other than drug use is associated with a lower risk of relapse for drinking, drug use, and smoking. Specifically, factors such as religious involvement, employment, having responsibilities in the workplace, good interpersonal relationships, and involvement in recreational pursuits predict sustained remission (for a review, see Moos, 2007). For example, in a large-scale study of rural and urban adults with or at high risk for an alcohol use disorder, the amount of time spent in religious activities (e.g., attending religious services, talking to religious leaders) was one of the largest and most consistent predictors of reduced use in the absence of treatment over a 2-year follow-up period, accounting for more variance in drinking behavior than factors such as negative life events, psychological diagnosis, or social support (Booth, Curran, & Han, 2004).

Treatment outcome studies also suggest that behavioral treatment approaches emphasizing client participation in enjoyable and meaningful nondrug-related activities result in better substance use outcomes than traditional therapies without this emphasis (for a review, see Carroll, 1996). For example, cocaine-dependent individuals who received the Community Reinforcement Approach, in which at least 50% of treatment is devoted to employment counseling and developing nondrug recreational activities, achieved significantly more weeks of continuous abstinence both during and following treatment than did those receiving a 12-step model of substance abuse counseling without such an emphasis (Higgins et al., 1993). With regard to alcohol use disorders, a literature review of behavioral and nonbehavioral treatments found that client employment was the factor most consistently related to abstinence at treatment completion (Adamson, Sellman, & Frampton, 2009). Similarly, in a review of outcome studies for treatment of opiate addiction, employment was a strong predictor of abstinence following treatment (Scherbaum & Specka, 2008).

GENERAL CLINICAL TECHNIQUES TO PROMOTE COMPETING BEHAVIORS

RBT therapists must go far beyond simply recommending that clients begin engaging in drug-free activities. Engaging in recreation that does not involve drugs and working are behaviors that have to be learned like any other. Clients often are not used to engaging in such activities and should not be expected to spontaneously do so on their own. Accordingly, the RBT therapist will need to provide a great deal of structure and support to clients if these skills are to be developed and reinforcement of these behaviors if they are to be maintained.

Introducing and Setting Goals for Competing Behaviors

To emphasize their importance, within the first two to three treatment sessions, specific goals should be set for various competing behaviors that the client can accomplish on a daily or weekly basis. The therapist should explain why such behaviors are so important to the client's larger goal of remaining drug free and use information obtained from the functional assessment of the client's longest period of abstinence (see Chapter 2, this volume) and other assessment tools previously completed in treatment to help the client see this information's relevance to him or her personally. To introduce the concept, the therapist can say something like the following:

> During our time working together so far we have talked about goals that you want for yourself. You have told me that it is important for you to [summarize the client's goals discussed to date as they relate to substance use, and acknowledge any goals already accomplished, such as completing detoxification; also summarize previous successes].
>
> We know that not using is your number one goal. But to accomplish this we need to replace your drug use with other behaviors that will satisfy your time. You told me that 3 years ago, when you were able to stay abstinent for about a year, you [summarize what the person was doing during periods of abstinence, e.g., church attendance, a satisfying romantic relationship, jobs].
>
> For you, having a job and being part of a religious community all helped you remain drug free 3 years ago. Doing these kinds of activities again is going to help you meet your ultimate goal of abstinence now.
>
> To support recovery, we generally recommend that clients set goals for activities in two areas—recreation and a productive activity such as work or school. Research with drug treatment programs indicates that having success in these areas greatly increases the chances that you will remain drug free after treatment ends.
>
> Let's start with recreation. As I said, one of the things that is going to be really important for you is to find ways to fill your time that are enjoyable and that do not involve drugs. So far in our work together you have told me that you enjoy [describe some of the client's interests]. What I would like to do is to set engaging in these and other recreational activities as a goal for you to work on each week. Engaging in more rewarding activities will help to keep you drug free. How would you feel about having a goal of engaging in more recreational activities?

Determining the number and type of activities the client will engage in each week is an iterative process based on the client's input regarding preferences and the therapist's feedback regarding the functions that drug use served for the client that need to be addressed. The most important task for the therapist is to help the client set goals for competing behaviors that (a) are or have the potential (with some time or support) to be truly reinforcing for the client and (b) will occur with sufficient frequency and duration to actually compete with the client's individualized pattern of drug use behavior (e.g., setting a goal for one 2-hr recreational activity a week will be insufficient to compete with a daily use pattern). Goals for competing behaviors should be highly specific (e.g., engage in five individual and two social recreational activities this week) and be clear to clients. Additional guidance for helping the client set goals in each domain appears in subsequent sections of this chapter.

Monitoring, Modifying, and Reinforcing Progress on Goals

A detailed conversation with the client about progress on these goals should occur almost every session (once each week is a minimum). Therapists should inquire as to what specific activities happened on what days during the week and what the experience was like for the client. On the basis of the information obtained, competing behavior goals should be modified from week to week to ensure that they are maximally effective in competing with drug use. For example, the number or type of recreational activities to complete in a week may need to be increased or changed if the client is experiencing cravings or does not find certain activities enjoyable.

Relapses are one indication that the alternative behaviors are not adequately competing with drug use. The client may not have actually enjoyed the activities, in which case new activities must be identified and targeted. Alternatively, the client may have enjoyed the activities but did not do them frequently enough or at key times in the day or week when he or she was most vulnerable to relapse. In addition to relapses, therapists should be alert to other signs that competing behavior goals need to be modified to better support a client's recovery. For example, a client who falls far short on goals each week (e.g., completes two but not five activities) may need to have any barriers that prevent goal attainment (e.g., skill deficits, monetary constraints) addressed explicitly in treatment.

When clients meet their weekly goals for competing behaviors, therapists (and, ideally, members of the client's nonusing social support network) should positively reinforce this accomplishment using various methods (e.g., through the behavioral monitoring graphing process; see Chapter 5, this volume). In addition, therapists should use motivational interviewing techniques (Miller & Rollnick, 2002) as much as possible during these conversations.

Techniques such as having the client elaborate on change talk and linking the competing behaviors to the client's goals and values can help to bolster the client's commitment to the competing behavior and to abstinence (see Chapter 3). The following is an example of how a therapist might ascertain whether a particular activity was reinforcing to a client and incorporate motivational interviewing techniques while discussing competing behaviors.

Therapist: Wow, I'm really impressed; you exceeded your recreational goal again this week. I commend you for that. What was it like for you to attend the family reunion?

Client: The first half hour or so was hard, you know. I was nervous to face everybody. Most of my cousins know about my DWI and about me being in jail earlier this year. And I had to stay away from the keg they had—that was a bit of a challenge.

Therapist: How were you able to stay away from the keg? [elaborating change talk]

Client: Well, you know, I just talked with my aunties, kind of stayed away from the younger folks who were doing most of the drinking.

Therapist: That was a great strategy. What else did you do? [reinforcing change talk; elaborating change talk]

Client: Well, I made sure I had some sweet tea in my hands at all times. Or coffee.

Therapist: That's terrific—what else did you do to avoid having a drink at the reunion? [elaborating change talk]

Client: You know, I just kept telling myself that I'm doing the right thing, that I don't need to go down that road again. And actually, one of my uncles, he told me straight up that I was a better man than the rest of them, not needing to get drunk and all that nonsense.

Therapist: It felt good to get that acknowledgement from your uncle. [reflecting change talk]

Client: Yeah, it really did. You know, my mother has cried on his shoulder a lot of times about my drinking and drugging. There were times when I wasn't his favorite person.

Therapist: So not drinking at the reunion really showed everyone that you've changed. And that was very meaningful for you— you've told me how important your family is to you. [summarizing change talk; linking to goals and values]

Client:	Yeah, it did feel good. I feel like I made my mother happy too. You know, she didn't have to answer tough questions about me. Like, I was just there and people could see that I have straightened up.
Therapist:	What do you think it will be like the next time you see your family? [looking forward]
Client:	Well, if I keep doing what I'm doing, I will be able to hold my head up high. Hey, maybe next year I'll even have a job that I can brag about at the reunion. [laughs]

Removing Barriers to Goal Attainment

It is important for therapists to help clients overcome any difficulties they may have meeting competing behavior goals. First, using a non-confrontational, supportive stance, therapists should explore the reasons goals are not being met. Therapists might broach the topic by saying something like the following:

> I really appreciate your good attendance to our sessions, and the fact that you've stayed drug free for 20 days now is fantastic. I am concerned though that you are not being as successful in meeting the goals that we talked about for ways to fill your time—goals for recreational activities and getting a job. I am concerned that if we do not work toward some of these goals, it will be more difficult for you to maintain your abstinence in the long run. I would like to talk some today about what we can do to make those goals more manageable or enjoyable for you. Tell me what you think is happening with these.

Clients may have difficulty meeting competing behavior goals for various reasons, each requiring different strategies to address. Common reasons for not meeting these goals include logistical challenges, skills deficits, a lack of buy-in as to the goal's importance, and opposition to the goal(s) from members of the client's social network.

Logistical Challenges

Many potential logistical barriers can get in the way of clients meeting weekly goals for competing behaviors. For example, a client's work or child-care responsibilities may leave limited time for recreation. Or clients may not have sufficient money to pay for their preferred recreational activities or access to a computer to download job applications. When clients acknowledge the importance of competing behavior goals but face logistical challenges in meeting them, therapists should use problem-solving techniques with the client to remove barriers. For example, therapists can help clients identify recreational activities that do not cost money or family members who might be willing to assist with child care a few times each week. Often, providing clients with more extensive case management support is necessary (e.g., linking the client to an employment support center; see Chapter 7, this volume).

Skills Deficits

Activities that seem straightforward to the therapist may be quite challenging to some clients who have limited experience with the suggested behavior. For example, a client may identify reading as a recreational activity that they would enjoy but not know how to go about getting a library card. Because clients are often reluctant to admit to not knowing how to do something, therapists must probe carefully to assess whether a skills deficit is impeding goal attainment. The conversation that follows provides an example.

> *Therapist:* You've mentioned that reading is a recreational activity you enjoy. Have you considered getting a library card?
>
> *Client:* Yeah, that's a good idea. I guess there's a library somewhere in my neighborhood.
>
> *Therapist:* Let's look it up together now on my computer. It says here that the closest one to you is at the corner of Maple and Elm Streets. Do you know where that is?
>
> *Client:* Yeah, that's across the street from the McDonalds.
>
> *Therapist:* Great. They are open every day from 10 a.m. until 9 p.m. When do you think you might be able to drop in and get a card?
>
> *Client:* It's on my bus ride home. I could go today when I leave here, but I don't have any cash on me right now, only bus tokens.
>
> *Therapist:* Actually, it says here that all you need to get a card is a photo ID. Checking out books is free unless you are late in returning them, then they charge you 20 cents for each day that they are late. When you go, just look for the front desk when you first get there. Someone there will take your information and give you a card. And they can give you an idea of where various kinds of books are. It's sometimes confusing to find what you're looking for in the bigger libraries. When you're ready to leave, you just take the books to the front desk again, and they will scan them and give you a date for when you have to return them.

Lack of Buy-In Regarding the Importance of Competing Behaviors

Occasionally clients will not agree that incorporating competing activities into their routines is important. When therapists encounter this stance, they should first try to determine whether the client's reluctance is really due to fears or misconceptions about certain activities. Helping clients build needed skills and modifying goals so that activities are more manageable or rewarding are two possible interventions when reluctance seems to be due to a low sense of self-efficacy. In some cases, avoiding pleasurable activities may be a sign of depression or other mental health issues that will need a specific focus in treatment.

When clients voice opposition to setting and meeting competing behavior goals, several interventions are useful. First, ask the client if there is any single recreation or work activity that he or she is willing to commit to, even if only for a short time. The idea that clients can benefit from even the smallest possible behavior change is a part of many behavioral treatments. Obtaining a commitment from a client who has not been doing any competing behaviors to engage in a single activity is a therapeutic success that can be built on in subsequent interactions. Another helpful way to frame competing activities is to ask the client to sample a new behavior on a single occasion. The therapist is not asking the client to make a long-term commitment, only to try the new behavior one time to see if he or she might like it after all. Reluctant clients might also benefit from hearing accounts from others receiving RBT about their experiences engaging in employment or recreational activities. Such conversations can be facilitated in any of the group components of RBT (e.g., during Job Club or a group recreational outing). As with all interventions within RBT, encouraging clients to set goals for competing behaviors should be undertaken following motivational interviewing principles (e.g., remaining nonconfrontational, avoiding advice giving or lecturing; see Chapter 3, this volume).

Social Network Members Oppose Competing Behaviors

Occasionally, members of the client's nonusing social network do not support or even actively discourage clients from engaging in competing activities. For example, we have seen spouses who, after putting up with the negative effects of the client's drug use for many years, view recreational pursuits as just more evidence of the client's self-centeredness. Similarly, we have seen spouses and parents of clients discourage a client from working, fearing that it will be too much for the client and threaten his or her tenuous abstinence. It is common for people unfamiliar with the nature of substance abuse to undervalue the role that competing behaviors play in abstinence, and the idea that people with addictions just need to "decide" to quit is prevalent in American culture.

If the network member(s) opposing the client's competing behavior goals is not a primary source of support to the client, the most straightforward way to address this barrier may be to simply ask the client to avoid contact with this individual for a period of time until the client has had a chance to sample the new activities and form an objective opinion about them. When opposition comes from a more central network member, such as a spouse or parent with whom the client lives, the therapist should communicate directly with the individual and listen carefully to his or her concerns. Often, simple psychoeducation regarding the role that competing behaviors play in sustaining abstinence is sufficient to convince the network member and gain his or her support of the client around these goals. In other cases, the network member has legitimate concerns that need to be addressed in the treatment plan. For example, a spouse may reveal that the bowling alley her husband has begun to frequent has a reputation for drug dealing. In cases in which a central network member's opposition is justified or his or her concerns about the activity are not easily allayed, the therapist should invite the member to sessions with the client to negotiate an arrangement that is suitable to all parties. Interventions with spouses and other important family members are discussed in more detail in Chapter 8.

DRUG-FREE RECREATIONAL GOALS

Recreational goals are essential in RBT treatment plans. When a client is no longer using drugs, replacement behaviors are necessary. Exposure to recreational activities (sampling) on a regular basis also helps to take up time previously spent using drugs and increases self-esteem (e.g., I am more than a drug user. I have other interests and skills.). In this section, we provide specific suggestions for helping clients increase their recreational activities at times of the day when they are not in treatment and discuss the program-sponsored recreational activities provided as part of RBT.

Recreational Activities Outside of the Treatment Context

The most straightforward way to find activities that are reinforcing to clients is to ask them. Another source of information is the functional assessment of the client's longest period of abstinence. Therapists can have clients construct a list of activities that they know they would like to participate in and another list of activities they are willing to try (called *reinforcer sampling*). The RBT therapist should help the client prioritize as goals those activities that (a) are most reinforcing to the client, (b) were present during the client's most recent period of abstinence, and (c) are something the client is willing and able to engage in on a regular day-to-day basis. For example, although going to a professional football game may be very reinforcing to a client, it is something that can only be done infrequently. In contrast, going to the public library, checking out novels, and reading each day is a recreational activity that can be done frequently and that is sustainable.

Therapists should not assume that they know what is reinforcing to a client. Instead, therapists should always verify with the client that any agreed-on activities are truly enjoyable to him or her. For example, taking her young daughter to the park may be enjoyable or highly stressful to a client (e.g., because of having to monitor or discipline the child). On the other hand, encouraging the client to try new activities that have the potential to be reinforcing is also important for expanding the list of activities that compete with drug use. Because it is uncertain whether a new behavior will be reinforcing, the client's specific recreational goals should include a mix of new (potentially reinforcing) and established (proven reinforcing) behaviors. Ideally, new reinforcing behaviors are added to the client's recreational repertoire all the time.

Clients should also be encouraged to create a broad repertoire of behaviors for different occasions and circumstances and to diversify their recreation within a given week. For example, clients need to have ideas for activities that can be done both alone (e.g., reading, self-care activities such as bubble baths) and with other people (e.g., lunch with a friend), in good weather (e.g., taking walks) and bad (e.g., putting together a puzzle), when they have money (e.g., going to a movie) and when they do not (writing letters to friends), and both inside and outside of their homes.

Activities conducted on the client's own time should be planned explicitly (e.g., spend two evenings a week with your neighbor watching movies), monitored (i.e., graphed in the client's chart), and discussed with the client throughout the course of treatment. The ultimate goal is for the client to learn to perform recreational behaviors outside of the program after treatment completion. To increase the likelihood that recreational behaviors will generalize to the natural environment, the client's social support network should be included in these activities as much as possible. Although recreational goals are a constant part of treatment, the nature of the recreation can change over time as clients' interests expand.

Program-Sponsored Daily Recreational Activities

Clinics providing RBT also can provide program-supported recreational activities to allow the process of learning how to have fun without drugs to start early in treatment, when clients lack ideas or sources of income to support their own activities. The behavioral principle involved is reinforcer sampling; the program introduces clients to new activities that they might not have tried before. Clients often report a sense of surprise that they enjoyed a particular activity (e.g., visiting a museum) that they had imagined would be inhospitable to "someone like them." Such experiences are critical for broadening clients' views of themselves as more than drug-addicted individuals and developing an identity as a mainstream citizen engaged in his or her community. Accordingly, RBT program staff should not stereotypically assume that certain activities are inappropriate because of a client's race, age, religion, drug use history, or socioeconomic situation.

At the Baltimore Cornerstone Clinic, where RBT was developed, participation in clinic-supported recreational activity is offered to clients who are drug abstinent on the day of the activity. On weekdays, a specific 2-hr time slot is reserved for the activity as part of the program day's itinerary, and all clients who test negative for drug use have the opportunity to participate. Activities are designed by the team on a weekly basis and are chosen to appeal to a diverse range of interests. Recreation includes a wide variety of activities, including hobby development (e.g., origami, scrapbooking, painting, knitting, woodworking), board games, trivia, storytelling, and writing assignments (poetry)—to name a few. Clients should be regularly involved in selecting activities through the use of recreation surveys. The point of involving clients is to teach skills for finding affordable activities (e.g., through local newspapers) and to engage in discussion and compromise regarding the activity that will be selected. As noted, sampling new activities is an important component of the intervention, so 100% consensus is not necessary or desired for every activity.

While leading the recreational activity, RBT therapists provide structure regarding the intent of the activity and the importance of leisure development generally. Group time also is spent identifying barriers to individual recreational goals, including identification of local low-cost activities. During the recreational activity, the therapist should monitor group interactions and intervene as necessary if conflicts erupt or a particular client seems agitated or upset. Asking each new cohort of clients to negotiate and agree on basic rules for conduct while at recreational events (e.g., losing is a part of playing games and is nothing personal) can help prevent any problems from occurring and ensure that all clients feel comfortable at the activity.

Social Club

Social Club is a program-sponsored activity offered once each week that provides a forum for clients to receive positive social reinforcement for abstinence and to be exposed to role models of clients who are further along in their recovery. Social Club is an important setting for clients to receive reinforcement not just from the clinical staff but also from their peers. This peer social reinforcement is a different and important form of reinforcement that must be regularly and consistently provided. Social Club provides a meaningful structure for providing such reinforcement, which may be particularly important early in treatment when clients may not yet have peer or family support in their natural social networks.

A specific time (about 2 hr) should be set aside each week for Social Club. Lunchtime on Friday is a time that works particularly well; it concludes the program week and gives clients an extra boost going into the weekend (a time when temptations to use drugs are greatest for some clients). Like all program-sponsored activities (except for individual counseling), clients must have a drug-free urine test that day to participate.

Format and Structure

The format of Social Club is as follows:

- The meeting begins with a 15- to 20-min review of clients' schedules, called *day planning*. Each client completes day plans that correspond with weekend days (see Appendix F). These day plans are essentially planners that detail the client's upcoming schedule of activities for the weekend. This plan serves to organize the client's time and to ensure that the client is engaged in meaningful activities (e.g., downtime is eliminated). The group discusses appropriate activities and brainstorms ideas for spending time productively. Often, the group exchanges information on upcoming events (e.g., Narcotics Anonymous [NA] marathons).
- Lunch or party food (cookies, hors d'oeuvres) is provided while clients socialize (unstructured) with one another. Ideally, the choice of the meal (carryout or other convenience food, such as a grocery store deli platter) is negotiated by clients earlier in the week. Music helps to set a festive tone.
- An awards ceremony is held in which each client receives a certificate indicating the number of days they have remained abstinent. Certificates should look nice (see Chapter 5, this volume) and be prepared by program staff ahead of time. The staff member will formally read each certificate and hand it to the client while other staff members and clients clap and acknowledge each person's efforts. Other client goals in addition to abstinence (e.g., getting a job, resolving a legal matter) that have been met during the week also should be reinforced. To make the awards ceremony as meaningful as possible, it is essential that as many clinic staff (therapists, supervisors, administrative staff) attend each week as possible, even if they only dash in for the awards ceremony segment (which usually lasts only 5–10 min). Clients also comment on their view of their own progress.
- A lottery drawing is conducted in which clients compete for a single prize worth approximately $10. The lottery drawing interjects some fun into the proceedings and inspires some friendly competition between clients. In conducting the draw-

ing, the number of slips placed in the can equals the number of clients in attendance that day. Each client draws a slip, but only one ticket designates a winner. The winner will have the opportunity to pick out one prize from a prize cabinet, which should be kept filled with a range of prizes each having an approximate value of $10. Items in the prize cabinet should be ones that are valued by clients (e.g., a gift certificate to a local store, nail polish, umbrella). Clients report enjoying these low-cost methods of abstinence reinforcement very much.

Graduates of Reinforcement-Based Treatment at Social Club

Social Club also functions as a way of providing some limited aftercare support to clients who have completed RBT. Clients should be told that they are always welcome to return to Social Club after their time in the program ends. In our experience, former clients who have terminated treatment successfully are usually too busy with work and recreational pursuits to attend, but appreciate the "lifeline" back to the program that a standing (unchanging) meeting time provides. Those who do return are asked to say a few words about how they are doing and how the program helped them, which often is an inspiration to current clients who are early in their recovery. For this reason, RBT staff may wish to extend personal invitations to former clients to drop in on specific weeks if doing so would not interfere with their work or other responsibilities. All RBT graduates who show up for Social Club must be screened for drug and alcohol use prior to having any contact with current clients and are only allowed to participate if they are drug free.

EMPLOYMENT GOALS

Every client should have an employment or education goal and receive extensive assistance from the therapist in meeting that goal. A focus on job skill development is a critical component of RBT in part because it directly competes with drug use. Working on vocational skills and obtaining and maintaining a job serve many functions for recovering individuals. Participating in these activities boosts self-esteem and self-efficacy, gives clients something meaningful to work on, and helps to take up large portions of the day previously devoted to drug use. In addition, procuring a job will lead to other behaviors that compete with drug use, such as having money for better housing and gaining respect from family members.

The nature of the job or educational goal depends on the client. Some clients are employed but dissatisfied with their work or have jobs that place them at risk for continued drug use (e.g., an exotic dancer who uses drugs at work, a person who takes cocaine to stay awake on a night shift). Other clients have never been employed and need to consider training experiences and entry-level positions. Employment goals that involve part-time or volunteer work or returning to school for a general education degree (GED) also are appropriate for some clients. Balance in the client's schedule should be maintained (e.g., not working so much that he or she cannot work on other treatment goals or becomes exhausted and thus susceptible to relapse), and the association between hours at work and abstinence and relapse should be examined using graphs (see Chapter 5, this volume).

Much of the information provided in this section comes from a chapter on vocational skills training for people who abuse substances in a treatment manual published by the National Institute on Drug Abuse, *A Community Reinforcement Plus Vouchers Approach: Treating Cocaine Addiction* (Budney & Higgins, 1998), available for free download at http://www.drugabuse.gov/TXManuals/CRA/CRA1.html.

Providing a Rationale for Job Goals

Clients should be given a rationale for having and working on job goals. Therapists must initiate a discussion about the role of a satisfying vocation in the short- and long-term maintenance of drug abstinence and in meeting other life goals. A therapist might say the following, for example:

> In drug abuse treatment, one of the predictors of long-term success is stable, satisfying employment. This relationship between abstinence and employment exists for the following reasons:
>
> - When you work at a job you like, you are unlikely to use drugs while working.
> - You are less likely to jeopardize that job by coming in late or missing work because of late-night partying.
> - The job makes you take pride in and feel good about yourself.
> - The job provides you with the financial means to access other positive things, such as social and recreational activities and desirable housing and transportation.
> - Sometimes the job also provides a source of social support, friendship, and social activities that are unrelated to drug use.

Setting Job Goals

Therapists must first conduct a thorough assessment of the client's work history and interests, then collaborate with him or her to set appropriate behavior-change goals. The goals of vocational counseling vary greatly depending on the individual client's situation. For example, many clients have difficulty initiating job-seeking behavior. For these clients, initial goals might involve filling out applications with the therapist's help or spending 30 min a day using a job-searching website that the therapist has taught the client how to use. Following are examples of goals that are commonly set in different client situations (Budney & Higgins, 1998).

For the unemployed client, these job-seeking behaviors are suggested:

- develop a resume,
- make eight job contacts per week (e.g., call managers to inquire about hiring),
- send out two resumes with a cover letter each day,
- go to a job service program twice a week,
- enroll in a job training program, and
- collect and consider information on educational possibilities.

For the client working in an environment that is high risk for drug use, or for a client who is dissatisfied with his or her job, these behaviors are suggested:

- submit applications for alternative employment while continuing to work,
- modify the work environment to reduce the risk of drug use or improve working conditions, and
- enroll in job skills or alternative career-related educational classes.

For the client who works "too many" hours or has an irregular schedule, these behaviors are suggested:

- keep work to 35–50 hr each week,
- establish a more regular schedule, and
- explore alternative work schedules.

Within the first few sessions of RBT, the client should have a long-term vocational goal (e.g., full-time employment as an administrative assistant) and specific, short-term attainable goals (e.g., five job contacts per week, employment with a temporary agency, enrollment in a computer skills class). These goals should be monitored and changed as needed until clients achieve their long-term goals. Thus, vocational counseling is typically an ongoing component throughout treatment.

Types of Job Assistance Provided by the Therapist

RBT staff should provide the following vocational counseling services to clients (from Budney & Higgins, 1998):

1. The therapist encourages clients to treat the job search as a full-time job. The suggested schedule for this is to eventually spend half of each workday looking for job leads and setting

up interviews and the other half going to interviews. Clients are to continue with this schedule each day until they find a job.

2. The therapist advises clients to systematically contact friends, relatives, and acquaintances for job leads.

3. The therapist provides standard scripts and forms to follow when making contacts with potential employers, for writing letters, for making telephone calls, and for keeping records.

4. The therapist provides the supplies and services necessary for a job search. Clients should have access to a work area, telephone, computer, photocopier, postage, and newspapers.

5. The therapist encourages clients to seek job interviews and applications for jobs that are not advertised. For example, the client could call all the manufacturing plants, all the car dealerships, or all the haircutting establishments in the yellow pages.

6. Clients are encouraged and taught to use the telephone for basic inquiries as to whether jobs are available. This is a more efficient method than letters or visits.

7. The yellow pages section of the telephone book is used to make lists of potential employers.

8. The therapist helps clients learn how to promote strengths other than work skills (i.e., social and personal skills). These skills can be highlighted in a resume when making job contacts as well as during interviews. In addition, the therapist helps clients identify and list marketable work-related skills that were not necessarily acquired during previous employment (e.g., babysitting for several children in the neighborhood, taking care of an elderly grandparent).

9. The therapist helps clients learn how to make the most of unsuccessful job contacts, that is, learn how to ask that source for other job leads.

10. Clients learn to recontact a potential job source following an interview. This can help demonstrate their interest and enthusiasm for the job to the employer. Also, after an unsuccessful contact with a very desirable job source, clients learn to call that employer back after a period of time in search of future opportunities.

11. The therapist helps clients learn how to arrange transportation to job sites that are difficult to get to for whatever reason.

12. Clients are encouraged to contact previous employers for jobs or job leads.

13. Clients are encouraged to get names of people who can serve as references. These can be used when submitting applications

or when interviewing to expedite the employer's decision. Make sure that the person will say positive things about the client.

14. The therapist helps clients build an effective resume. This includes inquiring about any positions held by the client (i.e., under the table work), helping the client present experience and skills in the best possible manner, ensuring that there are no typos on the resume, and minimizing gaps in employment when possible (clients should be prepared to address any gaps in employment in the interview).

15. The therapist provides advice and instruction on how to effectively fill out an application (e.g., emphasize personal skills).

16. The therapist provides training on how to effectively present oneself at interviews.

17. The therapist provides a list of effective behaviors that should occur during an interview (e.g., making eye contact, thanking the interviewer). After each interview, the therapist reviews the behaviors with the client and helps the client learn and practice any behaviors not performed.

18. The therapist encourages clients to create a structured job-seeking schedule. A datebook or form is used to schedule each day's activities.

19. Clients engage in record keeping of job-seeking behaviors using such tools as job lead lists, callback dates, and outcomes of phone calls.

20. The therapist encourages clients to contact job supervisors rather than personnel staff. Sometimes the supervisor has an important role in making hiring decisions.

21. The therapist instructs clients in how to discuss handicaps (e.g., physical limitation, prison record) with a potential employer and how to turn them into strengths.

22. The therapist encourages clients to consider a variety of jobs so they do not restrict themselves to the extent that they do not find employment.

23. The therapist provides continued assistance until a job is obtained.

Job Club

Because many clients will need similar kinds of vocational assistance (e.g., resume development, Internet-searching skills), clinics providing RBT may wish to provide this component of the intervention using primarily a group approach. At Cornerstone, this portion of the program day is known as

Job Club. Job Club meets for 2 hr a day Monday through Thursday and is usually led by a single RBT therapist (rotated among all therapists), although several therapists can be involved depending on the size of the group and needs. As with all group components within RBT, clients must test negative for drugs to participate. The first hour of Job Club is spent in structured activities such as didactics (e.g., how to search an online job posting site) or group discussions (e.g., ideas for how to answer difficult interview questions). In the second hour of Job Club, clients engage in individual activities, such as typing cover letters or role-playing an interview with a therapist or peer.

The room(s) in which Job Club is held should have as many resources to assist in job searching as possible. At minimum, there should be a computer (several computers are preferable to accommodate multiple clients at once) with Internet access and word processing software, a printer, a telephone, several yellow pages phone books, office supplies (e.g., envelopes, pens), and the most recent classified section of the local newspaper(s). Other helpful resources include a whiteboard, a bulletin board to post job-related information (e.g., locations and dates of upcoming GED classes), a photocopy machine, an area for clients to store materials (e.g., extra copies of resumes) from day to day, and vocational books (e.g., a GED test study book). The logistics of having large groups of clients share materials during the second hour of Job Club can be a challenge. We recommend limiting the size of the group to 12 clients maximum. Therapists can also flex the program schedule to ensure that all clients get access to the resources they need. For example, some clients can use the job resource room in the morning and have their individual session with their therapist during the second hour of Job Club.

Monitoring and Reinforcing Progress

Progress toward job goals should be monitored closely and reinforced in individual sessions several times each week using graphs (see Chapter 5, this volume). Any barriers to gaining employment should be removed (e.g., getting a copy of a Social Security card). Clients should not be expected to remove barriers on their own but should receive assistance (e.g., task analysis) and instrumental support (e.g., bus tokens) from the therapist (see Chapter 7). Each therapist should maintain a table of his or her clients' job status (known as a *job grid*) to be shared with the supervisor during weekly supervision sessions (see Chapter 9).

OTHER GOALS TO COMPETE WITH DRUG USE

In addition to engaging in recreational and vocational activities, clients may also benefit from having goals for other behaviors to compete with drug use that are based on the functions that drug use serves for the individual and clues about behaviors that have supported abstinence in the past (from the functional assessment interview of the client's longest period of abstinence). Common goals include attending recovery support group meetings, engaging in mental health treatment, and addressing health concerns.

Attending Recovery Groups

Research suggests that participation in a 12-step style recovery support group such as Alcoholics Anonymous (AA) or NA is associated with reduced alcohol and drug use, especially when such participation occurs as part of drug treatment and begins early in that treatment (for a review, see Moos & Timko, 2008). Individuals also are more likely to attend such groups when actively encouraged to do so (e.g., connecting clients to specific meeting groups) by drug treatment providers (Donovan & Wells, 2007; Timko, DeBenedetti, & Billow, 2006), even when they have histories of AA or NA participation. From the RBT perspective, attending such groups directly competes with drug use by serving as a substitution behavior, particularly if clients attend groups at the times of the day or week when they are most vulnerable to drug use (e.g., Friday evenings). Attending groups may also effectively compete with substance use if a function of the client's use was for friendship and social connection to others. Through participation in recovery support groups, clients can meet drug-free peers, practice social skills in a forgiving and drug-free context, sample new recreational behaviors, and experience efficacy by serving in the role of helper to others. Although the tenets of some recovery support programs are inconsistent with those of behavioral treatments (e.g., that the client has little control over the drug addiction), the potential benefits of involvement are so great that we recommend that RBT therapists discuss this option with all clients.

Clients vary in their willingness to attend support groups. Some are willing to attend meetings every day, whereas others are hesitant to try them at all. When clients are reluctant, RBT therapists should ask them to sample a meeting or two before deciding and assist the client in finding a meeting that suits his or her needs (e.g., times, location, group composition). Meetings themselves are highly variable, so some care should be taken in selecting appropriate ones for clients when there are multiple options in a community. Women, for example, often feel uncomfortable in groups that are composed primarily of men. Other RBT clients are good sources of information about the feel of different groups that the community has to offer. For those clients who reject AA and NA because of their spiritual focus, several nonreligious abstinence support groups also exist and are usually available in larger metropolitan areas (e.g., the SMART Recovery program; see http://www.smartrecovery.org/).

Addressing Mental Health Needs

It is estimated that as many as 60% of substance-abusing individuals also have a mental illness (U.S. Department of Health and Human Services, National Institute on Drug Use, 2009). For many clients, the functions of substance use are directly linked to mental health symptoms, such as using drugs to reduce chronic anxiety, avoid intrusive traumatic memories, or cope with depression. For such clients, finding other ways to meet these functions will be critical for sustaining abstinence. Attending mental health counseling sessions and/or taking psychotropic medications can effectively compete with the benefits of substance use by serving functions previously achieved through drugs and alcohol in ways that are safer and more effective, socially acceptable, and sustainable.

It is not always clear to the therapist if or how a psychological disorder contributes to a client's substance use. However, even if there is no evidence that substance use functions to mitigate symptoms of mental illness, left untreated such illness has a high likelihood of undermining the client's abstinence and interfering with success in other treatment goals such as finding a job and forming new relationships. For these reasons, we recommend that all clients who report histories of psychological disorders such as depressive disorder or bipolar disorder and who are not receiving treatment have an explicit goal of beginning mental health interventions. The mental health treatment goal should be tailored to individual client needs and can vary from week to week. For example, initially, clients may have weekly behavioral goals to select a provider, make an appointment, and fill prescriptions. Later, the treatment goal might be to attend mental health counseling sessions each week and take psychotropic medications every day.

Addressing Physical Health Needs

Clients with substance use disorders also often have physical health needs that either contribute directly to substance abuse or present significant barriers to engaging in competing behaviors. Prescription drug abuse, for example, often originates from the treatment of a legitimate health issue such as chronic back pain. Clients may fear that problems with physical pain, fatigue, or sleeplessness will return if they stop drug use. In these cases, as with mental health treatment, finding medically appropriate ways to address these issues will be an important task for the RBT therapist. The therapist should first help the client understand the association between his or her medical condition and substance use and provide a rationale for addressing this within RBT. Then, the therapist should obtain a release of information and speak with the client's physicians to better understand the client's needs and to make sure that the recommendations made within RBT are consistent with the client's medical treatment. On the basis of these consultations with health care providers, the therapist can help the client set specific weekly behavioral goals, such as setting and attending doctor appointments, getting regular exercise, or adhering to dietary recommendations.

Chronic and acute health issues also threaten overall progress in treatment by impeding a client's ability to engage in recreational activities or work, contributing to a sense of hopelessness about the future, and limiting social options (e.g., a chronic cough makes conversation difficult). Thus, even if the client's health condition is not directly related to the substance use, it should be addressed by the RBT therapist through an explicit goal to obtain treatment for the problem, monitoring and reinforcing of behaviors related to addressing the problem, and case management interventions to facilitate access to medical care and compliance with medical interventions. Cognitive behavioral and motivational techniques may also be necessary if clients are reluctant to seek medical treatment (e.g., to address a cognitive distortion that the disease is too far gone to address).

Several health conditions are common among those who abuse substances, including liver disease, chronic pain conditions, emphysema, sexually transmitted diseases, and kidney damage (Mertens, Lu, Parthasarathy, Moore, & Weisner, 2003). Dental problems also are common and can be debilitating and humiliating to clients (Metsch et al., 2002). All clients who have used drugs intravenously should have a treatment goal to have an HIV test and, if positive, to comply with an antiretroviral treatment. Beginning to address these problems is an essential goal that will facilitate the client's ability to remain abstinent, work, enjoy life, and assume the identity of a competent, healthy person.

CONCLUSION

A great deal of time in RBT is spent helping clients develop a repertoire of drug-free behaviors and encouraging them to engage in these behaviors frequently to ensure that abstinence becomes increasingly reinforcing over time. Clients must find alternative ways to fill the time previously spent in drug activity, and many very specific daily behaviors will be necessary to fill the gap left by giving up the former lifestyle. Especially early in treatment, clients are encouraged to sample a wide range of different activities to maximize the chances that the client will experience positive reinforcement from at least some of their drug-free behaviors. Once engaging in the drug-free activities that are most reinforcing becomes part of the daily routine, clients will have "something to lose" if they resume use, and the client's cost–benefit ratio for use versus nonuse will shift toward abstinence. Thus, engaging in an appealing repertoire of drug-free activities effectively competes with the client's former lifestyle.

Research suggests that the best activities for competing with drug use are drug-free recreation and employment. Each of these has been linked to better abstinence outcomes following substance abuse treatment. Clients should have weekly goals to engage in a variety of inexpensive recreational activities to be performed alone and with other people. Daily program-sponsored recreational activities are another way that clients experience positive reinforcement for being abstinent and provide a means for reinforcer sampling of activities that clients may not have attempted on their own. Every client receiving RBT also should have an employment or educational goal. Job Club, a group-based component of the RBT treatment program day, is a mechanism for providing extensive job-seeking and other job skills assistance to supplement activities performed by the client outside of treatment. Other competing behavior goals, such as attending peer recovery support groups and addressing physical and mental health needs, are important for many clients. RBT therapists help clients reach these goals by outlining specific weekly (or daily) action steps, building motivation for competing behaviors, removing barriers to goal completion, providing positive reinforcement for client progress, and enlisting family members to support the client in these activities.

5

BEHAVIORAL MONITORING OF TREATMENT GOALS: GOAL GRAPHING

After treatment goals have been clearly defined, a method for determining the occurrence frequency (and potentially the intensity, duration, and/or latency) of the behavior is developed. This information is recorded in the form of the behavior graph.

Behavior graphs are a primary tool in behavior modification procedures (Miltenberger, 2001) and have been used effectively as a self-management technique across a variety of populations and settings. In fact, a popular weight loss program, Weight Watchers, uses graphs to reinforce weight loss goals. Graphs provide a visual depiction of the changes (or lack thereof) in a client's targeted behaviors. They signal to the therapist that the treatment goals are either working to initiate or maintain abstinence or, conversely, are not adequate or appropriate to compete with the client's substance use. Behavior graphs also can serve as an intervention because the act of reporting and monitoring one's own behavior can produce behavior change. As Figure 5.1 illustrates, the functional assessment informs treatment planning, which is then translated into measurable goals that are graphed.

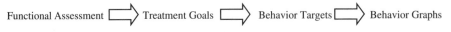

Functional Assessment ⟹ Treatment Goals ⟹ Behavior Targets ⟹ Behavior Graphs

Figure 5.1. From functional assessment to behavioral graphs.

Graphing in the context of Reinforcement-Based Treatment (RBT) serves multiple purposes:

- to evaluate the efficacy of treatment goals;
- to provide a form of client self-management that may increase adherence to treatment goals;
- to provide a mechanism for treatment staff to regularly reinforce client behavior change, both verbally (through praise) and tangibly (through stickers and other incentives);
- to keep abstinence goals and sub goals tangible and salient to the client;
- to help clients understand the ongoing relationship between substitution behaviors (e.g., work and recreation) and abstinence;
- to be a source of pride to clients; and
- to help to predict relapses and teach clients to know when they are vulnerable to relapses (if a client begins to decrease participation in important goal activities, this is a red flag for potential relapse).

In this chapter, we describe the use of behavior graphs as a clinical tool in substance abuse treatment. We begin with a review of the basics on how to construct behavior graphs and follow with a discussion of which behaviors to graph (on the basis of the functional assessment). Additionally, we discuss the types of graphs (e.g., line vs. bar) best suited for particular target behaviors. A brief description of the principles of behavior graphing is provided. Finally, in this chapter, we provide a discussion of how to use behavior graphs clinically, including examples of how to present graphs to clients.

DIRECT VERSUS INDIRECT ASSESSMENT

Before behavior graphing can occur, the target behavior must be clearly defined, and methods for recording and reporting behaviors also must be decided. There are two methods for the assessment of behaviors that will be graphed: *direct* and *indirect assessment* (Iwata, Vollmer, & Zarcone, 1990). Direct assessment involves directly observing and recording the target behavior (e.g., recording the number of outbursts for a child during math class). However, in some cases, direct observation is not feasible or safe. Because drug use occurs outside of the treatment context (and it would not be safe or appropriate for staff members to conduct direct observations of drug use in the community), indirect assessment must be used for counting problem behaviors. In RBT applications, urinalysis is the primary means for determining the occurrence of drug use. Clients are tested regularly (at least twice per week) for a variety of substances, and the urinalysis results are then recorded on the graph as either drug use or absence of drug use. Self-report also is used to supplement the information obtained from urinalysis results. For example, a urinalysis conducted on a Monday may indicate that the person has relapsed, but it does not indicate when the relapse occurred (e.g., on Saturday or Sunday). The individual's self-report of when the relapse occurred is used to mark the starting date of the relapse. When the client is absent from treatment without prior approval, and thus urinalyses are not conducted, the client is presumed positive.

CONSTRUCTING BEHAVIOR GRAPHS

Graphs are composed of an x-axis (horizontal) and a y-axis (vertical). Figure 5.2 depicts a line graph of cumulative days abstinent. The y-axis represents the days abstinent (target behavior), and the x-axis represents the client's days in treatment. For each day in treatment, the RBT therapist records a zero (indicating lack of abstinence) or a line indicating a one-unit increase (one unit/day of abstinence on the corresponding day). Figure 5.3 depicts a graph

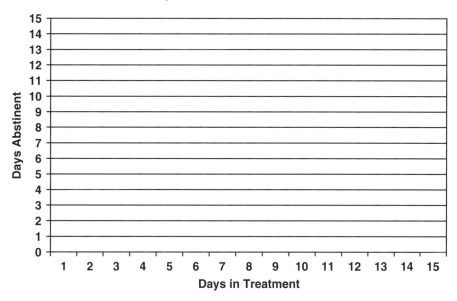

Figure 5.2. Line graph with title and labels for x- and y-axes.

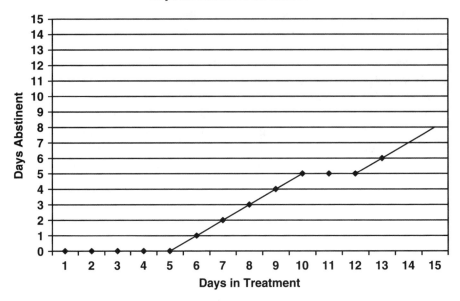

Days Abstinent From Heroin

Figure 5.3. Line graph with abstinence data.

with client data. The client tested positive for Days 1–5, tested negative on Days 6–10, tested positive on Days 11–12, and then negative on Days 13–15. The cumulative days abstinent are 8 for this client, meaning that the client has been drug free for 8 days total since the start of treatment. The graph also shows that the client was abstinent for 5 days total for the first period of abstinence and 3 days for the second period of abstinence. Figure 5.4 illustrates a graph with accompanying reinforcers and notes.

Abstinence is graphed as a goal for each client. Additionally, RBT therapists graph each client goal derived from the functional behavioral assessment (see Chapter 1, this volume). For each goal that is graphed, the RBT therapist should be able to argue for how the behavior targeted is functionally related to the particular client's ability to initiate or maintain abstinence, both with the client during individual sessions and when meeting with the supervisor and other therapists. During supervision meetings, the RBT therapist describes each goal and how it relates to the individual's ability to maintain abstinence and how the constellation of goals will adequately compete with the function(s) that drug use has served for the individual. As mentioned in Chapter 1, behaviors that were effective during periods of abstinence are automatically included in the treatment goals (and thus on the graphs) for the client. These goals were effective in the past, and thereby there is evidence that they actually work for the client.

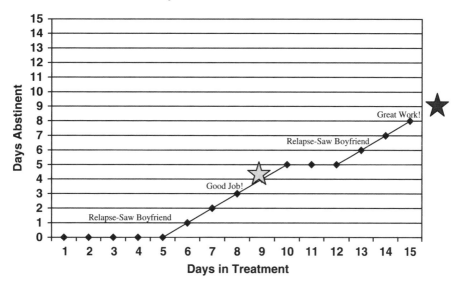

Days Abstinent From Heroin

Figure 5.4. Line graph with title, labels, abstinence data, notes, and reinforcement.

LOGISTICS OF GRAPHING

Graphs are kept in the client chart and are placed in order of importance for maintaining abstinence. This organization helps to maintain the logical argument for how the goals relate to abstinence and how they are prioritized (an important reminder for the therapist and the client). For example, if the client primarily uses heroin to "self-medicate" depression, taking prescribed antidepressant medications and attending psychiatric counseling sessions are two graphs that should be prioritized and thus placed after the initial goal of abstinence. By placing these graphs at the front of the line, the priority given to them is especially clear. The therapist also emphasizes this point verbally with the client by indicating such when the graphs are reviewed.

> The first graph we will review is your medication graph. This graph comes right after your abstinence graph because we agree that treating your mood symptoms is really critical to helping you to maintain abstinence. You took your medication [use name of medication] every day in the past 2 weeks. It is really good that this has become a consistent thing for you and that you recognize the need to not skip doses. Your consistency with the medication is helping your mood (as you have told me) and also is helping you to meet your goals with abstinence and in other life areas, too.

Although choice of graphs is highly individualized, as determined by the functional assessment, there are a number of behavior goals (and graphs) that we have found are particularly effective at competing with the functions of drug use (for a review of these goals, see Chapter 4). Two essential goals that should be graphed for every client are abstinence from drugs and attendance to treatment. In addition to these basic goals, we recommend that therapists start with a set of five essential goals unless there is a compelling reason why one of the goals is not consistent with the functional assessment. The goals include abstinence, attendance, recreational activities, employment-seeking activities, and attendance at Narcotics Anonymous (NA) or Alcoholics Anonymous (AA) or the equivalent. Other goals that are client specific include taking medication (e.g., methadone, psychiatric medications), attendance at outside appointments (e.g., psychiatric appointments, medical appointments), and self-care goals (e.g., exercise, relaxation). Additionally, goals that specify time away from a particular area or with particular people are especially useful. For example, the therapist might consider the following script:

> You have agreed that you will not go to [provide name] neighborhood because this is the area where you used to get drugs. To give you the best chance of success with your recovery, it will be important that you not spend time in areas where you have used previously. We are graphing your time away from the high-risk area for you (which we have depicted here in a map). The more time you spend away from this area, the more abstinence you are likely to accumulate.

TYPES OF GRAPHS TO DEPICT VARIOUS TARGET BEHAVIORS

The type of graph used will depend on the frequency and type of behavior being recorded. Typically, line and bar graphs are the most useful visual presentations of progress because they do not require a lot of interpretation (e.g., the higher the bar, the better the progress). The following is a list of goals and the types of graphs that correspond with them.

- Abstinence graph: Line graphs should be used to depict cumulative days abstinent. These should be labeled *Days in treatment* (and/or dates) on the x-axis and *Days abstinent* on the y-axis. A client who fails to give a breath or urine sample for a specific period also should receive a straight line for those days (presumed positive). Graphs for each drug of abuse and for alcohol should be depicted separately (see the Guidelines for Graphing section).
- Attendance graph: This graph can be depicted either as a line graph or as a bar graph, depending on the frequency of the attendance requirements. If attendance is required daily, then a line works well. If the attendance goal is less frequent, such as three

times per week, then a bar graph would be a better fit. The bar graph should depict the maximum level that is feasible for the behavior (e.g., 7 days of treatment each week).

- Recreational activity graph: Bar graphs work best for depicting the number of recreational activities the client engages in per week. The x-axis should be labeled *Weeks in treatment*, depending on the needs of a particular client. The y-axis should depict a reasonable number range for the behavior (e.g., 0–10), depending on the goal for each client. For example, if the goal behavior is three recreational activities per week, the client's y-axis may go up to 7 to indicate that the client can do more than the targeted number. Separate blocks representing each day are drawn on the bar graph, and the activity (e.g., went to movie) is recorded in the box. The criteria for what constitutes a recreational activity needs to be explicit, and activities that do not meet the criteria should not be counted (e.g., doing chores, going to the store). For a discussion of recreation as a treatment goal, see Chapter 4.
- NA and AA meetings: Bar graphs work well for recording the number of NA and AA meetings attended per week (same design principles as the recreational activities graph).
- Job graph: Bar graphs generally work best to depict progress on job goals. The x-axis is again weeks in treatment. The y-axis will vary depending on the client's particular needs. For clients who are already working, the y-axis might be *Number of hours worked each week*, whereas for clients who need to find a job, *Number of job contacts made* is more appropriate. For a discussion of employment as a treatment goal, see Chapter 4.
- Time away from drug cues (people or places) graph: A line graph works well for depicting the number of days away from particular people or drug cues (e.g., time away from a particular geographical location, time spent away from person with whom the individual has used drugs).

GUIDELINES FOR GRAPHING

The following is a list of principles and guidelines for effective graphing.

- Graphs should be directly related to the client's abstinence. To make the connection between particular behaviors and abstinence abundantly clear, graphing should be limited to the abstinence and abstinence-related behaviors.

- Only one target behavior should be depicted on each graph. One graph equals one behavior. Different behaviors may serve different functions for the individual; thus, each behavior is recorded separately. For example, if the client uses cocaine and alcohol, these two drugs are graphed separately. They likely serve different functions for the individual, and the client may well be abstinent from one and not the other (in which case reinforcement is given when the client is abstinent from cocaine, even when he or she continues to use alcohol). The graphs might reveal that the treatment goals are effective at treating one goal but not the other; in this instance, treatment would be modified to more adequately treat the drug still being used.
- Graphs should commence at the onset of treatment. Early treatment is a vulnerable time for relapse, and treatment gains should be reinforced immediately (e.g., Day 2 attendance at the clinic should be graphed and reviewed with the client to stress the importance of early steps in the treatment process and to commend the client on accessing and participating in the process).
- Graphs should be reviewed with clients at least once per week. Graphs work best in settings with clinical contact of at least once per week because the idea is to provide ongoing and timely feedback. If clinical contact occurs less frequently than this, it is not likely that the monitoring (say every 2 weeks) has much of an impact on the behavior. The feedback or reinforcement is simply too delayed to impact the behavior. Clients should become accustomed to reviewing their graphs routinely during individual sessions and have a clear understanding of what behaviors are being monitored and what success looks like on the graphs.
- Graphs should include a *goal line* for every graphed behavior other than cumulative days abstinent (which is ongoing). For example, if the client is expected to perform three recreational activities per week, a line can be drawn at the 3 level across multiple weeks. The goal line makes it clear when the client meets, exceeds, or falls short of the target goal.
- Graphs should line up in terms of dates so that progress can be compared across multiple graphs. Therapists need to keep the time periods depicted across graphs synchronized with each other. Using actual dates is one effective way of doing this, although for some behaviors the therapist might find it easier to use the week of treatment, counting from the first session, instead of dates (e.g., Week 15 of treatment rather than 08/15–08/30). The goal is to be able to explain changes, to link the behaviors on one graph

to those on another. The therapist should be able to clearly depict these links and be able to say things like the following:

See this period of relapse here [refer to abstinence graph]? Let's take a look at what your recreation was like during those weeks [flip to recreation graph]. See how you were below your goal of three recreational activities on the week that you relapsed and also on the week before your relapse? What that says to me is that whenever you do not take care of yourself by making some time for recreation, you are vulnerable to using drugs again. Let's find some ways to increase the recreational things you're doing on a daily basis.

■ Milestones, changes, relapses, and relevant notes should be depicted on graphs. For example, relapses are indicated by a horizontal line depicting the number of days of a positive drug test. On this horizontal line the therapist should write any relevant brief information related to the relapse (e.g., "went to see Charles"). To indicate times that the client could not provide a drug test to the therapist, the therapist can write "visiting brother in NC" on this horizontal part of the graph to indicate it as a stop-test period rather than necessarily a relapse. A big increase or drop in mood can be indicated with a quick explanation such as "moved into new housing" or "lost job" to explain that portion of the graph.

■ Actual graphing of behaviors can occur both inside and outside of sessions. It is not necessary that all graphing occur during the session itself. For example, therapists probably should set up the graphs (e.g., make the x- and y-axes and labels) prior to client sessions to make sure that they look professional. Also, for example, tallying the number of days drug abstinent or drug free since the last time the abstinence graph was reviewed with a client may take several minutes of work to look up urinalysis results, reconstruct the dates involved, and more. This work can be done by therapists prior to the session, and the new portion of the line that the therapist drew can be shown to the client in the session itself. For simpler graphs such as bar or thermometer graphs, it is better to color in the behavior with the client present as he or she describes his or her actions on that goal in the previous week.

■ Graphs need to look tidy and show careful attention to detail. The quality of the graphing is a reflection of the degree to which the therapist takes the activity seriously and respects the client. Graphs need to be easily readable and not overly complex; the handwriting should be neat and clear; the graphs should not be torn, stained, or otherwise messy. Colorful pens and markers and stickers are used to make the graphs vibrant and visually appealing to clients.

- Stickers, stars, smiley faces, written compliments, and more should be used liberally (but genuinely) on client graphs to reinforce client progress. Therapists should be providing lots of specific, genuine verbal praise directly linked to client behavior for progress made toward treatment goals when discussing graphs. For example, the therapist might say, "Wow, 35 days abstinent— that's really a lot, especially considering that your last period of abstinence before I met you lasted only about 2 weeks. I am really proud of you." As much as possible, these statements should be accompanied by so-called tangible rewards placed directly on graphs, such as stickers, stars, actually writing the words "nice job!" on the graph, and more, especially for particular milestones or accomplishments. In the preceding example, after making the statement to the client, the therapist might say, "I just have to give you a star for this. We need to emphasize here what you have accomplished and how these behaviors are all related to your success" and place a star on the chart at the 35-day point in the graph. Using such simple tangible reinforcers is a novel application in a population of individuals with substance use disorders; as such, therapists may assume that such praise is unnecessary, unwarranted, or unwanted. It is important to keep in mind that many clients have had very few opportunities to receive such specific positive praise in their lives. We have found that if the objective of giving such tangible reinforcers is explained accurately (e.g., "We use these notes and stickers to put a 'stamp' on your behavior; the point is to emphasize when you are meeting your goals."), clients value and appreciate the gesture. In fact, they look forward to it. It is also important to note that vast ranges of stickers are available, including self-designed stickers that can be tailored to the tastes of the individual client.

- Graphs should be added as necessary during treatment and discontinued when they are no longer important. Once a graph is started, it does not necessarily have to be maintained for the full course of treatment. For example, an older job graph depicting the number of job contacts made might be "retired" (and moved to the back of the chart) and replaced with a graph depicting the number of hours at work once a client gets a job. As another example, a therapist would graph a behavior that was part of a *sampling contract*, such as "Attend NA (Narcotics Anonymous) meetings," but would stop graphing this behavior after a few weeks if the therapist and client agree that the meetings are not helpful to the client (i.e., when a behavior is dropped from the list of treatment goals). Conversely, new graphs might be needed during the course of treatment as new information emerges, such as adding a graph with cumulative days not smoking for a client who determines that smoking cigarettes triggers his or her marijuana use. A graph should not be discontinued because the client is having success with the target behavior. For example, if the client has been abstinent from cocaine for 3 months, the graph remains in place for the treatment duration. In other words, graphs that work are never discontinued because the client needs and deserves ongoing praise for continued success.

INTRODUCING GRAPHING TO CLIENTS

The following is an example of a script for how graphing is introduced to clients (it includes mention of goal setting).

During our time working together we've talked about goals that you want for yourself and your family. We have also talked about the specific things you can do that will give you the best chance of remaining abstinent. You've told me that it is important that you are around other non-drug-using people, that you not isolate yourself, that you come to treatment 3 days a week, that you get back to the kind of work schedule you had before when you were successful, and that you start attending church again because that also helped you in the past.

We agreed that your treatment goals are abstinence from heroin, attendance here at least 3 days per week, at least two weekly recreational activities, daily attendance at NA, submission of three job applications per week, attendance at church each Wednesday evening and Sunday morning with your aunt. Does that sound like what we agreed on?

I want to show you a technique that we'll be using in our work together from here on out called graphing. Graphs are basically just pictures of how well you are doing with your treatment goals. We've found in working with other clients that having pictures of your progress toward goals can be really helpful. They sort of bring to life the progress you are making and help us to determine ways to keep you successful. Drug use is not an accident. It happens because you access drugs—often after going through quite a bit of effort to get the money for them. Abstinence is not an accident either. It happens when you purposely put effort into this new way of living. The graphs we will use tell us if goals we have agreed on are working for you. We are going to start using these pictures for all of your individual goals pertaining to staying abstinent. If we find that the goals are not working, we will change them. We will do whatever we can to make sure that your treatment goals are the ones that will help you to be abstinent. How does that sound?

After introducing the concept of graphing, the therapist should show the client a graph of the client's abstinence to date, based on urinalysis and/or breathalyzer results. This graph should be filled out prior to the session.

What I've done here is I've made a graph of your days abstinent so far in the time that we've been working together. On this side of the graph is the number of days that you've been abstinent, and down here on this part of the graph is the number of days that you have been in treatment. This line shows that you've been substance free for 3 days now, which is really terrific. I'm going to keep recording your urinalysis results on here so that we can watch this line continue to go up and up. You reported that heroin is the drug that you are struggling with and that you have not used other substances in many years, so we are targeting heroin. However, if that changes, please let me know so that we can update your graph to include any substance with which you are struggling.

One of the things that will be really important for you is to find ways to fill your time that are enjoyable and that do not involve drugs. You told me that you enjoy watching movies and sports, going to dinner at your sister's, and playing board games. What I would like to do is to set engaging in these recreational activities as a goal for you to work on each week. Engaging in more rewarding activities will help to keep you drug free. We talked about a goal of two recreational activities per week for you. Does that goal still seem reasonable?

Here is a recreation graph. You will see that it says "Weekly Recreational Activities" at the top. I will ask you each week what activities you have done so far, and then we will fill in each activity here. So, let's say for Week 1, you engaged in four recreational activities, I would draw a bar to the number 4, and then I would fill in the types of recreational activities you are doing. You will have a goal line like this (draw line at 3) to remind us of what your goal is. When you meet or exceed your goal, I will mark your success on the graph with a sticker or a note.

Do you have any questions about the recreation goal? When do you think you can schedule some recreational activities this week? [Discuss and engage in problem solving to find ways of making recreational activities fit into the client's schedule.] So, next week, I will ask you about your progress on your recreation goal, and I will fill in the graph with you.

To introduce job goals, the therapist might continue with the following (for more information on employment as a treatment goal, see Chapter 4, this volume):

Another important way to fill your time so that you are not tempted to use drugs is to get a job that you like. You told me that one of the big reasons that you did not use much last year was that you were working regularly, but that when you lost that job your substance use got worse. So you can see how steady employment can really help to structure your time so that you are not as tempted to use. Of course, getting a job has lots of other benefits too. It's likely to make you feel good about yourself and give you the opportunity to afford things that you want, like a nicer apartment or a car. We're going to be talking quite a bit about developing your employment skills, and I'm going to help you do that in any way that I can. We discussed that a goal for submitting three job applications per week is reasonable for you. What do you think about that goal? So, similar to the recreation graph, I will fill this graph in each week so that we are monitoring how you are doing. We also will work with you individually and in group to help you get employment. Do you have ideas for where you can apply for jobs next week? [Discuss ideas with the client. The client will also be attending Job Club, so specific recommendations for job searching will be provided at this time, if they have not been already.]

Also, you told me that last year when you were able to quit using for so long you also were attending NA meetings regularly. It sounded like going to those meetings really helped you to stay abstinent and that you felt you were also contributing something back. We agreed that daily NA attendance would be something that would make it much more likely that you can be successful now. We know that past successes are really good predictors of future successes, so I could not agree with you more that this is a smart decision on your part. Do you know where the meetings are near your house, and what times they meet? [Discuss logistics; provide the client with information; and engage in problem solving to get the behavior started if necessary.] Starting next week, we will record here your daily attendance at NA. If you are attending daily, the graph should go up to 7 here.

Each of the remaining goals and graphs is discussed in the same fashion—with a summary of the purpose for the goal (i.e., how the goal will help the client initiate or maintain abstinence), the frequency of the behavior expected, and how the graph will look when the behavior is recorded. After the essential goals and graphs (i.e., days abstinent, NA and AA [Alcoholics Anonymous], recreation, and job) have been discussed and agreed on, the therapist can discuss with the client other important goals that are unique to the individual.

TELLING THE STORY OF THE CLIENT'S PROGRESS IN TREATMENT: ONGOING BEHAVIOR GRAPHING

After the initial session in which the graphs are explained to the client, the follow-up reviews are focused on "telling the story" of the client's progress. Although each graph is reviewed and updated individually, the set of graphs, collectively, represents this story. The following is a script for how the graph might be reviewed with the client to most effectively present his or her progress and reinforce any successes.

> You have been in treatment for just about a month now. We have reviewed your progress on each of your treatment goals. I would like to take a moment to pull together the information further by summarizing what has happened during the past month. [The same activity should happen on a weekly basis as well.]
>
> You tested positive for about the first week of treatment, and you indicated that this was a rough period for you because you were still feeling withdrawal symptoms and adjusting to treatment. But you came to treatment nearly every day—more than you had to—but as often as you needed. Your attendance has been excellent for the entire first month of your treatment. You are here 4 days per week, and you stay for at least two groups on those days. There was only 1 day when you did not attend because you were sick, and you called me to let me know about that. Your first week of treatment, you also started attending NA. You went to one meeting that first week, but since that time you have attended NA almost daily—at least five times per week. You have been working hard on getting a job, even though it is a rough market right now. You have always submitted three applications a week, and many times you have exceeded that. One week you submitted nine job applications. You have worked really hard on this goal, and I commend you on your efforts. You have an upcoming interview, which is the result of all of your hard work. You also have been engaging in recreational activities on a regular basis, at least two times a week on most weeks. Mainly you have been watching movies with your girlfriend and going to your sister's. You also have started to do some recreational activities with your children, like going to the park, which I know means a lot to you. Last, you have been attending church every Sunday with your aunt. Our initial goal was for you to attend church on Wednesday and Sunday, but we adjusted that because the Wednesday meetings were not what you expected. But you go to church each Sunday, and that has meant a lot to you because you see spirituality is such an important part of your recovery. Your efforts in each of these areas—your regular attendance here, your participation and contribution to NA, your engagement in recreational activities (especially the time with your sister and your kids), your efforts toward meaningful employment, and your involvement at church—all have contributed to one really important goal, abstinence. There is a reason why this graph [refer to abstinence graph] looks so good for the past 3 weeks. It is because these other goals are being met. What do you think about the connections I am making? [Discuss the connection between the client's positive behaviors and abstinence. Explore what would happen if any of the abstinence-related goals were to drop off—What do you think would happen if you stopped doing these things?]

CONCLUSION

Goal graphing is an important clinical tool for making treatment goals salient and concrete for the client. Goal graphing also allows the therapist to reinforce client success, to predict relapses, and to intervene early to avoid relapses. Though behavior graphs are widely used in behavioral treatments, they are rarely used in substance abuse settings. Given the ability of graphing to allow for greater monitoring of important treatment goals, we feel that graphing holds intuitive appeal for clinicians who often struggle with getting clients to focus on measurable goals and to stay on task with treatment. Graphs demystify the reasons for drug use. Graphs also serve to accentuate the positive gains that clients make while in treatment by providing a consistent framework during which therapists routinely evaluate the progress that client's make (which often includes some successes as well as setbacks or difficulties). One barrier to implementation of behavior graphs may be that graphs require a skill set that is not widely emphasized in counselor education programs. Behavior graphs may, on first impression, appear to be data tools rather than clinical tools. Truthfully, the technique of graphing behavior does take time to master, and clinicians and supervisors must be diligent in implementing this technique for it to be effective (i.e., behavior graphs that are infrequently reviewed are not likely to have an impact on behavior). However, with consistency and diligence, clinicians can become proficient in behavior graphing, and once this skill is acquired it becomes an indispensable tool with clear benefits to therapist and client alike.

6

CONTINGENCY MANAGEMENT TO IMPROVE TREATMENT OUTCOMES

The primary objective of Reinforcement-Based Treatment (RBT) is to shift contingencies in the individual's environment such that non-drug-using behaviors (e.g., spending time with friends and family, employment) are more reinforcing than drug use. Although this objective appears simplistic, a host of interventions are needed to make this shift in environmental conditions. Contingency management (CM) is an essential component of RBT for reinforcing abstinence and abstinence-related behaviors (e.g., attending treatment, accomplishing treatment goals). CM is "the systematic delivery of reinforcing or punishing consequences contingent on the occurrence of a target response, and the withholding of those consequences in the absence of the target response" (Higgins, Heil, & Lussier, 2004, p. 444). The goal of CM techniques is to provide incentives—typically in the form of gift certificates or other items of monetary value—following the occurrence of specific target behaviors (e.g., drug-negative urine samples), thereby reinforcing the likelihood that the behavior will reoccur.

The use of contingencies (i.e., reinforcement and punishment) is common practice in substance abuse treatment. Examples of contingencies include take-home methadone doses for individuals who meet specific behavioral targets (typically a certain period of abstinence), certificates of achievement, prize ceremonies or celebrations, decreases in methadone for poor attendance or drug use, stepped-down requirements for group attendance following a particular threshold, and discharge from the program for rule violations or noncompliance. Although contingencies often are used in treatment programming, well-designed and systematic motivational incentive programs with well-thought-out contingencies, appropriate documentation, and consistent application remain uncommon in substance abuse treatment. Fortunately, dissemination efforts spurred by dedicated academicians and practitioners, with the support of the National Institute on Drug Abuse (NIDA) and the Substance Abuse and Mental Health Services Administration (SAMHSA), are making incentives more accessible and more palatable to community providers.

CM plans follow three simple guidelines (Petry, 2000):

1. The environment is "arranged" so that target behaviors (e.g., attendance, abstinence, medication taking) can be observed and measured.
2. Tangible reinforcers (incentives) are delivered when the target behavior goal is met.
3. Tangible reinforcers are withheld when the target behavior is not met.

For example, rapid drug testing (i.e., on-site drug testing that provides immediate results) is conducted three times weekly, on Monday, Wednesday, and Friday (Guideline 1). The target behavior is drug abstinence. Gift cards are provided each Monday, Wednesday, and Friday that the sample tests negative for drug use (Guideline 2). When the client tests positive for drug use, incentives are not given (Guideline 3).

These basic guidelines are a good framework for creating CM programs and for maintaining focus on the behaviors targeted for change. The use of CM in RBT has included several different types of incentive programs from paid recovery housing contingent on drug abstinence (e.g., Jones, Wong, Tuten, & Stitzer, 2005) to a constant voucher schedule for drug abstinence (e.g., Building Stronger Families application as described in Chapter 12, this volume) to low-cost lottery-style incentives for group attendance (e.g., currently being used in community program setting). We do not espouse a single type of incentive program; rather, the CM program should be evaluated on the basis of the impact it has on the target behavior(s). That is, the test of the CM program's value is whether it is effective at modifying the specified target behaviors (e.g., increasing attendance). Because many different schedules and types of CM programs are effective, including low-cost incentives, we describe in this chapter the use of CM in substance abuse treatment generally rather than focus narrowly on the use of incentives that have been used in RBT applications.

In this chapter, we review (a) the uses for CM in the context of substance abuse treatment, (b) example populations in which incentives have been studied, (c) the evidence base for using incentives (including low-cost incentives), (d) the steps for successful implementation of incentives, and (e) pitfalls to avoid when implementing incentive programs.

USES OF CONTINGENCY MANAGEMENT

More than 3 decades of research supports the efficacy of CM (also known as *motivational incentives*) for improving drug treatment outcomes, most notably increased retention in treatment and increased rates of abstinence. Motivational incentives have been used to effectively treat a wide variety of substance use disorders including marijuana (Budney, Higgins, Delaney, Kent, & Bickel, 1991), cocaine (D. H. Epstein, Hawkins, Covi, Umbricht, & Preston, 2003; Higgins et al., 1993; Silverman et al., 1998;), opiates (Bickel, Amass, Higgins, Bager, & Esch, 1997; Preston, Umbricht, & Epstein, 2002), alcohol (Petry, Martin, Cooney, & Kranzler, 2000), cigarette smoking (Heil, Tidey, Holmes, Badger, & Higgins, 2003; Roll, Higgins, & Badger, 1996), supplemental benzodiazepine or cocaine use while on methadone (Silverman et al., 1996; Stitzer, Iguchi, & Felch, 1992), stimulants (Petry et al., 2005), and polysubstance use (Carroll, Sinha, Nich, Babuscio, & Rounsaville, 2002; Downey, Helmus, & Schuster, 2000).

In addition to drug abstinence, behaviors targeted for incentive programming include attendance in treatment (Stevens-Simon, Dolgan, Kelly, & Singer, 1997), activities related to the client's treatment plan (e.g., discrete activities such as filling out job applications or attending medical appointments; Kadden & Mauriello, 1991), and compliance with medication (Grabowski et al., 1979; Liebson, Tommasello, & Bigelow, 1978). Other potential targets include completion of a certain threshold criteria (e.g., attendance at a full day of treatment), coming to group on time (punctuality), engagement of significant others in treatment, and group participation, to name a few.

PROGRAM VARIATIONS

The types of incentives provided in studies of CM have included vouchers or gift certificates, cash (Rosado, Sigmon, Jones, & Stitzer, 2005), clinic privileges such as methadone take-home doses (Stitzer et al., 1992), employment (Silverman, Wong, Umbricht-Schneiter, Montoya, Schuster, & Preston, 1998), housing (Jones et al., 2005; Milby et al., 1996), refunds or rebates (for clinic fees; L. H. Epstein & Wing, 1984), payment of bills or rent (Gruber,

Chutuape, & Stitzer, 2000; Katz, Gruber, Chutuape, & Stitzer, 2001), and participation in program-sponsored activities such as recreational outings (Jones et al., 2005). See Petry (2000) for a comprehensive review of the types of incentives used in CM interventions.

A variety of methods have been used for distributing incentives. The *fishbowl* technique, developed by Nancy Petry, was specifically designed to reinforce target behaviors while minimizing costs (Petry, Martin, Cooney, & Kranzler, 2000). A client who has met a target behavior (e.g., attendance at treatment, drug abstinence) draws from a bowl containing slips of paper representing prizes with an assigned monetary value, such as no value (e.g., a "good job" slip or affirmation), small (e.g., $1–$5), medium (e.g., $5–$20), large (e.g., $20–$50), and jumbo (e.g., $75–$100) amounts. The dollar amounts assigned to these designations (small, medium, large, jumbo) are example ranges; however, the amounts used for these designations vary as determined ahead of time by the program. The fishbowl technique serves two important purposes: (a) to reward the client immediately for emitting a target behavior and (b) to contain costs by using simple probability (e.g., costs are contained because a prize is not given each time a draw occurs).

The fishbowl technique also uses an intermittent schedule of reinforcement rather than a continuous schedule of reinforcement. This intermittent schedule means that behaviors are reinforced only a portion of the time that they are emitted (intermittently), whereas a continuous schedule of reinforcement means that the behavior is reinforced each time that it occurs. Behavior that is reinforced intermittently persists more readily when generalized to reinforcers in the natural environment (Martin & Pear, 1998), thus adding another benefit of the fishbowl technique.

RESEARCH SUPPORT FOR CONTINGENCY MANAGEMENT

CM is one of the best-studied and efficacious interventions for treating substance use disorders. Higgins, Wong, Badger, Haug Ogden, and Dantona (2000) randomized 70 individuals to receive either abstinent contingent incentives or noncontingent incentives in addition to counseling based on the Community Reinforcement Approach (CRA). The abstinent-contingent condition had higher rates of continuous cocaine abstinence (42%) compared with the non-contingent condition (17%).

In another study comparing abstinent-contingent incentives versus noncontingent incentives, Silverman et al. (1996) randomly assigned 37 cocaine-abusing methadone clients to receive (a) an escalating voucher schedule (amount earned increased with each consecutive negative urine sample) contingent on submission of cocaine-free urine specimens or (b) vouchers noncontingent on urine toxicology results. Individuals in the two conditions earned similar numbers of incentives. However, the contingent group had significantly more continuous abstinence compared with the noncontingent voucher group. Of the contingent voucher group, 47% maintained at least 6 weeks of continuous cocaine abstinence compared with 6% in the noncontingent group.

Higgins et al. (1994) in a 24-week study randomly assigned 40 cocaine-dependent individuals to one of two treatment conditions: (a) the CRA or (b) the Community Reinforcement Approach With Vouchers (CRA-V) earned during Weeks 13 through 24. Individuals receiving the CRA-V condition were retained in treatment at 24 weeks significantly longer than the CRA-only group (75% vs. 40%). The duration of continuous cocaine abstinence also differed (average of 11.7 weeks in the CRA-V group vs. average of 6.0 weeks in the CRA-only group).

In a study of the magnitude of reinforcement, Silverman, Chutuape, Bigelow, and Stitzer (1999) examined a population of methadone participants ($N = 29$) who had failed to achieve sustained cocaine abstinence prior to study enrollment. Participants sampled three incentive schedules, each for a period of 9 weeks, a zero-earning condition, a low-magnitude condition (maximum earnings $382), and a high-magnitude condition (maximum earnings $3,480). Analyses of outcomes for participants who were retained for all three conditions ($n = 22$) showed that the high-magnitude schedule significantly increased rates of cocaine abstinence. Nearly one half of the participants in the high-magnitude condition achieved 4 weeks of sustained cocaine abstinence, whereas only one participant in the low-magnitude condition and none in the zero-magnitude condition achieved more than 2 weeks of continuous abstinence.

Petry et al. (2000), in a study of 42 alcohol-dependent individuals, showed that participants who received incentives in addition to standard treatment (12-step-oriented groups, relapse prevention, coping-skills training, daily planning, recreational and vocational training) were more likely to be retained in treatment at 8 weeks than those who received standard treatment only (84% retention in incentive group vs. 22% in the community-treatment-only group).

CONTINGENCY MANAGEMENT IN COMMUNITY SETTINGS AND FEDERAL INITIATIVES TO EXPAND IMPLEMENTATION

Unfortunately, the results of trials examining CM are largely unknown to practitioners. Additionally, the costs associated with many incentive programs (the magnitude of reinforcement used) are prohibitive for community treatment providers. Community providers are in need of low-cost methods for engaging and retaining clients in treatment. Although some studies have shown low-cost incentives to be effective (for a review, see Petry et al., 2000), large-scale studies were needed to further evaluate lower cost methods for reinforcing positive treatment outcomes. To this end, NIDA funded a large scale study, Motivational Incentives for Enhanced Drug Abuse Recovery (MIEDAR), to evaluate the potential benefits associated with the use of low-cost incentives in a sample of 800 stimulant abusers. Petry et al. (2005) examined a subsample of stimulant abusers (methamphetamine or cocaine) from the MIEDAR study ($n = 415$) assigned to one of two groups: usual care or usual care plus motivational incentives. The fishbowl method for distributing incentives was developed in an effort to contain costs and to improve the generalizability of study findings to community settings. Study results indicated that, on average, participants who received incentives were retained in treatment longer than those participants in the usual care group and achieved longer durations of continuous abstinence—49% of the incentive group was retained at the end of the 12-week study period compared with 35% of the usual care group. On the measure of continuous abstinence, nearly 19% of the incentive group maintained abstinence throughout the study period (12 weeks of continued abstinence) compared with approximately 5% of the usual care group (Petry et al., 2005).

Based in part on the MIEDAR study findings, NIDA, SAMHSA, and the associated Addiction Technology Transfer Centers have spearheaded an awareness campaign, Promoting Awareness of Motivational Incentives, to educate clinicians, providers, and policymakers about the benefits and logistics of implementing motivational incentives. The Promoting Awareness of Motivational Incentives website (http://www.nattc.org/pami/pami_home.html) contains valuable information including slides on motivational incentives that review the history of incentives, the research support for the approach, and the mechanics of implementing incentive programming. Programs and/or practitioners interested in using CM now have an impressive amount of information and resources available to assist them. The use of these resources, along with formal training, will enable practitioners to implement the approach most effectively.

BASIC STEPS TO FOLLOW WHEN IMPLEMENTING AN INCENTIVE PROGRAM

The following is a summary of the key steps used when designing and implementing CM. This information is taken largely from the slides developed by the blending initiative of NIDA and SAMHSA, "Promoting Awareness of Motivational Incentives: Successful Treatment Outcomes Using Motivational Incentives" (available online at http://www.nattc.org/pami/presentations.html), and an unpublished chapter by Kellogg, Stitzer, Petry, and Kreek (n.d.). Optimally, programs will develop incentive programs that explicitly address each of the following principles prior to implementation. A written procedure that addresses each of the principles will be most useful so that there are clear instructions and guidelines for staff implementing the procedures and so that clients can receive clear information on what to expect. Another benefit of written procedures regarding each of the principles is that if the incentive programming performs poorly, program staff can evaluate the protocol and determine which of the principles was not followed or which procedures were not well designed.

Identify the Behavior That Needs to Be Increased

The target behavior is the focus of the written or unwritten behavioral contract between the provider and the client. This behavioral contract outlines what changes need to occur in the target behavior and what incentives will be provided when the change occurs (Petry, 2000). The demands placed on the client's behavior need to be explicit, understandable, and mutually agreed on to optimize success. A very important consideration regarding target behaviors is the level of difficulty involved with emitting the behavior. An understanding of behavioral principles is very useful when making this determination because behavioral demands that exceed an individual's abilities are unlikely to succeed. For example, in a population of methadone clients in the first week of treatment, medication taking might be a more attainable goal than abstinence (reinforcement can be used to increase medication taking, and compliance with medication is associated with increases in abstinence).

Choose the Group or Subgroup That Will Receive the Incentive Program

Programs with limited financial resources designated for incentives may choose to target a specific subgroup in particular need of incentives. This approach is cost saving and also acknowledges that behaviors that occur naturally do not need additional reinforcement. Examples of target groups include those first entering treatment (to reduce early dropout); individuals with whom the treatment has not been successful either initially or in past treatment episodes, including individuals who use multiple substances (e.g., cocaine in addition to methadone, benzodiazepines) or a substance for which there are not medications available to treat the disorder; individuals with comorbid psychological and medical disorders; and particularly high-risk populations (IV drug users, pregnant women). It is also important to consider groups that are at critical time points in treatment when dropout or risk of relapse may be higher (e.g., early treatment, transition from intensive outpatient to outpatient, at the 90-day mark).

Choose the Reinforcer That Will Be Used

The choice of the incentive that is used in the contingency program is a key element in the success or failure of the program. To have the most impact on behavior, incentives need to be items or privileges that a client actually values. The best way for determining the types of incentives that will be effective is to ask clients. Client surveys that assess the desirability of various incentives are useful for this purpose. Surveys can include check off boxes or rankings (e.g., "Please number the following incentives in order of preference with 1 being the *most desirable* and 10 being the *least desirable*") as well as open-ended questions to assess items that program staff have not considered (e.g., "Please list other ideas you have for incentives").

The most frequently used types of incentive programs include

- contingent access to clinic privileges (e.g., access to recreational activities are contingent on submission of a drug-free urine sample);
- on-site prize distribution (e.g., prizes are immediately available for distribution at the time the behavior is emitted); and
- token economy systems in which tokens, cards, or points are earned and then exchanged for prizes at a later time (e.g., after the client has earned five tokens, the tokens can be exchanged for a prize from the prize cabinet).

Exhibit 6.1 lists 50 low- or no-cost incentives that could be used.

Determine the Value of the Incentive

The magnitude of the incentive chosen should be consistent with the level of demand being placed on the client's behavior. The question to ask is, What magnitude is necessary to increase the target behavior? The answer depends largely on how difficult the target behavior is to emit. Programs and practitioners must bring their clinical and programmatic knowledge to the forefront when making this determination. For example, presume that the target behavior is total drug abstinence in a population of polysubstance users, a group with whom your program has had little success. If the incentive for 1 week of abstinence is a draw from the fishbowl at the end of the week, the magnitude of this incentive appears inconsistent with the demand on the behavior. In other words, it does not seem, at face value, that a chance to earn a prize would have much of an impact on daily drug use in polysubstance users. The magnitude appears insufficient to compete with drug use. A more competitive reinforcer magnitude for this population might be $10 per day per negative urine sample submitted. Stitzer et al. (1984) provided some considerations

EXHIBIT 6.1
Ideas for 50 Low- or No-Cost Incentives

1. Gift certificates to restaurants, online outlets, or stores or for services (e.g., manicures)
2. Tickets to events or activities (e.g., zoo, movies, bowling, museums)
3. Tokens that can be traded in for prizes
4. Key chains with designation of target behavior (e.g., 30 days abstinence)
5. Mugs
6. Photo frames
7. Journals and books
8. Alarm clocks
9. Calendars and planners
10. Stuffed animals
11. Toiletries
12. Fishbowl distribution of tickets that are exchanged for small, medium, or large prizes
13. Assistance in paying for driver's license fee
14. Family portrait (taken on-site or gift certificate for professional photography services)
15. Pizza party at treatment program (or off-site)
16. Movie night at treatment program
17. Donated toiletries
18. Donated cosmetic makeover session
19. Candy with affirmation slip
20. Clothing closet (client can pick from donated items that are new or like new)
21. Designation as on the "A-list" with particular clinic privileges (i.e., facilitates portion of the group)
22. Bus tokens
23. Meal tickets to on-site cafeteria
24. Arts and craft supplies
25. Food snacks
26. Spa day at low-cost programs (e.g., massage school)
27. Certificates of achievement
28. Inspirational stones
29. Disposable cameras
30. Medallions (with program contact phone numbers)
31. Special privileges at the clinic
32. Scrapbooking workshop
33. Membership to a gym
34. Children's books
35. Moving in kits (for clients who are moving to new housing)
36. Board games
37. Community donations
38. Dollar store items
39. Ceremonies
40. Candles
41. Magazine subscriptions
42. Take-home methadone
43. Privilege of first in line for lunch or other service at the clinic
44. Privilege of extra computer time at the clinic
45. Participation in recreational activities

(continues)

EXHIBIT 6.1
Ideas for 50 Low- or No-Cost Incentives   *(Continued)*

46. Lessons at the clinic or in the community (e.g., computer skills training)
47. Help with bill payments
48. Positive letter from program staff to probation or court (documenting progress in treatment)
49. Congratulation cards signed by staff commending client for meeting target behavior
50. Stickers (good job, A +, etc.)

when determining the magnitude of the incentive needed. These considerations include (a) the level of drug use; (b) the client's treatment history, specifically, his or her history of successes and failures; (c) the presence or absence of antisocial personality disorder; (d) the nature and vitality of the client's social networks; and (e) the client's personal responsiveness to reinforcements for behavior change.

Determine the Frequency at Which the Incentive Will Be Given

Also known as the *schedule of reinforcement* (Kazdin, 1994; Petry, 2000), the frequency of the incentive distribution should be compatible with the target behavior and the resources available for distributing incentives (e.g., staffing, record keeping). Clinic staff must decide whether a behavior can be reinforced each time that it occurs or whether reinforcement occurs on a less frequent basis. Tokens that are redeemable for prizes may be a useful type of program for delaying incentive distribution (e.g., actual prizes) while still providing the client with a tangible symbol of success (e.g., token). In this scenario, the client still receives an incentives (the token), but staff can organize the distribution of the prizes (e.g., allowing clients to choose among prizes from a prize closet) weekly so that the distribution is more manageable.

Ensure the Appropriate Timing of the Incentive

This step has to do with how close in time the incentive is given following the emission of the target behavior. To be most effective, reinforcement needs to occur close in time to the behavior (as immediately as possible).

Determine How Long the Incentive Program Will Operate

Another consideration when implementing incentive programming is how long the program will run. This consideration must take into account the financial resources of the program as well as the duration most likely to provide therapeutic benefit to clients. Incentive programs that target the early phases of treatment may ensure that the client has the opportunity to sample what the treatment program has to offer and may allow for the development of a greater reserve of intrinsic motivation for treatment; thus, incentives may not be as needed or as valuable to clients in later phases. Another approach is to provide incentives for the entire duration of treatment.

COMMON PITFALLS IN DESIGNING AND IMPLEMENTING INCENTIVE PROGRAMS

The following pitfalls should be avoided:

- The magnitude of the incentive is not compatible with the behavioral demand. For example, a $1 reinforcer for 1 week of continuous abstinence is not likely to serve as a reinforcer for abstinence.
- The target behavior is vaguely defined or understood. For example, behavioral targets such as "attitude," "showing commitment to your recovery," or "complying with treatment plan" are not readily measurable and observable.
- The target behavior frequently changes. For example, a clinician may start with one behavioral demand (i.e., drug abstinence) and then change the goal the next week to abstinence and attendance and then change the goal again to include abstinence and attendance for full treatment days.
- The distribution of prizes is inconsistent or infrequent. For example, prizes are distributed when a staff member is available to do so, rather than on a set and time-sensitive schedule.
- Prizes are undesirable. For example, donations may not be reinforcing or useful to the client (e.g., used videotapes donated from a store that is closing, only providing baby items as reinforcers for pregnant women).
- The duration of the incentive program is inadequate (giving up too soon). For example, implementing an incentive program for a few weeks without making revisions to the program to ensure it is effective. Programs often need to be modified to ensure that the aforementioned steps are being followed and are likely to be successful when modifications are made.
- Record keeping is poor. For example, observable behaviors (attendance, abstinence) are not tracked, so that it is unclear when reinforcers are earned.

CONCLUSION

There is a strong and continually growing evidence base that CM is effective for improving substance abuse treatment outcomes. The efficacy of lower cost incentives provides justification for the use of incentives in community settings. In the context of RBT, incentive schedules have ranged from higher cost incentive schedules in randomized trials (abstinent-contingent recovery housing) to the less costly fishbowl technique used in community practice.

The efficacy of an incentive program depends on many factors. Incentive schedules and methods must take into consideration the populations being treated, the demand on behavior (i.e., incentive magnitude consistent with behavioral demand), and budget constraints. It is clear from the research on CM that a variety of reinforcers and methods can be effective. The seven principles of CM provide a guiding framework for implementing effective CM programs.

7

THE ROLE OF CASE MANAGEMENT IN SUBSTANCE ABUSE TREATMENT

Nonclinical interventions that actively and directly address barriers to the primary clinical goals of abstinence, employment, and meaningful social relationships can be broadly classified as case management services. Case management involves supporting clients to access the resources they need to function in the community and coordinating and integrating these services with substance abuse treatment (Vanderplasschen, Wolf, Rapp, & Broekaert, 2007). Examples of case management interventions include linking clients with a medical assistance program, providing clients with access to a computer to complete job applications, helping to solve a legal problem (e.g., finding locations for community service work), or planning how clients will attend treatment sessions (e.g., determining bus routes, transfers, and schedules).

Case management is a common component of substance abuse treatment programs and a central tenet of Reinforcement-Based Treatment (RBT). Although findings from empirical studies of the effectiveness of case management with substance abusing clients are mixed, a recent systematic literature review has concluded that high-quality, well-specified, and strength-based case management approaches are associated with better treatment retention and sustained abstinence following treatment (Vanderplasschen et al., 2007). Emerging evidence also suggests that the inclusion of such services is likely to be cost beneficial, at least when interventions are delivered as a part of residential treatment (French, McCollister, Cacciola, Durell, & Stephens, 2002).

In this chapter, we discuss how case management services are delivered within RBT. First, we outline a rationale for providing case management interventions by reviewing the empirical literature on the common needs of individuals presenting for substance abuse treatment and outcome studies examining the effectiveness of case management interventions. We then provide an overview of how case management interventions are delivered within RBT and how they are integrated, through the use of a sole provider (i.e., the RBT therapist), with clinical interventions. Next, we describe how to assess case management needs using formal and informal sources of information. Finally, we review the core domains of case management interventions offered within RBT, including facilitating detoxification interventions; helping clients structure their time; reaching out to members of the client's network; facilitating abstinent housing; providing job and financial assistance; and addressing the client's legal, medical, and mental health needs. We also present guidelines for task analysis (a technique for breaking complex tasks down into component parts) and maintaining program resources to facilitate case management interventions.

EMPIRICAL BASIS FOR PROVIDING
CASE MANAGEMENT SERVICES

In the sections that follow, we discuss the empirical literature related to needs of those who seek treatment for substance abuse and the effectiveness of case management interventions.

Needs of Individuals Who Abuse Substances

It is common for individuals seeking substance abuse treatment to experience multiple other life problems. For example, 28% of men and 54% of women who meet criteria for substance abuse or dependence also experience serious psychological distress (defined as having multiple symptoms of serious mental illness including anxiety disorders and depression; U.S. Department of Health and Human Services, Substance Abuse and Mental Health Services Administration [USDHHS, SAMHSA], Office of Applied Studies, 2009). In addition, 39% of adults with a substance use disorder and 75% of those seeking treatment for a substance use disorder are unemployed (USDHHS, SAMHSA, Office of Applied Studies, 2008). Even when treatment-seeking clients are employed, the majority (61%) lack any type of health insurance (USDHHS, SAMHSA, Office of Applied Studies, 2008). Health problems such as liver disease, chronic pain, emphysema, and kidney damage are common (Mertens, Lu, Parthasarathy, Moore, & Weisner, 2003), and as many as 25% of clients seeking methadone maintenance treatment are HIV infected (Puigdollers et al., 2004). Although it is difficult to determine how many clients seeking substance abuse treatment are involved in the criminal justice system, a national survey of drug treatment facilities indicates that probation officers and drug court counselors are the single largest source of referrals to treatment (USDHHS, SAMHSA, Office of Applied Studies, 2008). Homelessness and substance abuse also go hand-in-hand; approximately one half of all homeless people meet criteria for a substance use disorder (McMurray-Avila, 2001).

The legal, financial, mental health, medical, and housing problems faced by clients with substance use disorders contribute to their patterns of use and threaten the success of substance abuse treatment. Most directly, as noted in Chapter 2 of this volume, the functions of drug use may be related to these issues. For example, in the absence of adequate mental health care, a client's heroin use may function to help reduce anxiety and posttraumatic stress disorder symptoms. As another example, in the absence of stable employment, dealing (and, by association, using) drugs may function to provide income to a client. Less directly, unresolved problems in other areas of the client's life may hamper motivation for change or impede participation in treatment. For example, a client may feel there is no reason to sustain abstinence if they have (or suspect) a serious medical condition for which they cannot afford treatment. In addition, meeting the demands imposed by such problems (e.g., doctor appointments, court appearances) can threaten the client's ability to attend treatment or to engage in activities that compete with drug use.

Given the high proportion of clients who have challenging life circumstances and the negative impact these problems can have on treatment effectiveness, case management interventions to address these concerns is an essential element of RBT. Anecdotally, we have found that clients often appreciate the assistance they receive for their other life problems, which frequently feel overwhelming, more than the substance-use-specific RBT interventions. Early progress in case-management–related treatment goals is particularly effective in reducing clients' overall stress level and preventing the risk of early relapse. Attending to other life problems early in treatment also facilitates a strong alliance with the RBT therapist (e.g., I am obtaining tangible benefits from engaging in treatment) and can help prevent dropout if the client is initially ambivalent about giving up drug use.

Effectiveness of Case Management Interventions

Empirical examination of the effectiveness of case management interventions has been limited by variations in the definition of case management and the failure to specify or document the fidelity of such services within treatment studies. Studies have typically examined counselors using their own clinical judgment to provide whatever assistance they feel the client needs, with no manualized guidelines regarding the type, amount, or frequency of case management services or the relative emphasis that should be given to these versus core clinical interventions. Without good documentation of the type, intensity, or quality of the case management interventions delivered, it is difficult to determine empirically whether such interventions are helpful. This variability in case management interventions is the likely reason for conflicting evidence regarding its effectiveness in promoting positive substance abuse treatment outcomes (Vanderplasschen et al., 2007).

Several initiatives have attempted to better specify case management interventions and to set practice guidelines for delivering such services (e.g., National Association of Alcoholism and Drug Abuse Counselors, 1986; National Association of Social Workers, 1992; USDHHS, SAMHSA, Center for Substance Abuse Treatment, 1998). From this work, four general approaches to providing case management services have been identified: the *brokerage or generalist model*, the *assertive community treatment* (ACT) or *intensive case management model*, the *clinical model*, and the *strength-based model*. The brokerage model is the least studied of all the models but is the most common type that occurs in practice settings. In this model, case management interventions are usually limited to a relatively small number of sessions during which a counselor identifies the client's needs and arranges for ancillary services for the client (setting up appointments, giving clients lists of resources). Staff persons providing case management services tend to be different from those providing clinical interventions. In ACT or intensive case management, counselors work in teams to provide many services to clients, including outreach for engagement and treatment retention, skills training and coaching (e.g., interviewing), and crisis intervention (e.g., after hours on-call support). As the name implies, clinical case management integrates psychotherapeutic interventions with brokered services. In this model, the therapist responsible for the client's substance abuse treatment also delivers case management interventions, and each contact with the client involves aspects of both treatment aims. Finally, in strength-based case management, the primary emphasis is on the emotional support the counselor provides to the client to be self-directive and to use primarily informal support networks (e.g., family, neighbors) to get needs met. This model also emphasizes client advocacy and empowerment, encouraging clients to assert their rights when interacting with public systems.

Vanderplasschen et al. (2007) conducted a systematic review of the case management intervention literature as it pertained to substance abuse populations and outcomes, classifying the model of case management examined in each study as fitting one of these four categories. The review consisted of

48 empirical studies dating from 1993 to 2003 and examined the relative effectiveness of each model on a range of outcomes (e.g., retention in substance abuse treatment, diversion from more intensive services such as inpatient hospitalizations, substance use). Vanderplasschen et al. concluded that there was no evidence that case management delivered using the brokerage model is effective on any outcome of interest, whereas there is at least some evidence that each of the other three models can positively affect treatment outcomes. Specifically, case management that uses an ACT, clinical, and/or a strength-based approach is associated with better treatment retention, increased use of community-based supportive services (e.g., legal aid or outpatient health clinics), avoidance of "deep end" services such as inpatient hospitalization, and abstinence following treatment. The impact of case management on abstinence appears to be mediated by improved retention in broader treatment services, suggesting that case management in the absence of traditional therapeutic interventions is insufficient to achieve substance abuse outcomes.

Vanderplasschen et al. (2007) concluded that across categories, the characteristics of case management that are associated with more positive outcomes include (a) intensive training of staff in case management interventions; (b) effective communication between case management and clinical staff, such as having a shared treatment plan and frequent team meetings whenever different counselors provide these services; (c) regular supervision of staff regarding case management issues; (d) provision of administrative support to clients for case management needs (e.g., bus tokens, supplies); and (e) use of protocols and manuals specific to case management interventions. These recommendations, based on the empirical literature, confirm and expand on best practice guidelines set forth by the Center for Substance Abuse Treatment's Consensus Panel on Case Management (i.e., representing practitioners and administrators working in the area of substance use disorders from treatment programs, the criminal justice system, and child welfare agencies around across the country; USDHHS, SAMHSA, 1998).

CASE MANAGEMENT WITHIN REINFORCEMENT-BASED TREATMENT: AN OVERVIEW

Case management interventions within RBT contain aspects of the clinical, ACT, and strength-based models. Although RBT goes far beyond the brokering of services for clients, it is similar to clinical case management models in that clinical and case management interventions are delivered by a sole provider and are highly integrated. RBT therapists themselves provide all case management interventions during individual counseling sessions and during the group-based components of RBT (e.g., during Job Club; see Chapter 4, this volume). In this regard, RBT differs from most substance treatment programs in which case management interventions typically are delivered by separate staff. This structure for the provision of case management is possible because RBT therapists hold low(er) caseloads (i.e., no more than 15 clients each in outpatient RBT).

We have found the single unified provider approach to be the best model for the provision of case management interventions for several reasons. First, in our experience, the other life problems faced by clients with severe substance abuse problems are so complex and interconnected with their drug use that a highly integrated approach is necessary for achieving abstinence. The use of a single RBT therapist (supported by the other therapists on the team) to deliver all model components provides the best possible integration. The therapist knows all of the issues the client faces, how they interrelate, and how best to prioritize needs across areas. Second, because the therapist is highly skilled in clinical techniques such as motivational interviewing and cognitive restructuring, he or she is well suited for addressing any ambivalence about change that the client may experience regarding a case management issue (e.g., making an appointment with a mental health care provider) or intervening with distortions that interfere with progress on case management goals (e.g., "taking antidepressants means that I am crazy"). Finally, clients themselves seem to prefer an integrated approach. They do not make distinctions between the various needs they are experiencing and appreciate having a single point of contact for all of their concerns and goals. Not having to repeat their story to numerous individuals also reduces client frustration.

Like the ACT model, RBT case management is intensive (i.e., a large portion of treatment time is devoted to case management interventions), comprehensive (i.e., addresses all broader life needs), uses many outreach techniques (e.g., going to the client's home when sessions are missed), and emphasizes directive client skill building in various areas (e.g., how to fill out a job application or set up a bank account). In addition, RBT case management incorporates aspects of strength-based models, such as a strong therapeutic relationship with the client, a focus on client self-sufficiency, and use of natural supports (e.g., family sponsor, nonusing peers) whenever possible. As with the delivery of the clinical interventions described in other chapters of this volume, all case management interventions are delivered using a nonconfrontational motivational stance, and goals are set in full collaboration with the client on the basis of the client's broader treatment goals.

In the following sections, we further discuss the integration between case management and clinical interventions within RBT and how to provide case management so that client gains are sustained after treatment is completed.

CHALLENGES OF INTEGRATING CASE MANAGEMENT AND CLINICAL INTERVENTIONS

As noted, integrating clinical and case management interventions has numerous advantages. However, this approach also presents several challenges, including developing therapist case management skills and maintaining sufficient intensity of both treatment components.

Therapist Skill Level

Therapists working within a standard outpatient substance abuse treatment setting are unlikely to have much knowledge of or experience in delivering case management interventions, given that this topic often is not a focus of graduate training programs in psychology and or even in clinical social work. Accordingly, without agency-provided training and ongoing supervision specifically around case management issues, therapists are likely to do what they know best (i.e., provide clinical interventions) with clients and avoid case management components, which often are less straightforward. (Although, occasionally, we have seen therapists who lack confidence in their clinical skills gravitate toward providing only case management support.) Therapists who know they are supposed to provide case management interventions but who are inexperienced in doing so also are unlikely to go beyond merely brokering services (e.g., providing the client with phone numbers of mental health care providers with no follow-up).

In Chapter 9, we provide general tips for how to hire, train, and supervise therapists to maximize the effectiveness of all RBT components. Briefly, with regard to training in case management, we recommend that a 1- to 2-hr segment of initial training be devoted to this topic, using this chapter as a guide. Therapists should be clear that providing case management interventions is an essential part of the RBT model and an expectation of their position. They also should understand the importance of case management interventions for sustaining abstinence and be familiar with the range of specific interventions RBT provides (outlined subsequently). More experienced therapists can share their case management experiences with new therapists and describe how they have used structured techniques (e.g., problem-solving interventions and task analysis, which are discussed subsequently) to resolve case management issues with their clients. In weekly supervision, supervisors should ask therapists about the status of the case management needs of each of their clients, what the therapists' ideas are for helping the client meet case management goals, and whether therapists need help in resolving problems or locating resources. Supervisors also should help therapists prioritize how best to allocate session time in the upcoming week to best meet clinical and case management needs.

Sometimes therapists are resistant to providing case management interventions because they feel they are not as important as the clinical work or that such interventions are beneath their skill level (unfortunately, some graduate training programs socialize therapists in this view). Hiring therapists who conceptualize the causes of clinical problems broadly and who are skilled at maintaining a strength-based approach goes a long way to avoiding this problem. Providing consistent oversight of the case management component and pointing out the interrelatedness of the problems therapists' own clients face also is helpful. Usually, once they experience directly how unresolved broader life issues interfere with clinical progress with their own caseloads, even the most reluctant therapists come to embrace the benefits of case management interventions.

Maintaining Sufficient Intensity of Both Components

Another challenge of the integrated approach is how to allocate session time so that neither aspect of RBT is short-changed. As noted, therapists tend to have preferences for one component or the other, and prioritizing interventions should be a topic of every supervision session. Occasionally, clients themselves show strong preferences for one component or the other, which can threaten the sufficiency of each piece. For example, a client may attempt to use individual counseling sessions only for help with nonclinical problems (e.g., how to get their car out of an impound lot) and avoid the therapist's attempts to deliver clinical interventions (e.g., to conduct a functional assessment of a relapse). This behavior is understandable when a client is in crisis (e.g., facing eviction) or is experiencing multiple crises at once (e.g., the client's phone service and utilities have been cut off and his or her car breaks down). Under such circumstances, it is probably in the best interests of all to devote considerable time to case management interventions to provide more stability in the client's life so that clinical progress can occur. Failing to intensify case management interventions at such times also runs the risk of losing the client's engagement in treatment. However, if a client shows a pattern of avoidance of RBT clinical interventions, the dynamic needs to be discussed directly with the client and the likely negative effects of avoiding clinical work (i.e., that the client will not meet his abstinence goal) explored using motivational interviewing techniques (see Chapter 3, this volume).

Occasionally, clients show a strong preference for clinical rather than case management interventions. One legitimate reason this may occur is that clients truly have few case management needs (e.g., client already has a job, health insurance, and a primary health care provider) and/or they already have the skills necessary to address any broader life problems they are experiencing (e.g., although they are facing drunk driving charges, they have secured legal representation on their own). In such cases, therapists should verify that broader needs are being addressed (e.g., by inquiring with the family sponsor or probation officer) and offer the client any additional assistance they need but otherwise feel free to focus primarily on the clinical aspects of RBT. One important caveat is that even high-functioning clients can benefit from getting reinforcement from therapists for how well they are managing their broader life concerns (e.g., having the group acknowledge the client's ongoing efforts during Social Club).

If a client seems to need case management interventions (e.g., the client is clearly physically ill, does not have health insurance, and has not taken steps to address the matter) but resists working with the therapist on broader life problems, this too should be addressed explicitly with the client and new goals for addressing these concerns renegotiated as an update to the treatment plan. Usually, this pattern is one of simple behavioral avoidance—talking about or taking steps toward solving broader life problems is aversive because of feelings of shame, guilt, or fear that the problems are unresolvable. Again, use of motivational interviewing techniques (see Chapter 3) can be helpful for getting clients "unstuck" on these issues, and a task analysis approach (described subsequently) can make problems feel more manageable and give clients a small success (e.g., client makes one call to a free health care clinic) that can be built on.

Because RBT is so highly individualized (on the basis of clients' unique needs), there is no one ratio of clinical-to-case management interventions that works for all clients. Clinical judgment, in conjunction with supervision and input from other team members as to the client's needs, should always drive the proportion and sequencing of interventions. The following are some general guidelines for ensuring that case management interventions are sufficiently intensive without impinging on clinical work.

- Retention in treatment should be a primary goal of RBT. Clients are unlikely to achieve abstinence if they do not attend. When retention is threatened, case management interventions such as outreach or resolving logistical barriers to treatment should be the top priority.
- The treatment day should always begin with a drug test and provide either reinforcement for a negative screen or a functional assessment if the client has relapsed. When clients are attending treatment, case management interventions should never be prioritized over these model components. One possible exception is if the client presents to treatment in crisis (e.g., has just been evicted) and failing to attend to a case management need immediately would threaten the client's abstinence or attendance and retention in treatment.

- Whereas all clinical components of RBT (i.e., functional assessment, behavioral monitoring and graphing, motivational incentives, feedback, Job Club, and program-sponsored recreation) are administered to all clients, case management components (outlined in the sections that follow) are administered as needed on a case-by-case basis.
- Case management interventions should be intensive enough that goals are met as quickly as possible while still requiring the client to do as much as he or she is capable of doing. Developing the client's own skills to address life concerns is critical for gains to be sustained posttreatment.

Sustainability of Case Management Gains

The central dilemma of all case management services is how to make swift progress on needs identified (so that clients can better benefit from clinical interventions) while at the same time empowering clients to address concerns on their own. Drug-abusing clients often have led chaotic lives, with the primary focus being on obtaining and using drugs. They therefore may find it difficult to follow through with behaviors that lead to goal accomplishment, even if they agree that meeting these goals would be desirable. In the RBT model, the therapist is expected to actively participate in problem solving with the client and to accept some of the responsibility for ensuring that behavior change occurs. This sometimes means that goals should be pursued during the session by using the telephone or by personally accompanying clients into the community to ensure that goals are accomplished (e.g., important appointments kept, adequate progress on job search activities made, engagement in new activities). In general, RBT counselors should plan to spend about 25% of their time out of the office performing case management activities.

There is sometimes a concern that clients will become dependent on this type of help. However, it is more important that clients accomplish their goals. One good rule of thumb is for therapists to provide more structure and support early in treatment as a way of getting clients moving in a positive direction and get some early successes under their belts. Issues of dependency, if they arise, can be dealt with later by gradually withdrawing help and shaping self-efficacy. Even in the early stage, therapists should avoid fully completing tasks for the client (e.g., filling out a housing application on their lunch break) if possible and instead complete tasks alongside the client (e.g., doing the application together during a session). In addition to getting tasks moving quickly, this "doing with" approach helps the therapist to directly observe the client's skills and motivation to complete tasks as part of getting to know the client.

ASSESSING CASE MANAGEMENT NEEDS

Therapists should use a variety of formal and informal assessment tools to determine issues faced by the client for which case management interventions are warranted. Regarding formal tools, most clinic intake procedures involve gathering a lot of information about the client's living situation, health needs, and information about mental health history, all of which can point to case management needs. In addition, we recommend the use of a standardized instrument such as the Addiction Severity Index (McLellan, Carise, & Kleber, 2003). The Addiction Severity Index assesses the client's functioning and needs in numerous domains relevant to people who abuse substances (e.g., legal involvement, health needs) and can also be used to assess changes from pre- to posttreatment. Information obtained from the functional assessments of drug use (see Chapter 2, this volume) can also point to case management needs (e.g., a client's relapse was related to hitchhiking instead of taking a city bus).

Informal assessment procedures include talking with clients, family sponsors, and other people who know the client well (e.g., a probation officer) about the client's needs. Therapists should ask clients directly what goals other than abstinence they would like to pursue in treatment and explain to clients that case management interventions are a part of RBT. As noted, therapists also can determine clients' needs and skills for getting needs met by pursuing tasks with them directly in the community. For example, during an escort home following the first day of treatment, a therapist might notice that the client does not have any bedding at their primary residence or a lock on the front door. The client's behavior at group activities such as Job Club also provides insight into a client's case management needs (e.g., familiarity with and comfort using a computer).

COMMON CASE MANAGEMENT INTERVENTIONS PROVIDED WITHIN REINFORCEMENT-BASED TREATMENT

In this section, we discuss the broad range of case management interventions used in RBT. We first present interventions that are essential at the beginning of treatment, such as facilitating detoxification services, contracting for abstinence, engaging in outreach activities, and initiating day planning. Subsequently, we discuss case management techniques that are ongoing throughout treatment, such as providing job assistance and addressing medical needs.

Facilitating Pretreatment Detoxification

Some clients referred to RBT may have a need for detoxification before they can begin treatment. Detox should be suggested to any client who submits an opiate-positive urine during the first session or who self-reports regular current opiate use and has not yet experienced a detox. Many alcohol-dependent clients will require a detox as well. In our experience, clients know whether they will require a detoxification and often appreciate help procuring a bed. RBT program therapists should be highly familiar with detoxification facilities in the area and have strong working relationships with staff at these facilities.

In some cases, referrals to RBT may come directly from a detoxification facility, or RBT may be the primary aftercare intervention following the client's stay at a residential treatment facility. In these cases, we recommend that the RBT therapist make initial contact with the referred client in person at the facility itself. During the initial contact, the RBT therapist can inform the client about the program's intensive therapy schedule, obtain consent for RBT treatment, and talk with the client about plans and needs for the day of discharge from the facility.

In either scenario, when detoxification immediately precedes RBT treatment, the therapist should work with the new client and facility staff to ensure an immediate and seamless transition to the RBT program. Clients exiting residential and detox facilities are extremely vulnerable to early relapse. In a study of heroin abusers exiting a 3-day residential detox program in Baltimore, we found that 20% relapsed that same day; 50% relapsed sometime within the first week, and 80% relapsed by 10 days postdetox (Chutuape, Jasinski, Fingerhood, & Stitzer, 2001). Thus, the initial case management goal for these clients is to provide them with a highly structured new therapeutic environment immediately (i.e., on the same day) on leaving the facility to help prevent an early relapse. The RBT therapist should arrange with detox facility staff that discharge occur during regular RBT program hours and should escort the client directly to the program on the day of discharge to resume or begin intake procedures.

Clients may need help making arrangements so that they can start RBT on the day they leave a detox unit. They may need to cancel transportation previously arranged or take care of urgent business left until after the detox (e.g., checking in with a probation officer). Therapists should make every effort to problem solve these needs with the client so that he or she does not have to travel alone into the community on the day of discharge. To accomplish this goal, the therapist may have to do some tasks on behalf of the client or accompany the client as he or she completes them (e.g., go to the probation officer's office on the way to the RBT program).

Once at the RBT program, clients should receive as much treatment as possible on the transition day. At minimum, clients should receive an escort to the program and have an individual counseling session with their therapist focused on strategies for remaining drug free until the next program day and on arrangements for getting to the program the next day. In addition, depending on the time available on the transition day, clients can also be introduced to other clients and possibly even participate in group activities (e.g., Job Club or program-sponsored recreation). This protocol for the transition day places a safety net around new clients and helps them to feel a part of the RBT program as soon as possible.

Case Management Interventions During the First One to Two Sessions

Whether or not clients enter treatment directly from a detox facility, it is still important for the RBT therapist to do everything in his or her power to keep the client drug free for the first few days of treatment. Early return to drug use will dramatically increase the chances of dropout and/or greatly increase the difficulty of working with the client toward goals. Although obtaining specific information about the client's drug use behavior (i.e., through the functional assessment and other tools; see Chapter 2, this volume) as soon as possible is important so that an individualized treatment plan can be created, immediate case management needs may predominate the first sessions of RBT to minimize the risk of early relapse and to address barriers that may impede attendance to treatment. The following sections on early treatment priorities illustrate how case management and clinical tasks are especially highly integrated during these first days at the program.

Initial Abstinence Contracts

An abstinence sampling contract should be completed during the first session indicating the client's commitment to 24 hr of abstinence (for an example, see Appendix G). When this topic is broached, clients often want to set a goal of several weeks, months or indefinite abstinence (I will never use again). However, it is important to focus efforts on the short term early in treatment. That does not mean that the client's commitment to longer term recovery should be undermined; rather, the client's commitment is acknowledged and redirected to the first step toward this longer term goal. A sample way of focusing the client on initial sobriety is as follows:

> I am glad to hear of your commitment to a lifetime of abstinence. You have expressed to me that you are tired of using and that this time you want to get it right. I think that you will gain a lot from a new life without drugs. As you know, this commitment starts with one day and then one week and one month and so forth. I want to focus first on one day and then move forward with larger goals. This way we are breaking down a bigger goal into smaller parts, which is an important technique we will use throughout your treatment. One of the biggest reasons for doing this is so that the goals are manageable. Another important reason we do this is so that you can be rewarded for meeting smaller goals. We all need compliments and rewards

along the way to a larger goal. This contract, the abstinence sampling contract, requests your commitment to remain abstinent for the next 24 hours—until I see you tomorrow. So, if you can commit to that, sign here, and then we will review your success tomorrow. Do you have any questions?

In addition to this initial 24-hr contract, contracts for abstinence over longer periods and for other specific behaviors are used in RBT throughout the treatment process. More information about the use of contracts is provided in Chapter 11.

Initial Housing Plan

The RBT therapist should talk with the client about where he or she intends to stay during this first week of treatment. The role of the client's environment as a trigger for drug use should be discussed. Some clients are willing to agree not to return to a home where they have used drugs in the past during these first critical days. When this occurs, the therapist can facilitate alternative temporary housing, such as speaking on the client's behalf to family members or arranging for a stay at an emergency shelter. Other clients are reluctant to relocate, and additional interventions (described subsequently in this chapter) will be necessary. In these cases, the RBT therapist should complete an initial alternative housing plan (see Appendix H) with the client during the first session, which will be used in the event that the client cannot initiate or remain abstinent in his or her current living environment. The plan outlines where the client could stay temporarily if his or her abstinence were threatened in the current living environment.

Transportation Arrangements and Other Logistics

The therapist should ask the client how he or she will get to the RBT program the next day and discuss options with the client. At the Cornerstone Clinic in Baltimore, a program van is used to transport clients during the early weeks of treatment. Because most programs will not have such a resource, the therapist should discuss bus routes, taxi services, and rides from supportive network members as options. Any barriers to returning to the clinic should be discussed and resolved. Some other areas that the therapist should explore include (a) how the client gets up in the morning (e.g., alarm clock), (b) any questions the client has about the route of transportation chosen (e.g., which bus to take, when to catch the bus, how long it will take to get the program), (c) what time to leave the house to get to the clinic in the morning, and (d) any remaining questions about the program schedule. A verbal commitment to return the following day should be obtained.

Day Planning

After leaving the treatment program, the client will return to the natural environment in which drug use has occurred. This natural environment consists of many stimuli for drug use, cues that will be particularly hard to resist if the client experiences boredom, has mental health issues (e.g., anxiety, depression), or engages in illegal activity (e.g., drug dealing, prostitution). In this context, it is easy to understand why structured use of time is so critical during the early stages of treatment. The use of day plans can head off a potential relapse and increase the likelihood that the client will return to treatment on Day 2. A day plan is simply a calendar with time slots for all waking hours of the day (see Appendix F). In conversation with the therapist, the client fills in what exactly he or she intends to do (i.e., substitutes for drug use behavior) during all time slots on a given day. The therapist then encourages the client to keep the day plan on hand at all times and adhere to the schedule developed. This intervention helps clients to anticipate times of day when they will be particularly vulnerable to relapse and to plan ahead by having ideas for what to do to cope with cues and cravings.

The following is a sample script for introducing the idea of day planning:

> One really important thing you can do to keep from returning to drug use is to fill your time. We know this from working with many clients, most of whom tell us that boredom or downtime or not having plans is a real trigger for drug use. And that makes a lot of sense. If you have things to do that are not related to drugs, that will help you cope with urges to use. I have told you about all the things that you can do during the day when you come here to our program. Do you think it would help you to keep from using drugs if you were to come here every day? [Respond to the client's opinion about treatment, and offer alternative perspectives if applicable.] Even if you come to our program every day, there is still free time to deal with outside of treatment. I would like you to begin learning to plan your time so that you can feel you have some control over your life and the way you spend your time.
>
> We use day plans for this purpose. This is what a day plan looks like. Basically, it is just a calendar of how you are spending your time. We will complete one together for how you will spend your time tonight until you get here tomorrow. I will ask you what things you plan to do, and I will make some suggestions for things that can help to keep you on track until I see you tomorrow. How does that sound?

The focus should generally be on very concrete activities, such as spending time with family, preparing a meal, calling a friend, or showering. Often, clients do not yet have meaningful activities to include in their day plans. In these cases, the therapist should make recommendations that will supplement the client's activities. For example, the therapist should recommend that the client attend a Narcotics Anonymous or Alcoholics Anonymous meeting and get the client's commitment to sample a particular meeting on a given day and time. Spending time with a non-drug-using member of the social network is another excellent early activity to put in the day plan. These activities are likely to encourage abstinence more than watching television, sleeping, or hanging out. A well-developed day plan includes mostly tasks that reduce boredom and directly promote abstinence. Thus, the therapist should not let the client leave with a day plan that involves sleep or watching television for large chunks of the first evening home. As noted, the client should be given a copy of the day plan to take home, and a copy also is kept in the client's chart. At the next session, the therapist can talk with the client about his or her success in following the day plan and reinforce adherence to it. Having a day plan every day is critical during the first week of treatment, and this intervention can be continued or resumed at any point in RBT treatment (e.g., if the client is abstinent but having trouble structuring time to accomplish job-seeking tasks).

Escorts Home and Initial Outreach to Support Network Members

In addition to completing the day plan, we recommend that therapists escort clients home after the first day or two of RBT. For individuals who live in a private residence, the client should be asked whether it is OK for the therapist to come in and meet the person(s) with whom the client lives. When this is possible, it can be very useful to establish an early link with a potential family sponsor or other community support resource. With the client's permission, the therapist informs the community support person that the client has entered a treatment program. The individual should be told the time that the client is expected to return to the clinic the next day as well as the transportation plans. If acceptable to the client, the individual should be shown the client's day plan and specifically requested to spend time with the client during the rest of the day and evening to help him or her carry out that plan. These steps help to ensure that the client returns to treatment on Day 2. The therapist should give the community support person his or her card and ask whether it is OK to contact them again in a few days.

Ongoing Client Outreach: Interventions to Promote Treatment Attendance and Retention

Missed sessions are a serious problem because they send a warning signal that treatment engagement is weak and relapse may be imminent. When a session is missed, the therapist should use that time to initiate a vigorous search for the client. The therapist should immediately initiate a search that includes calling all known contacts and traveling to the designated safe housing location identified in the alternative housing plan. Therapists should inquire and leave messages with contact people and, if it is safe to do so, go to look for the client using information obtained from contact people regarding the client's whereabouts. The search should be continued until the client is contacted. Arrangements should be made to pick them up for a session immediately if possible or on the next day at the latest. The goal is to find the client and bring him or her into the clinic either for full treatment participation or for an abstinence reinstatement counseling session.

Facilitating Safe and Abstinent Housing

Making sure that clients have a safe place to live is a primary concern within RBT. Clients are judged to be in need of housing assistance if they (a) have nowhere to live, (b) live with other active drug users, (c) live alone or with non-drug-abusers but in a neighborhood where drugs and/or drug-using friends are readily available (e.g., the client's drug dealer lives across the hall or the dealer periodically comes by unsolicited and offers the client drugs), or (d) have used drugs in the home where they reside. The last criterion is important because as a result of classically conditioned cues, drug use will be more likely in an environment where drugs have been used before. Clients who meet any of the criteria should be encouraged to live in a recovery house as their best option for avoiding relapse in the early weeks of treatment. Alternatively, clients should be encouraged to relocate to the next best option available to them, which usually involves staying with family or abstinent peers.

The following is an example of how a therapist might approach the need for new housing with a client:

> If you have used drugs in the place where you live, that place is going to remind you of using every time you go there. However, if you were to move to a new city or even a different house, there would be fewer reminders there. At this time, you can make some important decisions that will help to determine whether or not you will return to using drugs. Living in a safe environment where drugs are not available is one of the smartest things you can do for yourself. What do you think about the idea of living in a safe environment at least for a while?

Clients may be reluctant to relocate from their current home, on either a temporary or a permanent basis, and may deny the impact of their living environment on their use. RBT therapists should provide the client with evidence for the link between the client's environment and his or her use. If the client is still uncertain, the therapist should first assess the client's ambivalence regarding moving to new housing. Is the client reluctant to move because he or she does not really have as a goal for him- or herself to remain abstinent? Is the client worried that he or she will be isolated in the new environment or will not be able to make friends? Does the client feel uncomfortable with the housing that has been identified (e.g., an African American client feels uncomfortable moving to a predominantly Caucasian neighborhood)?

Once the ambivalence is understood, the therapist can address the client's concerns directly. In general, the therapist should emphasize to the client that the new housing arrangement will greatly reduce the likelihood that the client will use substances again and that moving is something healthy that the client can do for him- or herself. If the family sponsor or other key members of the client's social support network agree with the housing plan, they can be engaged to help persuade the client to move. The therapist should assure the client that RBT staff will serve an important supportive function during the transition to new housing and will help the client get established (e.g., make friends, find work) in the new setting.

Linking Clients to Recovery Houses

Recovery houses provide a very structured and supportive environment to facilitate a client's abstinence. They require that clients be drug free to stay at the house and conduct routine drug tests to verify abstinence. They also can do random or spontaneous drug testing if use is suspected. Many recovery houses also require that clients participate in structured activities, such as attend house meetings, abide by a curfew, or attend Narcotics Anonymous meetings. Given the high level of structure and monitoring they provide, recovery housing is the preferred option for clients immediately on leaving a detoxification facility and is a good option for clients in other circumstances or at other points in treatment as well.

RBT therapists should be familiar with the recovery house options available in the community and have personal, strong working relationships with house managers. Developing these relationships requires that therapists visit homes regularly (e.g., visit each home twice a year), whether or not they have clients living there, so that they are familiar with their condition and policies. Ideally, the RBT team has a rough idea of which houses have openings at any given time and can make informed suggestions to clients as to which ones might meet their needs. If a client agrees to move into a recovery house, the therapist should be prepared to take him or her to the home following the session while the client is feeling committed to this plan.

Clients may be quite reluctant to stay at a recovery house. When such a stay is warranted given the client's pattern of use, relapses, or lack of other housing options, persuading the client to just visit the home before making his or her decision often is an effective strategy for allaying the client's fears. Therapists can take clients to visit or drive past homes before they have agreed to move in to give them a sense of what it would be like and help allay their misconceptions. The RBT therapist also can present a stay at a recovery house as a temporary option that can "buy some drug-free time" prior to the client's deciding whether he or she ultimately wants to remain drug free or work out a more permanent living arrangement. Even a brief stay (e.g., 1 week) at a recovery house can be beneficial for the client to sample abstinence in a safe, supportive setting.

Linking Clients to Other Temporary Housing

Living with extended family members (e.g., parents, siblings) is a good option for many clients with housing needs, provided that the new household is drug free and emotionally supportive of the client's recovery. RBT therapists should work with extended family members to prepare everyone for such a move and to increase the chances that the transition will be successful. Many clinical issues often need to be addressed in these circumstances, including, for example, (a) making amends for damage done by the client toward family members during the client's history of use (e.g., addressing lingering resentments about stolen money, behavior), (b) educating family members regarding signs of substance abuse, or (c) ensuring that other users (e.g., other family members) will not have access to the home.

Linking Clients to More Permanent Housing

Clients often face many barriers to permanent relocation, including financial constraints and the difficulty of finding affordable housing in drug-free neighborhoods. In addition, client reluctance to undergo a permanent move is likely to be more pronounced than when considering a move that is only temporary. In our experience, clients who agree to live elsewhere temporarily (e.g., in a recovery house, with a family member) are more open to changing their living arrangement permanently after a few weeks in the new environment than those without such a "trial run." When the RBT therapist feels strongly that continuing to live in or returning home will severely threaten the client's abstinence, the therapist should encourage the client to try an alternative environment if he or she has not already done so and should provide extensive case management assistance in locating new housing. Doing some of the legwork for the client (e.g., printing off a list of available apartments in the client's price range, investigating what housing benefits the client qualifies for) can get the ball rolling and help the client visualize what the new housing would be like.

In helping a client locate new permanent housing, it is obviously preferable that he or she move to a place that is not known for drug activity. However, even a new neighborhood that is only marginally better than the current living situation (e.g., there is some drug activity, but the client is not known to the dealers) can facilitate abstinence because the specific cues for the client's drug use (e.g., a particular dealer, a corner where drugs were obtained or used in the past) will not be present. Thus, RBT therapists should help the client find "good enough" alternative housing that is sustainable financially and should provide the client with skills for being successful in the new environment (e.g., drug refusal skills to use if drugs are offered in the new environment, not telling neighbors about his or her history of drug abuse, avoiding signaling behaviors such as gang paraphernalia or clothing with drug logos).

Providing Job Assistance

Details regarding the job assistance provided within RBT are outlined in Chapter 4. From a case management perspective, interventions provided within the context of Job Club can be supplemented to meet client's unique needs using community outreach or other interventions as warranted. For example, a client may benefit from having the therapist drive him or her to the first day of work to help reduce the client's anxiety or to ensure that transportation plans do not fall through. As another example, a therapist might telephone an associate of the client on the client's behalf (advocacy) to share the progress in treatment and request that the person be listed as a reference who can vouch for the client.

Addressing Financial Barriers

In addition to employment, clients often have other financial needs that RBT therapists can address as part of case management. When warranted (i.e., when failing to address these issues could threaten the client's abstinence or engagement in treatment), we have assisted clients in setting up checking accounts, arranging for direct debit child support payments, budgeting monthly finances to be able to afford rent on a new apartment, and filing bankruptcy proceedings. Group didactic time blocks can be used to address these topics (e.g., money management) as well, followed up with individual work with the client around his or her specific needs. Sometimes, clients may feel particularly motivated to get a financial problem behind them, such as gradually paying off an old utility bill or victim restitution monies, as a symbol of putting past problems associated with drug use behind them. Providing case management interventions in these situations is completely justified given the reinforcement value they hold for the client. Thermometer graphs (see Chapter 5, this volume) are a nice way to track and reinforce clients' progress toward such goals.

Addressing Legal, Medical, and Mental Health Needs

Clients are likely to need case management assistance in meeting their goals to improve health or mental health functioning or address legal problems. Regarding health and mental health interventions, RBT therapists should be knowledgeable about community resources such as free health care clinics and mental health care professionals who accept Medicaid. Ideally, a mature RBT program would have strong links to such resources that involve personal contacts and the ability to refer clients to specific providers. As with all case management activities, therapists should be willing to help clients access health and mental health care by providing direct support in the community to do so (e.g., accompany the client on the first visit) when necessary.

In providing case management for legal issues, one of the most important tasks is for the therapist to have a good grasp on what the client is going through and who the key players are in the client's situation. Clients may have (or need) probation officers, victim advocates, defense attorneys, child protection case workers, or legal aid case managers. Therapists should make contact with each of these individuals (after obtaining appropriate releases of information). Navigating the legal system is complex, and therapists should always offer clients help in this area, even if the client is already receiving help regarding the issue elsewhere. The RBT therapist should assume that only he or she will go the extra mile to ensure that interventions are coordinated and consistent across systems and that any inconsistencies in demands get resolved.

Facilitating Detoxification Later in Treatment

For clients who relapse to opiates or alcohol at some point after treatment is underway, clinical judgment is needed to decide whether physical dependence has been reinstated. For example, heroin use on more than 3 days per week will eventually lead to dependence. The client may be encouraged to try stopping heroin use for 1 day to see whether withdrawal symptoms appear. Those who experience withdrawal or who are concerned that they will experience withdrawal should be encouraged to return to detox. Often, clients who relapse stop coming to the clinic, so outreach efforts may be needed to contact them and offer the detox reentry option.

Clients often want to try stopping on their own before they commit to another detox. In this case, the counselor should not argue with the client. However, an alternative plan should be presented for use if the client fails to sustain abstinence on his or her own. This should be in the form of a written contract that says that the client agrees to return to a detox program if he or she fails to give an opiate-free urine by a specified date (usually within 1 week of signing). The alternative of enrolling in a methadone program should also be explored for clients who relapse on opiates.

As soon as a client has agreed to initiate or return to detox, whether immediately or after trying first to stop on their own, the therapist should begin arranging for his or her detox entry. If a returning client, the most desirable option is to have the client return to the same detoxification program from which he or she came. However, the highest priority should be given to having a bed available at the time the client is ready to enroll rather than waiting for a bed to become available in the formerly used facility. Clients should be escorted to the detox whenever possible, either from their home or from the clinic. As noted previously, clients should be escorted from detox back to the RBT treatment facility on day of discharge.

The client can reenter the RBT treatment facility as soon as he or she completes detox. If it is a redetox, the client will return to the same level of service he or she had before the detox, according to the number of days in treatment to date. However, therapists should schedule intensive (daily) contact with such clients for 1 to 2 weeks after the relapse even if they are attending on a 3-day per week schedule.

Providing Task Analysis

Task analysis is a clinical and case management tool used when clients have difficult, complex tasks to accomplish that may feel overwhelming or unsolvable. It is similar to shaping in that the steps that a client takes along the way to an ultimate goal are reinforced by the therapist. However, task analysis teaches clients to break down complex tasks into manageable components so that the client knows how to achieve a large, complex goal. Unlike the shaping technique, in task analysis the client is capable of doing all the components of the task, but does not know where to begin or how to best sequence the tasks for success. Task analysis is a way of building client's problem-solving abilities, a skill that will, it is hoped, be generalized after treatment is completed.

Clients present with complex "circular" problems all the time. For example, a client may not be able to get a driver's license until a fee is paid and she obtains a copy of her birth certificate. To get money for the fee, she needs to visit her former employer about a check that she failed to pick up that has now expired. To contact the employer, she needs a car, and so forth. Task analysis is a way to break this complex problem down into manageable components and decide where to begin. Basically, the therapist teaches the client to analyze the task to be accomplished.

Therapists should have clients describe the problem they are having or the goal they wish to achieve. Using Socratic questioning (e.g., "OK, so what do you think needs to happen first to solve this problem?") and other problem-solving probes (e.g., "Could your brother give you a ride to your employer's office? You told me that he is off of work this Wednesday; maybe you could ask him"), the therapist guides the client toward an initial plan for mastering the task. Steps should be agreed on with the client and written out in their logical order. The therapist should set a goal with the client as to when the first task will be accomplished and/or assign the task component as homework. Clients should keep a copy of their task list, and a copy should be placed in the client's chart. Once the client has successfully completed a component, he or she should be reinforced heavily for the accomplishment, and a new goal should be set for when the next component will be undertaken.

THE IMPORTANCE OF RESOURCE LIBRARIES

Given the broad array of case management support provided within RBT, clinics need to have organizational structures in place to manage information and share resources across RBT team members. These structures can take many forms, including binders and file cabinets full of written materials, bulletin boards, data spreadsheets, and website bookmarks. Clinics providing RBT should devote some resources to setting up and maintaining these resources (e.g., updating phone numbers and eligibility requirements for various programs), including staying abreast of local resources by attending resource fairs, conferences, and open houses. In addition, clinics should require that each RBT team member play a role in sharing and modifying information whenever new resources or rules are discovered.

CONCLUSION

Clients with serious substance abuse problems more often than not have numerous other life problems that interfere with engagement in treatment and sustaining abstinence over the long run. Case management services are an essential component of RBT to help clients address these problems in sustainable ways. Case management interventions are provided primarily by the client's lead RBT therapist (with the support of other RBT team members) and are highly integrated with the clinical components of RBT. These services must be intensive (i.e., comprising sizable portions of session time) and at times delivered within the client's real-world settings (e.g., home, medical clinic) to be effective. RBT therapists should not merely broker services for clients; rather, extensive problem solving, modeling, and skill building must be used to empower clients to resolve problems on their own when treatment ends.

Client dependence on case management services is less concerning than the risk that tasks critical to sustaining abstinence (e.g., getting a job, moving to alternative housing) will not occur. Therapists should do whatever is necessary to accomplish case management goals, especially early in treatment. Clients can be taught to become more independent in addressing broader life concerns during the later phases of treatment. Therapists should provide whatever types of case management support are necessary for abstinence, health, and safety to be achieved. The most common areas for case management interventions involve arranging for detoxification (when warranted), linking to family members, arranging physical and mental health care, addressing housing needs, and resolving financial and legal problems a client may face.

8

THE ROLE OF SIGNIFICANT OTHERS AND FAMILY MEMBERS IN SUBSTANCE ABUSE TREATMENT

The majority of adults who have substance use disorders report having a significant other.[1] Because significant others and family members can serve as powerful influences in either helping a client maintain abstinence from drugs or setting the occasion for substance use, Reinforcement-Based Treatment (RBT) involves these people in clients' treatment whenever possible. The involvement of the significant other can take several forms. For example, a significant other can be involved simply as a coach to support the client's behavior change. Alternatively, the significant other can be encouraged to change aspects of his or her own behavior, which may function to maintain the client's substance use behavior.

In this chapter, we review the empirical basis for involving significant others and family members in substance abuse treatment and outline common treatment considerations for this involvement. Specifically, we review how to effectively apply RBT treatment principles when working with significant

---

[1]In Reinforcement-Based Treatment, a *significant other* is defined either as a spouse, a common-law partner, or a person with whom the client is romantically and/or sexually involved and with whom there is an emotional attachment.

others who are either drug free or drug dependent. Last, we present the concept of a family sponsor of abstinence who can be enlisted to provide specific social support to clients that promotes abstinence.

EMPIRICAL BASIS FOR INVOLVING SIGNIFICANT OTHERS AND FAMILY MEMBERS

At least two lines of research support the argument that significant others and family members should be involved in clients' substance abuse treatment. First, reviews of the treatment outcome literature (e.g., E. E. Epstein & McCrady, 1998; O'Farrell & Fals-Stewart, 2003) and a recent meta-analysis (Powers, Vedel, & Emmelkamp, 2008) have established that behavioral couples therapy (BCT)—an evidence-based couples therapy intervention for a substance abuser and his or her substance-free married or cohabitating partner—produces better outcomes than individual-based treatment for alcoholism and drug abuse problems. BCT includes two essential assumptions. First, significant others can reward drug abstinence. Second, a reduction in relationship stress decreases the likelihood of substance abuse and relapse (O'Farrell & Fals-Stewart, 2006). More broadly, a second line of research highlights the critical role that social support plays in abstinence. Social support from non-drug-using individuals is a central reason why those who stop drug use without treatment are successful in sustaining abstinence (for a review, see Moos, 2007) and is a primary predictor of positive outcomes following treatment for drug abuse (Scherbaum & Specka, 2008).

A randomized clinical trial of RBT focused on the non-treatment-seeking opioid-using male partners of pregnant women enrolled in a comprehensive drug treatment program. To help maintain drug abstinence, male partners had rapid facilitation into either opioid detoxification with aftercare or methadone maintenance. Interwoven into the RBT treatment for the men was couples counseling. Results of this trial showed that compared with a usual care condition in which men received a weekly support group, the men receiving the intervention with couples counseling had significantly increased treatment retention, decreases in heroin use, increased involvement in recreational activities, less reliance on public assistance, and increased social support for their pregnant intimate partners (Jones, Tuten, & O'Grady, in press).

Similar improvements in treatment retention and drug abstinence relative to a usual care control group were found in a trial in the Republic of Georgia that focused on male drug users and their drug-free female spouses (Otiashvili, Kirtadze, O'Grady, & Jones, in press).

REINFORCEMENT-BASED TREATMENT VERSUS BEHAVIORAL COUPLES THERAPY

RBT draws on BCT principles but differs from BCT in important ways. Although a review of the theory, components, techniques and evidence-based support of BCT is beyond the scope of this chapter, it is important to note the similarities and distinctions between BCT and RBT. BCT and RBT share common assumptions that significant others can reward drug abstinence and that reducing the distress in this significant other relationship decreases the likelihood of substance use. However, unlike in BCT, in RBT the individual presenting for substance abuse treatment is the client, not the couple, and interventions that involve the significant other are solely to help the individual meet his or her treatment goals. This critical point should be emphasized to the significant other at the beginning of the first contact with him or her to avoid misunderstandings. When warranted, the RBT therapist can refer the couple to a couples therapy provider, preferably one who is familiar with substance abuse issues and who uses an evidence-based approach such as BCT. A referral to a couples therapy provider may be necessary because of the important distinctions between BCT and RBT. Another difference is that RBT can work with dual substance-using partners, whereas BCT requires one partner to be substance free. Finally, the "active ingredients" of RBT also extend beyond those ingredients of BCT, which includes a single focus on modifying spousal interactions to reduce substance-abusing behaviors.

CLINICAL CHALLENGES OF COUPLES INTERVENTIONS WITHIN REINFORCEMENT-BASED TREATMENT

Before describing how couples sessions coordinate with broader RBT interventions, two important clinical challenges involved in working with significant others are briefly discussed: (a) safety and (b) the possibility that partners may reinforce the client's drug use. These challenges can apply to couples in which one person is a drug user and the other is not as well as to couples in which both individuals are drug users.

Safety

One issue that is ever present is the need for safety and the determination of whether couples sessions are appropriate. Couples sessions should not take place unless both individuals in the couple have a voice and everyone can raise issues in a setting that provides safety during and after the exchange of communication. Thus, if there is evidence of domestic or intimate partner violence, couples therapy should in most cases be avoided. Engaging in couples therapy without first assessing the potential for violence may result in poor treatment outcomes and, most importantly, an increased likelihood of episodes of abuse. Guidelines for screening for violence can be found in *Substance Abuse Treatment and Domestic Violence: Treatment Improvement Protocol, Series 25* (U.S. Department of Health and Human Services, Substance Abuse and Mental Health Services Administration, Center for Substance Abuse Treatment, 1997).

Partner Reinforcement of Client Drug Use

The involvement of significant others is often critical for the success in treating many clients for substance use disorders. However, in the case of either type of couple (dual drug users or single drug user), the partner often consciously or inadvertently reinforces or supports the drug use. For example, the drug-free husband of a female drug-using client may have taken on additional roles in the family because of the vacuum left when his wife used drugs. The husband may want to retain control of these roles and to avoid the conflicts that arise when the wife is abstinent enough to advocate for herself and her children. When a partner becomes drug free, the relationship and communication in the couple must often change. It is normal for individuals to be fearful of such changes and ambivalent about making them. RBT has specific tools for helping partners work through those changes.

TREATMENT COMPONENTS

The following sections describe how RBT treatment principles are applied to working with significant others.

Assessment

When a client is admitted to an RBT program, one of the initial issues the therapist assesses is the social and family situation and support available to the client. As discussed in earlier chapters, one of the main treatment goals of RBT is for the client to have a strong positive social support system. The therapist queries the client to explore the family history. For example, is there a family pattern of substance use disorders and/or comorbid mental health disorders in the family members? What is the current status of relationships? Does the client have close relations with family members? Is there a significant other—spouse, romantic partner? Is there more than one close relationship of this type? Are there children and what is the status of the client's relationship with those children? The primary therapist contacts the family to orient them to the treatment process and invite their participation in it. Information about the program, the nature of addiction and the recovery process, and their family member's treatment is shared.

Atmosphere of Reinforcement

RBT creates a reinforcing treatment atmosphere. This supportive atmosphere helps drug-using partners to consider pursuing their own drug treatment by providing a model of the benefits they are likely to receive if they do so. Often, the partner lacks positive interactions in his or her own life. The reinforcing atmosphere also is very helpful for putting nonusing partners at ease with the idea of treatment for the presenting client and being involved in that treatment. The RBT therapist working with the couple will treat the client and partner with the utmost respect, caring, and positivity. The therapist will commend the client for bringing the partner and tell the client in front of the partner messages of hope and future success. The partner too will also hear words of encouragement and optimism for change. The couple is reminded that the focus of treatment will be on the here and now and is urged to not focus on why drug use occurred. When past behaviors are discussed, it is in the context of learning from them and not to inspire guilt or shame.

Ideally, when the client's significant other is drug free, he or she can be enlisted to extend this atmosphere of reinforcement for abstinence into the client's home. The therapist can provide psychoeducation to the partner regarding the fact that reinforcing abstinence-supporting behaviors is likely to be more facilitative of abstinence than punishing the client for drug use behavior (e.g., during times of actual use, when hungover). Also, the therapist can offer specific suggestions for how the partner can provide such reinforcement (e.g., specific verbal praise, a special meal) and for how to ensure that he or she is doing it contingent on targeted client behaviors (e.g., when the client attends a job interview) and accurate client information (e.g., drug testing results from the RBT program).

Functional Assessment

It is important to remember that the client is the individual whom the RBT therapist is treating. Thus, a functional assessment should in most cases be done only with the client. It is possible that the partner can help fill in the gaps or provide a different perspective on the antecedents or consequences of the client's drug use.

Goal Setting and Abstinence-Supporting Behaviors

For many couples, there is a need to establish more positive and supportive styles of communication with each other and also to develop shared recreational activities that are free of and not compatible with drug use. Often, specific goals need to be set about the avoidance of criticisms, put-downs, or other negative interactions as well as about positive supportive verbal behavior. These behaviors should be graphed at each therapist contact on the basis of the report of the client and partner. This can be a tricky issue to negotiate, and ground rules need to be set in advance to avoid arguing over the specific instances, which may derail the focus of the treatment session. Depending on the couple, it may be that the client needs to develop recreational activities that do not involve the partner. This type of recreation may be needed to strengthen the client's ability to be independent and enhance his or her self-esteem. This individualized recreation may be threatening to the partner and may take discussion and negotiation.

It also is important that the client has an employment goal. As discussed in previous chapters, maintaining consistent work behavior directly competes with drug use, increases socialization, and contributes to a sense of personal self-efficacy. The issues of identifying, obtaining, and remaining in employment have been discussed in previous chapters. In relation to couples, having the client employed may be threatening to the partner in one or more ways. For example, the partner may feel worried that the client will become financially independent and leave the partner or that the new social circle the client joins may result in the client spending less time with the partner. The hours devoted to work could also result in the partner now having to take on more of the responsibilities of the home and/or child care. Thus, the RBT therapist will need to engage the partner's support for the client's work activity and help the partner identify advantages of the client's employment to his or her own life (e.g., the partner also benefits from increased household income, the partner wants the client to stop using drugs).

Clearly a central goal of RBT is being and remaining drug free. This is likely the goal that bears the most discussion in the different ways to handle couples in which only the client uses drugs versus those in which both partners use. When a client's partner is also using drugs, it is critical to attempt to engage that person in exploring the need for drug treatment and agreeing to it. If drug treatment does not also engage the partner, the likelihood of its success for the client is reduced. The RBT therapist may need to spend some time working with the partner to identify and secure drug treatment.

For a couple in which only one individual is a drug user, the drug-free partner may be able to, with education, serve as a valuable monitor of drug behavior and help with providing support on days when the client does not attend

RBT. The many ways the drug-free significant other can help support an environment of drug abstinence are discussed in the next sections of this chapter regarding the family sponsor. For example, if the client has been diagnosed with major depression and drugs were used as a form of self-medication to alleviate depression, he or she might be prescribed an antidepression medication. The drug-free partner can help the client remember to take the medication daily and help the client keep track of and report to the RBT therapist about medication adherence. It is less likely that a drug-using partner will have the stability and consistency to perform this type of supportive behavior. Enlisting drug-free partners (also known as family sponsors and discussed in the section that follows) in the monitoring of client behavior is delicate and should only be pursued if it seems appropriate to the relationship dynamic of the couple. For example, many drug-free partners have "overfunctioned" for the relationship for many years, and treating the client like a child is a dynamic that needs to be changed. In this case, having the partner perform monitoring activities may exacerbate an already dysfunctional dynamic, foster resentment in the client, and ultimately undermine the client's abstinence. Whether or not monitoring by the significant other is established as a treatment goal, partners should be enlisted to provide consistent positive reinforcement to the client for his or her abstinence and engagement in abstinence-supporting behaviors.

ROLE OF THE FAMILY SPONSOR AND GOALS FOR FAMILY INVOLVEMENT

In this section, we outline ways to enhance the client's involvement with family members within RBT. First, we discuss the concept of a *family sponsor*, someone who, like sponsors used in Alcoholics Anonymous (AA) or Narcotics Anonymous (NA), can be called on to provide the client specific, targeted support for abstinence. This person may or may not be the significant other discussed previously. Next, we outline more general ways of helping clients to reconnect with family supports. Guidelines for helping clients access more intensive family-based services (e.g., a course of family therapy) beyond those provided within RBT can be found in Chapter 7. Issues to consider when clients are the caregivers for children and have been abusive to or neglectful of a child are discussed in Chapter 12.

Family Sponsor

The concept of having a specific sponsor to whom one can turn for support when experiencing cravings or other temptations to relapse is a central part of many substance abuse self-help programs (e.g., AA, NA). At least one study has found that clients who have sponsors have better abstinence outcomes following treatment (Johnson, Finney, & Moos, 2006). The model in most self-help programs is for group members who are farther along in their recovery from alcohol or drug addiction to serve as sponsors to those who are earlier in their recovery process. In RBT, clients select a family member to serve in this role. Family members as sponsors, by virtue of their proximity and concern, have the advantage of being able to closely monitor the client and provide consistent approval for nonuse. They also can be helpful with other tasks crucial to recovery (e.g., providing child care for the client to go on a job interview).

The family sponsor should be someone who is willing to give support (material and emotional) to the client surrounding his or her substance use issues but who disapproves of use and will not condone or enable the client's use. A drug-free person whom the client lives with (e.g., a spouse or parent) is the natural candidate for this role whenever possible. In our experience, there is almost always someone in the client's life who can serve in this role even when the client lives alone or is socially isolated. And we have rarely seen family members who are approached to be sponsors decline the role. Generally, close family members want to help loved ones who are struggling with substance abuse but are not sure what to do. The concept of a sponsor is familiar to many laypersons and provides a structure for how to be helpful. Family members also tend to feel supported themselves when approached to serve in this role. Instead of worrying about how their loved one's treatment is progressing, they can be actively engaged in the process and communicate regularly with the therapist. Also, their "expertise" on the client's situation is a resource the therapist values and incorporates into treatment planning.

Assistance Provided by the Family Sponsor

The help that family sponsors can provide clients is highly individualized on the basis of the client's needs. The following is a partial list of behaviors that may be requested of family sponsors:

- meet with the therapist and client periodically during treatment sessions;
- receive updates on the client's progress (including drug testing results) regularly from the therapist;
- provide praise and other reinforcement (e.g., a congratulatory dinner) to the client for remaining abstinent and for meeting recreational and job goals on the basis of objective information such as the program's drug testing results;
- receive phone calls and visits from the client at times when the client needs additional emotional support to stay clean (e.g., at times of cravings or other temptations);

- provide instrumental support for behaviors that support abstinence, such as driving the client to a job interview or engaging
  in regular drug-free recreational activities with the client;
- make some benefits the client receives from the sponsor contingent on abstinence, for example, allow the client to visit
  with the sponsor's children only when the client is drug free;
  and
- speak positively on behalf of the client to other family members
  and facilitate the client's connections to them (e.g., allow the
  client to meet with his estranged father at the sponsor's home).

Agreeing to a Family Sponsor

The following is an example of how the RBT therapist might request
the involvement of a family sponsor to the client:

> Another aspect of our program is the involvement of what we call a fam-
> ily sponsor, who is basically someone whom you would feel comfortable
> allowing to be involved in our work together and who can give you addi-
> tional support to remain drug free. Are you familiar with the idea of a
> sponsor in AA and NA? [discuss]
>
> Right, exactly, it is someone who is there for you not just in a general
> way but in a way that is specifically helpful in terms of staying clean. We
> think family members are great in this role because generally clients tend
> to see them a lot so they can get lots of support, and family members often
> are willing to do lots of concrete things that support abstinence, such as
> babysitting while you are on a job interview or giving you rides occasion-
> ally to our clinic.
>
> Whomever you would choose would need to be drug free, of course,
> and someone with whom you would not mind sharing some of the details
> about how your recovery is going. The person does not have to have a
> substance abuse history of his or her own. What do you think—is there
> someone in your life who you think might be good in a role like this?

Engaging the Family Sponsor in Treatment

Before approaching the family sponsor about assuming a role in the client's
treatment, the therapist should have the client sign a release of information
clearly stating that drug-screening results and other treatment information
(e.g., attendance, progress on weekly treatment goals) will be shared. Ideally,
the client also agrees to allow the therapist to contact the family sponsor to
determine the client's whereabouts or to deliver messages. As soon as the
family sponsor is identified and a release of information obtained, the counselor should request permission to call the person right there and then in the
session. In this initial phone contact, the counselor should identify him- or

herself and the program and request a meeting. A time should be specified, and the counselor should indicate that he or she looks forward to meeting the contact person at that time.

Having the client's permission for full disclosure is important for ensuring that the client does not fly "under the radar" with the sponsor (i.e., continuing to use while denying use) and for ensuring that the sponsor can provide positive reinforcement that is truly contingent on abstinence. Being honest also is important for regaining the trust of the sponsor and other family members. It is important that clients understand the rationale for full disclosure with the sponsor and the role that secrecy and lying plays in maintaining substance use patterns, drawing on examples from clients' own use history to make the point whenever possible. For example, clients often feel guilty about lying and then use drugs to escape their feelings of self-loathing. Or family members' feelings of betrayal and anger lead them to withdraw their support of clients, which, in turn, increases clients' risk of relapse.

Initial sessions with family sponsors require planning and an explicit statement that the scope of the sessions is limited to the client's use issues (i.e., that these sessions are not family therapy or couples counseling sessions). The goal of these initial sessions is to formulate an agreement between the family sponsor and the client and program that specifies that the sponsor will assist the client with meeting treatment goals. In this agreement, expectations are clarified for behaviors that the sponsor will perform to help the client remain drug free. These may include providing transportation, engaging in pleasant drug-free activities as a reward for abstinence and behavior change, offering emotional support as needed, and helping the client carry out treatment goals. The contract usually includes things that the client will do in return (e.g., remain drug free, attend treatment sessions).

An agreement also should be sought for the therapist to convey objective information about clients' progress on a regular basis and to seek information from sponsors periodically about how things are going from their perspective. Family sponsors then should be invited to attend the treatment regularly (e.g., at 1-month intervals) to check on progress and make any needed adjustments in the mutual helping agreement. The therapist should give family sponsors his or her card and encourage them to contact him or her at any time.

Goals for Family Reconnection

Unfortunately, many clients lack supportive family relationships and friendships and have social networks composed almost entirely of drug-using peers. When they stop having contact with people with whom they have used drugs, clients may find themselves socially isolated, making them vulnerable to relapse. Making new friends who do not use drugs is a critical long-term goal, addressed within RBT through individualized recreational goals that specifically target meeting new people (see Chapter 4, this volume). Also critical is helping clients reconnect to family members and improve relations with them. Family connections hold great meaning for most people and, when positive, are powerful rewards for abstinence.

The nature of the family reconnection goal is tailored to the client's situation and needs, which vary tremendously from client to client. The therapist should use his or her general knowledge of the client and information obtained from the functional assessment of the client's longest period of abstinence to assist the client in setting an individualized goal for family connection. For example, if the client indicates on the functional assessment of abstinence that during a previous period of abstinence she regularly attended church with her sister, one obvious family involvement goal would be to spend time each week with the sister, either at church or elsewhere (attending church could be an additional recreational goal in and of itself). The idea is to come up with a set of family-oriented behaviors for the client to engage in that will do all or some of the following: (a) directly compete with drug use (i.e., people tend not to use drugs while visiting their mother), (b) provide positive reinforcement for being abstinent, and (c) enhance motivation for the client to remain drug free in the future. The goals for family involvement will differ depending on individual circumstances.

Goals When the Client Has Generally Positive Relationships With Supportive Drug-Free Family Members

In this case, goals for family involvement are simple and straightforward:

- increase time spent in specific activities (e.g., going out to dinner, taking a walk) with particular people (e.g., a spouse or sibling);
- increase phone and e-mail contact with members who live farther away;
- share accomplishments with members, for example, telephone an out-of-town sibling to share the excitement of an upcoming job interview; and
- engage in behaviors that "signal" that the client is now drug free, such as inviting extended family over to see his or her new, drug-free apartment.

Goals When the Client Is Estranged From Key Supportive Family Members but Reconnection Would Be Beneficial and Is Possible

In this case, the client's substance abuse and other problematic behaviors (e.g., stealing money from a parent to purchase drugs) likely have contributed to the estrangement from family. In a supportive, constructive manner, the therapist should help the client understand how his or her behavior may have affected specific family members and engage in problem solving with the client as to what steps the client can take to reconcile with key individuals now. Possible goals under this circumstance include the following:

- write letters to family members apologizing for past inappropriate behaviors and acknowledging the effect that such behaviors likely had on the person (therapists should read drafts of letters and assist clients in revising them);
- ask the family sponsor to speak on behalf of the client to estranged family members, communicating the specific behaviors that suggest a commitment to abstinence that the client is now doing;
- develop and work toward a plan for paying back any debts owed family members (e.g., to repay money stolen or the value of property destroyed); and
- offer to help family members with their needs, for example, to assist a sibling in the care of an elderly parent.

Goals When the Client's Family Is Unlikely to Be Supportive of Abstinence

A sizable portion of clients come from families in which many members are engaged in drug or alcohol abuse or antisocial behavior. Some have experienced physical or sexual abuse from a parent or sibling or have been exploited by family members in other ways (e.g., providing money to a parent with a gambling addiction). Recommending that clients reconnect with family under these circumstances is ill-advised and could increase the client's risk of relapse. In fact, when clients have used drugs with such individuals or have family members who serve as cues for use (e.g., a brother who uses heroin and keeps paraphernalia in his house), the therapist should have the client commit to not seeing the person, using a behavioral contract for no contact (see Chapter 6, this volume).

The therapist should thoroughly explore with the client whether there is anyone at all in the family network who is a positive influence with whom the client could connect. Usually there are at least a few people in the network of extended family members who disapprove of the behavior of the deviant family members. Behavioral goals would then focus on reaching out to these individuals and getting to know them better. Alternatively, the client may need to focus on developing or nurturing close, supportive friendships or a romantic relationship that can provide the functions that are traditionally served by families of origin and extended families (e.g., people to spend holidays with, people to serve in aunt or uncle roles with the client's children).

Goals When the Client Is a Parent of Minor Children

Spending time with children can be a highly rewarding activity that competes with drug use. A common reason clients who are parents give for wanting to become abstinent is so that their children will not learn of their addiction or come to view them as "drug addicts." Thus, it often is appropriate for clients to have family involvement goals that include enhancing their relationships with their children. However, when setting behavioral goals that involve children, the therapist needs to be mindful of the child's developmental level and needs. First, it is critical that clients commit (through use of a behavioral contract) to being drug free whenever they interact with their children. Therapists also should make sure that clients understand that it is not appropriate for minor children to know the details of treatment progress or to provide support to clients regarding their substance abuse (e.g., the parent should never discuss cravings or other temptations with children). Finally, therapists may need to help clients understand that it is normal for children who have experienced negative effects from a parent's drug use (e.g., worry about the parent's health, witnessing marital conflict) to reject the parent's attempts to reconnect to them. In such cases, the therapist should recommend and assist clients in accessing family therapy services.

CONCLUSION

Most clients in substance abuse treatment have significant others, and almost everyone has at least some contact with family members or people who function like family members (e.g., a best friend who has known the client for 20 years). These individuals are important resources to use in substance abuse treatment and, if not engaged, may hinder clients' progress. Effective engagement of partners in particular, regardless of the partner's drug-using status, can optimize the drug treatment outcomes of the client. In addition to helping partners provide monitoring and reinforcement of the client for abstinence-supporting behaviors, couples sessions also can focus on improving the couple's communication styles. Partners or other family members also can be enlisted as family sponsors of the client's abstinence to provide specific support for abstinence. Helping clients increase contact and improve relationships with family members (e.g., siblings, parents) also helps reinforce abstinence in the short run and provides incentives for remaining drug free in the long term.

II

PROGRAM
ADMINISTRATION

9

TRAINING AND SUPERVISION

The decision to use an empirically supported intervention such as Reinforcement-Based Treatment (RBT) in a real-world practice setting is a laudable one. Making this commitment, however, is only a small part of what it takes to deliver the model effectively and achieve outcomes similar to those obtained in RBT clinical trials. The devil, they say, is in the details.

In this chapter, we provide guidelines for how the integrity and potency of the RBT model can be maintained through hiring appropriate staff and providing high-quality training and supervision to therapists. We first describe the professional and personal characteristics that make for effective RBT therapists and supervisors. We then provide guidelines for how to conduct initial trainings of new staff in the RBT model and the kinds of supplemental and ongoing trainings necessary for therapists to maintain and enhance skills. Finally, we discuss the purpose, structure, and content of supervision within RBT and how to provide supervision to ensure that the intensity and fidelity of the model is maintained.

HIRING

In the sections that follow, we describe the qualifications and personal characteristics that are most important in hiring and training effective RBT therapists and supervisors.

Therapist Qualifications

RBT is a complex, multifaceted intervention that incorporates the latest scientific advances in behavioral interventions for addiction. Accordingly, it is preferable for therapists who provide RBT to have a master's degree in clinical social work, psychology, or a related field. Having such a degree helps to ensure that the therapist has developed at least some basic proficiency in critical areas such as core clinical techniques (e.g., interviewing), professionalism (e.g., maintaining boundaries with clients), session time management, and treatment planning. Occasionally, a highly skilled and knowledgeable bachelor's level therapist also can deliver model components effectively. For example, an individual who has had years of experience providing case management services to substance-dependent populations may be able to implement the treatment elements with proficiency. However, in our experience, bachelor's level staff usually require quite a bit more training and hands-on instruction than those who have had didactic and supervised practicum experiences during graduate study.

Through background experiences and/or in-house training, the RBT therapist will need an in-depth understanding of the following topics to be effective with clients:

- basic drug and alcohol pharmacology (e.g., classes of drugs and their effects, drug urine detection windows),
- behavioral treatment principles and techniques (e.g., principles of shaping, rehearsing client behaviors through role playing), and
- motivational interviewing (MI) principles and techniques (e.g., the nature of client ambivalence, reflecting change talk).

Therapist Personal Characteristics

The most effective RBT therapists have the following personal characteristics:

- a belief that drug abuse is due to client learning and reinforcement histories, not personal character flaws;

- the ability to maintain a nonjudgmental stance in all clinical interactions;
- a belief that client outcomes are affected by the skill and empathy of the therapist (i.e., that outcomes are not simply the result of client characteristics but are influenced by the quality of the interventions used to treat them);
- a warm, engaging, and friendly style of interaction;
- a strength-based philosophy in conceptualizing and treating substance use disorders (i.e., even individuals with severe problems with substance abuse have areas of competence that can be built on for broader lifestyle change);
- comfort with the use of concrete methods for addressing complex problems (e.g., contracts, behavior graphing, task analyses);
- good professional boundaries;
- patience for setting and reinforcing small steps toward larger goals with clients;
- willingness to work with tardiness, relapses, client crises, and other challenges; and
- willingness to deliver interventions that fall outside of the traditional role of a therapist, such as case management services.

Supervisor Qualifications and Characteristics

RBT supervisors should have the same skill set as described in the preceding list for therapists. In addition, it is preferable for supervisors to be advanced-level clinicians (i.e., multiple years of clinical experience) who are well versed in behavioral principles and their application with a substance-abusing population. Ideally, supervisors would have experience in delivering RBT itself or other behavioral treatments that are closely related to RBT (e.g., MI). Supervisors should have a willingness to fill in and provide direct clinical services (e.g., conduct intakes and individual sessions) as necessary to assist the team or to assess clients' needs. They also should recognize issues often faced by therapists who work with challenging clinical populations, such as burnout or cynicism, assess therapists regularly for signs of such problems, and provide supportive interventions to relieve these problems. The best RBT supervisors hold therapists to high standards for model adherence without being authoritarian. They value the knowledge and insights of all team members and have warm, supportive relationships with them.

TRAINING

Training of new therapists involves three main components: (a) 2 days of RBT-specific training that involves both didactic and hands-on learning, (b) 1 to 2 days of training in MI, and (c) on-the-job training with oversight and support during the therapist's first 4 to 6 weeks of employment.

Specific Training in Reinforcement-Based Treatment: Didactics and Practice With Model Components

We have found that it takes 2 full days (about 6–7 hr each) of instruction to provide a basic overview of and foundation for providing RBT. These training sessions should be held before therapists begin work with clients. Ideally, this aspect of overall training is provided to small groups of three to six newly hired team members; therapists seem to benefit from the discussion and practice that group training provides, and the group approach is more cost-effective for clinics. However, providing didactic training to a single therapist at a time also is acceptable. It is valuable to invite to the training key community stakeholders with whom the clinic needs to have close working relationships (being mindful not to allow group size to exceed 12–15 attendees), such as probation officers, drug court judges, detoxification facility staff, and recovery house managers. These working relationships tend to be more beneficial to clients when all parties understand the treatment that clients are receiving and the rationale behind RBT techniques.

Ideally, attendees should be given a copy of this volume well in advance of the training day and asked to read the Introduction and core content chapters (i.e., Chapters 1–8) before attending. If this timeline is not possible, therapists should read these chapters as soon as possible after completing the initial training. In addition, therapists should bring this volume to the training sessions, and the trainer should point out pages on which more information can be found as each topic is discussed.

Qualifications for Trainers

Training should be provided by someone knowledgeable in RBT, usually the RBT supervisor. To be qualified to be a trainer, the individual should have (a) gone through a 2-day RBT training him- or herself, (b) had experience delivering RBT, and (c) been observed providing RBT training by a more senior RBT trainer prior to conducting the training independently.

Training Content

The content of the training should involve a thorough overview of the following topics in roughly the order presented here:

- Introduction and overview of RBT (45–60 min, didactic). We have found it valuable to provide a brief overview of the rationale for and principles of RBT and a cursory review of model components at the beginning of the training to set the stage for more in-depth coverage. The main focus of this segment should be on the *atmosphere of reinforcement* concept within RBT (a theme that should be revisited during most training segments throughout the day). An overview of the logistics of RBT (e.g., individual and group interventions, caseload sizes, program day schedule, how the provider organization manages outreach activities; see the Introduction, this volume) also should be provided. If time permits, the overview can also include a brief review of the evidence for RBT effectiveness (i.e., a summary of clinical trial outcomes). Laying out the "big picture" first is particularly valuable for community stakeholders who may not be able to attend the full training days.
- Basic drug education (30–45 min, didactic). Attendees should be provided with information regarding the main categories of drugs of abuse (e.g., opiates, hallucinogens), specific drugs within each category, their positive (e.g., euphoria) and negative (e.g., risk of cardiac arrest) effects on the body (both immediate and over time), drug tolerance information, modes of delivery (e.g,, injection, snorting), the interrelatedness of different drugs (e.g., a *speedball* is heroin and cocaine used together), and any other details about drug use that may be useful clinically (e.g., typical costs, how drugs are usually acquired, slang terms). The National Institute on Drug Abuse has excellent summary descriptions of the major drug categories available at its website (http://drugabuse.gov/drugpages/). Table 9.1 summarizes this information.
- Understanding behavioral principles (60 min, didactic). This component can be thought of as Behaviorism 101, a crash course to ensure a basic understanding of behavioral terms and concepts (e.g., the difference between positive and negative reinforcement, shaping behavior using successive approximations, extinguishing behavior). Drug use examples should be used to illustrate concepts.

TABLE 9.1
Commonly Abused Drugs

Substance category and name	Examples of commercial and street names	Drug Enforcement Administration schedule[a]/how administered[b]	Intoxication effects/potential health consequences
Tobacco			
Nicotine	Found in cigarettes, cigars, bidis, and smokeless tobacco (snuff, spit tobacco, chew)	Not scheduled/smoked, snorted, chewed	Increased blood pressure and heart rate/chronic lung disease; cardiovascular disease; stroke; cancers of the mouth, pharynx, larynx, esophagus, stomach, pancreas, cervix, kidney, bladder, and acute myeloid leukemia; adverse pregnancy outcomes; addiction
Alcohol			
Alcohol (ethyl alcohol)	Found in liquor, beer, and wine	Not scheduled/swallowed	In low doses, euphoria, mild stimulation, relaxation, lowered inhibitions; in higher doses, drowsiness, slurred speech, nausea, emotional volatility, loss of coordination, visual distortions, impaired memory, sexual dysfunction, loss of consciousness/increased risk of injuries, violence, fetal damage (in pregnant women); depression; neurologic deficits; hypertension; liver and heart disease; addiction; fatal overdose
Cannabinoids			
Hashish	Boom, gangster, hash, hash oil, hemp	I/swallowed, smoked	Euphoria; relaxation; slowed reaction time; distorted sensory perception; impaired balance and coordination; increased heart rate and appetite; impaired learning, memory; anxiety; panic attacks; psychosis/cough, frequent respiratory infections; possible mental health decline; addiction
Marijuana	Blunt, dope, ganja, grass, herb, joint, bud, Mary Jane, pot, reefer, green, trees, smoke, sinsemilla, skunk, weed	I/swallowed, smoked	

Drug	Street names	Schedule/how taken	Effects/health effects
Opioids			
Heroin	Diacetylmorphine: smack, horse, brown sugar, dope, H, junk, skag, skunk, white horse, China white, cheese (with over-the-counter cold medicine and antihistamine)	I/injected, smoked, snorted	Euphoria, drowsiness, impaired coordination, dizziness, confusion, nausea, sedation, feeling of heaviness in the body, slowed or arrested breathing/constipation, endocarditis, hepatitis, HIV, addiction, fatal overdose
Opium	Laudanum, paregoric: big O, black stuff, block, gum, hop	II, III, V/swallowed, smoked	
Stimulants			
Cocaine	Cocaine hydrochloride: blow, bump, C, candy, Charlie, coke, crack, flake, rock, snow, toot	II/snorted, smoked, injected	Increased heart rate, blood pressure, body temperature, metabolism; feelings of exhilaration; increased energy, mental alertness; tremors; reduced appetite; irritability; anxiety; panic; paranoia; violent behavior; psychosis/weight loss, insomnia, cardiac or cardiovascular complications, stroke, seizures, addiction
Amphetamine	Biphetamine, dexedrine: bennies, black beauties, crosses, hearts, LA turnaround, speed, truck drivers, uppers	II/swallowed, snorted, smoked, injected	
Methamphetamine	Desoxyn: meth, ice, crank, chalk, crystal, fire, glass, go fast, speed	II/swallowed, snorted, smoked, injected	Also, for cocaine—nasal damage from snorting; Also, for methamphetamine—severe dental problems
Club drugs			
MDMA (methylenedioxy-methamphetamine)[c]	Ecstasy, Adam, clarity, Eve, lover's speed, peace, uppers	I/swallowed, snorted, injected	MDMA—mild hallucinogenic effects, increased tactile sensitivity, empathic feelings, lowered inhibition, anxiety, chills, sweating, teeth clenching, muscle cramping/sleep disturbances, depression, impaired memory, hyperthermia, addiction
Flunitrazepam[c]	Rohypnol: forget-me pill, Mexican Valium, R2, roach, Roche, roofies, roofinol, rope, rophies	IV/swallowed, snorted	

(continues)

TABLE 9.1
Commonly Abused Drugs (Continued)

Substance category and name	Examples of commercial and street names	Drug Enforcement Administration schedule[a]/ how administered[b]	Intoxication effects/potential health consequences
GHB[c]	Gamma-hydroxybutyrate: G, Georgia home boy, grievous bodily harm, liquid ecstasy, soap, scoop, goop, liquid X	I/swallowed	Flunitrazepam—sedation, muscle relaxation, confusion, memory loss, dizziness, impaired coordination/addiction GHB—drowsiness, nausea, headache, disorientation, loss of coordination, memory loss/unconsciousness, seizures, coma
Dissociative drugs Ketamine	Ketalar SV: cat Valium, K, Special K, vitamin K	III/injected, snorted, smoked	Feelings of being separate from one's body and environment, impaired motor function/ anxiety, tremors, numbness, memory loss, nausea
PCP and analogs	Phencyclidine: angel dust, boat, hog, love boat, peace pill	I, II/swallowed, smoked, injected	Also, for ketamine—analgesia, impaired memory, delirium, respiratory depression and arrest, death
Salvia divinorum	Salvia, shepherdess's herb, Maria Pastora, magic mint, Sally-D	I/chewed, swallowed, smoked	Also, for PCP and analogs—analgesia, psychosis, aggression, violence, slurred speech, loss of coordination, hallucinations
Dextromethorphan (DXM)	Found in some cough and cold medications: robotripping, robo, triple C	Not scheduled/swallowed	Also, for DXM—euphoria, slurred speech, confusion, dizziness, distorted visual perceptions
Hallucinogens LSD	Lysergic acid diethylamide: acid, blotter, cubes, microdot yellow sunshine, blue heaven	I/swallowed, absorbed through mouth tissues	Altered states of perception and feeling, hallucinations, nausea
Mescaline	Buttons, cactus, mesc, peyote	I/swallowed, smoked	Also, for LSD and mescaline—increased body temperature, heart rate, blood pressure; loss of appetite; sweating; sleeplessness; numbness; dizziness; weakness; tremors; impulsive behavior; rapid shifts in emotion

Drug	Street names	Schedule/route	Health effects
Psilocybin	Magic mushrooms, purple passion, shrooms, little smoke	I/swallowed	Also, for LSD—flashbacks, hallucinogen persisting perception disorder Also, for psilocybin—nervousness, paranoia, panic
Other compounds Anabolic steroids	Anadrol, Oxandrin, Durabolin, Depo-Testosterone, Equipoise: roids, juice, gym candy, pumpers	III/injected, swallowed, applied to skin	Steroids—no intoxication effects/hypertension, blood clotting and cholesterol changes, liver cysts, hostility and aggression, acne; in adolescents—premature stoppage of growth; in men—prostate cancer, reduced sperm production, shrunken testicles, breast enlargement; in women—menstrual irregularities, development of beard and other masculine characteristics
Inhalants	Solvents (paint thinners, gasoline, glues); gases (butane, propane, aerosol propellants, nitrous oxide); nitrites (isoamyl, isobutyl, cyclohexyl): laughing gas, poppers, snappers, whippets	Not scheduled/inhaled through nose or mouth	Inhalants (varies by chemical)—stimulation, loss of inhibition, headache, nausea or vomiting, slurred speech, loss of motor coordination, wheezing/cramps, muscle weakness, depression, memory impairment, damage to cardiovascular and nervous systems, unconsciousness, sudden death
Prescription medications[d] Central nervous system depressants Stimulants Opioid pain relievers			

Note. This table is updated regularly by the National Institute on Drug Abuse. Reprinted from *Commonly Abused Drugs* (http://drugabuse.gov/DrugPages/DrugsofAbuse.html), by the National Institute on Drug Abuse, Bethesda, MD: National Institutes of Health. In the public domain.

[a]Schedule I and II drugs have a high potential for abuse. They require greater storage security and have a quota on manufacturing, among other restrictions. Schedule I drugs are available for research only and have no approved medical use; Schedule II drugs are available only by prescription (unrefillable) and require a form for ordering. Schedule III and IV drugs are available by prescription, may have five refills in 6 months, and may be ordered orally. Some Schedule V drugs are available over the counter.

[b]Some of the health risks are directly related to the route of drug administration. For example, injection drug use can increase the risk of infection through needle contamination with staphylococci, HIV, hepatitis, and other organisms.

[c]Associated with sexual assaults.

[d]For more information on prescription medications, please visit http://www.nida.nih.gov/DrugPages/PrescripDrugsChart.html

- Functional assessment of substance use (90 min, didactic and role play). The idea that drug use is logical and serves important functions for clients should be emphasized, and the common functions of drug use (e.g., peer interaction, anxiety reduction) presented. The trainer should provide tips on how to extract useful information for each question on the initial and relapse functional assessment of drug use interviews, and each trainee should be required to practice administering an initial functional assessment as part of a role play. Pairing up attendees and having them alternate playing the therapist and a client works well, and the trainer can listen in and provide feedback to the therapist about his or her interviewing technique.

- Feedback session (90 min, didactic and video). If training in MI has not yet been provided, the trainer should begin this segment with a basic overview of client ambivalence and the importance of maintaining a nonconfrontational and nondirective stance in the face of ambivalence. The rationale behind why objective information provided in the form of a feedback session can help clients overcome ambivalence and make positive changes should be articulated (i.e., it organizes the reasons for quitting drug use). Considerable time should be allotted to going through the feedback report itself and making sure therapists understand where the information within each field comes from. We have found it difficult to have therapists role play a feedback session because doing so requires an extensive understanding of a case. Instead, we prefer to present a video- or audiotape example of an experienced RBT therapist conducting a feedback session and engage attendees in a discussion of the session.

- Treatment planning (30 min, didactic). The idea that treatment plans flow directly from the information obtained on the functional assessment should be emphasized, with examples provided. How to phrase treatment goals in behavioral terms and break down overarching goals into weekly goals should be discussed. The main competing behavior domains (see Chapter 4, this volume) can be briefly presented as essential elements of the treatment plan, but details about how to help clients set and achieve competing behavior goals should be saved for a later segment (see the discussion that follows).

- Behavioral monitoring (graphing) and reinforcement of client goals (90 min, didactic, practice, and role play). The trainer should emphasize that the frequent assessment of client progress using objective behavioral measures is critical to the effectiveness of behavioral treatments and should present graphing as the primary way such monitoring occurs within RBT. The trainer should remind attendees of the concept of the atmosphere of reinforcement and how it relates to the tangible (e.g., stickers) and intangible (e.g., verbal praise) reinforcers that are provided during the graphing process with clients. Main graph types should be explained. Therapists should then have the opportunity to thoroughly peruse several examples of actual client graphs as the trainer "tells the story" of each set of graphs (see Chapter 5). Therapists should then be given the opportunity to practice setting up and adding data to example graphs of the key target behaviors that are monitored in RBT: abstinence (line graph), recreational goals (bar graph), and job activities (bar graphs).
- Other RBT treatment elements: recreation, Job Club, Social Club, use of contracting, and case management interventions (20–30 min each, didactic). These segments are generally straightforward to present and can be accomplished in small time blocks using primarily didactic techniques. The emphasis should be on the key "dos and don'ts" of each element. For example, important details about behavioral contracts are that they use as few words as possible, outline clearly what specific behaviors are to be accomplished in what time frame, and are used judiciously so that their value is not diluted from overuse.
- Details about drug testing and the voucher system (30–45 min, didactic and practice). We have found that new therapists who do not have experience in administering and observing urine drug tests sometimes have considerable anxiety about this component of RBT and appreciate the opportunity to learn and train with their peers. Stick-test cups should be provided and examples of abstinent and drug-positive sticks displayed. It also is important that therapists understand details regarding the voucher program so as to avoid misrepresenting this component to clients.
- Practice and role play. The need for therapists to practice RBT techniques during the training day and in on-the-job training

cannot be overemphasized. For most therapists, RBT will be the first highly specified intervention they have provided, and there are many details about the interventions to master for therapists to use them effectively with clients. Graphing, though seemingly simple, is a particularly difficult skill for therapists to master. New therapists tend to have difficulty depicting drug-testing data on abstinence graphs (e.g., depicting relapses as flat lines instead of streaks) and in keeping different graphs (e.g., for abstinence and work activities) lined up so that data on both for particular weeks can be compared. Having therapists spend a considerable portion of the 2-day training engaged in hands-on activities also begins to socialize them to the intensive, active nature of providing RBT and to the detailed nature of supervision.

Training in Motivational Interviewing

It is critical that RBT therapists adhere to the principles of MI in the delivery of all model components. MI is now widely adopted, and training in the technique is readily available. Clinics can arrange for an MI training by accessing the Motivational Interviewing Network of Trainers (an international collective of trainers available for hire) at its website: http://motivational interview.org/training/index.html. MI trainings vary in length (e.g., from less than a full day to multiple days) and depth of coverage; a full day of basic training is the minimum recommended for RBT. Large clinics that anticipate the need to frequently train therapists in this technique should consider investing in an in-house person to become a recognized trainer in the network and combining resources with other substance abuse treatment providers locally. To supplement their training and ongoing supervision in MI, therapists should be provided with a copy of the MI treatment manual (Miller & Rollnick, 2002) and allocated time for reading it.

On-the-Job Training

Learning to implement RBT is an ongoing process, and therapists should not be expected to be proficient from training sessions alone. The following are recommendations about how to support therapists in learning RBT during their first weeks of employment:

- Keep caseloads small initially. Therapists should begin conducting intakes with new clients and building a small caseload soon after their RBT and MI training so that they have the opportunity to use new skills after learning them. We recommend starting with a caseload of two clients for the first 2 to 3 weeks of employment to avoid overwhelming the therapist and to allow time for other training components (e.g., reading treatment manuals, shadowing more experienced therapists, assisting with the group components of the model) to occur. The ramp-up from two clients to a full caseload of as many as 12 clients should occur gradually because new therapists will be less efficient at delivering interventions until they are more familiar with them.

- Have new therapists shadow more experienced therapists. With the clients' permission, new therapists should sit in on several individual counseling sessions with different clients and therapists. Because RBT uses a team approach, existing clients and therapists are used to working with different team members and having their work observed by their peers. Therapists should observe (a) intakes, (b) staff escorts and other outreach (case management) activities, (c) initial functional assessment interviews, (d) graphing sessions, and (e) family sponsor sessions. Absent from this list is direct observation of a client confidential feedback session; having third parties in the room for this intervention is not recommended. Instead, new therapists should listen to several audiotapes of feedback sessions.

- Directly observe new therapists as they provide interventions. This observation can occur in sessions themselves (i.e., the supervisor shadows the new therapist) and by listening to audiotapes of sessions.

- Provide new therapists with specific feedback about both well-delivered and poorly delivered interventions. Behavioral goals should be set with therapists to develop skills in areas identified as needs.

- Assist new therapists in their initial setup of behavioral monitoring graphs. As noted, this component is particularly difficult for new therapists and can languish if direct support is not provided by either the supervisor or a more senior RBT therapist.

- Assist new therapists in compiling information for feedback reports. Compiling client information for the feedback report is complex, and it is easy to make mistakes, especially in the area of determining prevalence rates for drug use. The supervisor should sit with the therapist as he or she compiles his or her first report to ensure that the therapist knows where each data element comes from, that the data are accurate, and that none of the client's early accomplishments in treatment (e.g., completing detox) are overlooked.

SUPERVISION

Ongoing clinical supervision is an important component of RBT. Given the comprehensive nature of RBT, we have found that 2 hr of weekly group supervision with a team of no more than five therapists is sufficient to maintain close monitoring of client progress and to provide adequate clinical feedback to counseling staff. Group supervision should be held at a consistent time and place each week, and therapists should bring client charts to the session and be prepared to discuss each client's progress. The goals and agenda of supervision should be clear to all participants, and the feedback provided to the therapists should be concrete. Group supervision should be supplemented with informal (e.g., troubleshooting a client crisis) and formal (i.e., when therapists are new and learning RBT) individual supervision as needed.

Overarching Goals

The overarching goals of supervision are as follows:

- Ensuring supervisor familiarity with cases. To monitor progress effectively, supervisors must be highly familiar with all cases and ideally have met (e.g., provided an escort) or worked with (e.g., in Job Club) all clients personally.
- Ensuring fidelity to model components. Supervisors should monitor therapists' work with clients to ensure that they are (a) being proactive in promoting positive client behaviors across all model components (i.e., in individual clinical sessions, group didactic sessions, and case management interventions), (b) doing everything possible to minimize clients' relapse potential, and (c) maintaining a nonconfronational motivational stance at all times. A key question for supervisors to answer is: Are the interventions provided by this therapist intensive enough to sustain the client's abstinence in the short- and long-term?
- Prioritizing client goals and planning the sequencing of interventions. This is a dynamic process based on clinical judgment

as to the relevance of each goal to maintaining abstinence. Furthermore, the priority of goals is expected to shift over time as some are accomplished and placed on "maintenance" status and others emerge as more important. Finding a job is frequently the highest priority goal early in therapy. Once a job is found, the goal is modified to maintaining the job, and hours of work per week are graphed. Lifestyle balance then becomes important, and social recreational goals are moved into the foreground.

- Troubleshooting problems and sharing resources. Barriers to clinical progress are identified, and ideas for addressing barriers are generated from all team members. New resources relevant to case management activities also should be presented so that all team members can benefit from the new information.

- Anticipating relapses and barriers to treatment progress. Supervisors should be alert to signs of impending relapse even when cases are going well and sensitize therapists to them. Early warning signs that warrant discussion are tardiness and absenteeism, inconsistencies in clients' goal attainment, and clients' major life transitions (e.g., a client who receives his or her first paycheck may be tempted to spend money on drugs).

- Reinforcing therapist successes and self-care. Therapists should also be recognized and reinforced during supervision for treatment successes. Supervisors also can encourage therapists to engage in self-care activities (e.g., exercise, social support) to mitigate the stress inherent in providing treatment to complex client populations.

Structure

RBT supervision is conducted in a semistructured format consisting of the following components, in order.

Census Overview

The census provides an overview of program enrollment and is helpful in directing team members to specific clients in need of review during the supervision session. A copy of the census for the program is provided to each team member in table format. Some important information to include in the census table is client names, dates of intake, days in treatment, days spent in recovery housing, days since last relapse (if any), and employment status. A brief review of all clients also gives therapists a wider view of how clients are faring. Therapists are presented with a visual of client successes as well as areas in need of improvement.

Chart Review

After briefly reviewing the census data, the team should prioritize (triage) which cases will receive an extensive versus a limited chart review. Clients who are currently testing positive for drugs warrant the most discussion so that corrective action can be taken to get them back on track. After any clients who are relapsing are discussed, other client charts should be prioritized for review on the basis of specific needs. Team members may request a review of a specific chart on the basis of length of stay in treatment, counselor request for feedback in difficult cases, or to introduce a new client.

Chart review involves the therapist sharing with the team the client's progress toward goals, including abstinence, treatment attendance, job acquisition (number of resumes, interviews), recreational activities, Narcotics Anonymous attendance, and other client-specific goals (e.g., spending time with children). In presenting the client's progress, the therapist should show team members the client's behavioral graphs for all drug and competing behavior targets (and supervisors should verify that graphs are up-to-date, lined up with each other, and visually appealing). Each component of the client's treatment plan is reviewed to monitor whether the client is reaching his or her goals and to bolster reinforcement and clinical attention in areas in which goals are not being met. For example, a client may be attending Narcotics Anonymous meetings each day and participating in recreational activities but not following through with his or her job acquisition goals. The team will discuss the need to increase client behaviors in this area and how to deal with the barriers that have kept the client from following through with this goal (e.g., ambivalence about working). On the basis of the factors identified, interventions are modified or added to help the client resume progress on the goal. Therapists are expected to implement the new interventions within the next one to two sessions with the client.

After the prioritized cases have been reviewed, urine toxicology and competing behavior graphs for any client not yet discussed are briefly reviewed. Doing a cursory review of all cases each week, even those that are progressing well, ensures that supervisors stay familiar with all cases and safeguards against missing any relevant changes in the client's progress. Reviewing all client behavioral graphs also helps RBT team members to identify any overall trends in client retention, relapse, or progress in treatment domains. For example, a pattern may emerge across weeks that most clients are not meeting employment goals. Such a pattern may suggest that Job Club needs to be enhanced or expanded in addition to intensifying efforts in individual sessions. Conversely, a trend in successful treatment for clients highlights program strengths (i.e., are clients who attend more recreational activities faring better than those who do not?).

Guidance to Therapists

Although much of the supervision meeting is spent on a review of client graphs, as in traditional clinical supervision, the session should also provide a basis for therapist support and skill building. Supervision is a time for therapists to role-play interventions that they might need help with prior to implementing them and to get specific ideas from the supervisor and peer therapists. Supervisors and peers can refer therapists to materials (e.g., a chapter on shaping procedures from a core behavioral interventions book) in which they can learn more about particular techniques and determine how to provide the therapist time within the work day to review these materials.

Issues that are commonly addressed in supervision include the following:

- the role of the therapist in bringing about client change (what strategies can be used in individual and group sessions),
- working with challenging clients (those with mental disorders such as depression and antisocial personality disorder, those who are disruptive in group sessions),
- working with family members and creating social networks (how to involve family members, eliciting support from the community),
- recovery house issues (encouraging clients to move into stable housing, removing drug-positive clients from recovery housing),
- how to individualize treatment for the client (evaluating what works for which client and under what circumstances), and
- treatment dropout.

CONCLUSION

To obtain outcomes similar to those achieved in randomized clinical trials, clinics implementing RBT should follow the staffing, training, and supervision guidelines described in this chapter. Hiring well-qualified master's level staff who embrace a behavioral and strength-based approach to treatment helps to ensure that all RBT model components will be delivered with fidelity. Some personal characteristics that help to make RBT staff successful include flexibility, warmth, patience, tenacity, and openness to peer and supervisor feedback. Even highly skilled therapists will need considerable initial and ongoing training in RBT that includes didactics in RBT itself and its associated treatments (i.e., MI) as well as on-the-job training in the model components that tend to be most challenging for therapists to learn (i.e., feedback reports, feedback sessions, and behavioral graphing).

The primary goals of RBT supervision are to ensure that therapists deliver all RBT components with adherence to the guidelines described in this volume (i.e., to maintain fidelity to the model) and to troubleshoot barriers to client progress. Supervisors should be highly familiar with cases and be able to step in and assist in cases in times of therapist absence. During weekly group supervision, supervisors should help therapists prioritize client goals and plan how interventions will be sequenced in the coming week. Supervisors and other therapists can discuss ideas for addressing barriers to treatment progress and should anticipate client relapses based on case data. It is important for supervisors to reinforce the successes of RBT therapists and encourage staff to engage in self-care activities (e.g., using vacation time, impromptu supervision to discuss difficult sessions) to help prevent therapist burnout. Ideally, the RBT team of therapists and the supervisor operate as a cohesive unit in a climate of support, positivity about client progress, problem solving, and idea exchange.

10

IMPLEMENTATION CHALLENGES

In this chapter, we describe common challenges frequently encountered when treating substance use disorders and the Reinforcement-Based Treatment (RBT) methods used to address them. We do not attempt to cover the broad range of challenges faced; rather, we focus on some of the most commonly occurring challenges that we have encountered. The most common challenge for treatment substance use disorders—relapse—is discussed in detail.

MISSED SESSIONS

Clients in drug treatment may not have much experience with maintaining regular appointments because this behavior is incompatible with a drug using lifestyle. It should be expected that clients will experience difficulties with adjusting to the schedule that treatment requires. Flexibility and patience with clients as well as reinforcement for adherence will facilitate client progress in this area. Concrete tools to assist clients to keep appointments are also useful, such as appointment reminders (phone calls from the program or business card reminders), day plans (as discussed in Chapter 4, this volume), and planners. In any event, missed appointments and treatment days signal that treatment engagement is weak and relapse may be imminent (or may already have occurred). In the event of a missed appointment, the safest assumption is that the client is at risk of relapse, particularly if the missed appointment(s) occur early in treatment. Therefore, outreach procedures should be implemented immediately (ideally the same day of a missed appointment or within 24 hr).

When a session is missed, the counselor should use that time to initiate a vigorous search for the client. Outreach includes a set of activities ranging from phone contact to home visits that are specifically designed to ensure increased engagement with treatment. This starts with calling the client's residence and contacts (see Appendix I). This search should continue until the client is reached. Outreach, in its most effective form, includes multiple avenues—not only phone calls but letter writing and home or community visits as well. Once contact is made, arrangements should be made for the client to come into treatment as soon as possible (e.g., "Can you catch the bus or get a ride here right away?") or by the next day at the latest.

As indicated previously, outreach efforts should be initiated at the first sign of disengagement, for example, when a client who has been reporting for treatment every day does not show up after a long holiday weekend. Even if the client is not required to be in treatment on that day, lack of attendance is not his or her usual behavior pattern and thus could signal a relapse or risk for relapse. Contact with the client may help to head off a relapse.

Home Visits

Home visits should be attempted when phone contact has been unsuccessful. Home visits are likely the most powerful outreach tool available because they may allow for immediate therapeutic contact with the client. Even when the client is not at home, the therapist can leave a letter, which signals that the program staff was willing to go out of their way to reach the client. The Central East Addiction Technology Transfer Center (2007) has published a guide, *Outreach Competencies: Minimum Standards for Conducting Street Outreach in Hard-to-Reach Populations*, that provides a nice review of outreach techniques, including safety precautions.

Letter Writing

Although immediate contact with the client through phone calls and home visits is optimal, there are times when clients cannot be contacted through these means. Letter writing can be a potent technique for engaging with clients and alleviating any fears they have about returning to treatment. Letters that convey that the program wants to see the client in treatment and that program staff are available to help him or her improve the treatment process serve to decrease anxieties or guilt on the client's part. Motivational interviewing techniques are especially useful for this purpose, including affirming the client's successes in treatment, instilling hope that change can still occur, and maintaining a nonconfrontational and nonjudgmental stance about the client's disengagement from treatment. When receiving such a letter, clients often report that they felt cared for and less ashamed of a relapse. This effect is exactly the intent of outreach letters.

TARDINESS

Tardiness to treatment is common and should be expected until clients learn to adjust to a schedule. Tardiness is addressed through discussion with the client about barriers to getting to treatment on time (e.g., no alarm clock, bus takes over 1 hr to get to the program) and methods for overcoming them (e.g., take an early bus, borrow an alarm clock). Even when using problem-solving techniques, therapists should maintain reasonable expectations of client behavior (i.e., should expect that occasional tardiness will occur). The therapist should, if possible, see clients who are tardy rather than withhold treatment. If a client is receiving treatment on a regular basis (which therapist flexibility helps to ensure), it is more likely that he or she will become more adherent over time. But if these doses of treatment are withheld early on, the client's behavior may deteriorate because the goal of being on time for every appointment (or not be seen at all) is too difficult to meet.

POOR COMPLIANCE WITH DAY PLANS, HOMEWORK, OR TREATMENT GOALS

Clients may also experience difficulty adhering to the work required by treatment, such as day planning, homework, and treatment goals. The rationale behind these tasks should be reviewed on a regular basis so that the client is reminded of their relevance to treatment success. It is useful in these situations to reduce the requirements so that they are more attainable. For example, if the client is not completing homework assignments, efforts should be made to make the assignments less cumbersome. The client may, for example, prefer to complete homework worksheets by coming to the program half an hour early, when there is peace and quiet to focus on the activity. Time can be set aside at the end of the day to assist the client with completing day plans. Short-term goals can be broken down into smaller steps so that the client has a better chance of achieving the goal and can receive reinforcement for doing so. For example, if the short-term goal is to call three people to inquire whether they will serve as employment references, the goal can be revised to write down the names and phone numbers of three individuals whom the client might call about being a reference and bring the list to treatment the next day. The goal during the next day's individual session could be to call one person from the list so that progress on this goal is ensured. The new homework assignment then becomes to call the next person on the list and to report on the activity on return to treatment.

Another technique that can be helpful with ambivalent or "stuck" clients is to review the client's goals for the future and the reasons that he or she sought treatment in the first place. Such a review will help the therapist explain that the tasks of treatment are designed to help the client reach those important goals. Additionally, a cost–benefit analysis (typically conducted early in treatment) can be particularly helpful for reminding the client of the benefits to be gained from treatment (see Appendix J for an example cost–benefit analysis form).

DENIAL OF DRUG USE

On occasion, clients will deny drug use when urinalysis indicates that it has occurred. We have found that the best approach to handling this situation is to (a) indicate to the client that the result "is what it is" and that counselors go by what the test results indicate (i.e., a positive result will be recorded on the behavior graph) and (b) remind the client that counselors are here to treat substance use and do expect that relapse will occur. It is not possible to conduct a functional assessment of use if the client denies use. However, the counselor should explore any changes in feelings about abstinence or other life difficulties or drug triggers recently encountered. The therapist may also get a commitment from the client that if he or she continues to test positive, the client will agree to an exploration of the conditions for relapse at that time. When possible, daily urinalysis testing should be employed to evaluate the duration of the relapse (e.g., if the client does not test negative in a few days, there is more evidence of continued drug use that will need to be addressed).

EMERGENCE OF PSYCHOLOGICAL SYMPTOMS

Substance abuse frequently co-occurs with psychological disorders; thus, supplemental treatment for psychological symptoms on-site or off-site should be facilitated from the onset of treatment. However, sometimes symptoms can arise without forewarning, and plans have to be made to facilitate treatment for the client at the time of the symptom emergence. For suicidal or homicidal clients, crisis response teams should be contacted and emergency psychiatric admissions should be obtained. When the symptoms are not acute or life threatening, the therapist can work with the client to identify and procure ongoing psychiatric assistance, including counseling and medication management, if warranted. The RBT therapist can play an important role in facilitating not only access to psychiatric services but also compliance with these services (including medication taking) by graphing these target behaviors. Such monitoring is essential for ensuring that the client is functioning optimally emotionally because such functioning has a direct impact on progress in substance abuse treatment. Mood problems are frequently cited as one of the reasons that clients use drugs, so treatment of these symptoms can have an enormous impact on clients' ability to remain abstinent.

EMERGENCE OF CRISES AND CHALLENGING LIFE CIRCUMSTANCES

Many situations may trigger drug use for clients, particularly situations that are stressful and have served as precursors to drug use previously. Therapists need to be alert to behaviors and attitudes that could signal an upcoming relapse. Such behaviors include going into areas that are high risk, being around people with whom the client has used, and exhibiting stress or anger over conflicts at work or with family or friends. If changes in behavior and/or attitude are observed, it is important for the therapist to discuss such observations with the client and to problem solve coping mechanisms for dealing with them. Role play of interactions with individuals with whom the client is experiencing conflict can be useful for illustrating that the client controls how conflict is handled and influences the consequences of nonproductive conflict resolution (e.g., anger at work can lead to the loss of a job, and the person who loses in this scenario is the client).

RELAPSE TO DRUG USE

Relapse to drug use is expected during treatment for substance use disorders. Just as depressed individuals cannot be expected to remain depression free because they have begun treatment, individuals entering drug treatment cannot be expected to remain symptom free. One of the best ways to handle relapse actually occurs when the client first enters treatment. The program's approach to relapse should be explained from the outset so that the client has an awareness of what to do when he or she has relapsed. We believe that the client's perception of how the program will view this occurrence can have a great impact on that client's decision about whether to return to treatment. Our philosophy is that treatment is the best place for a client to be following a relapse. Our therapeutic response to relapse is nonjudgmental, objective, and proactive. Though relapse highlights that the client needs to make changes in how he or she is contributing to the recovery process, it also highlights that therapists need to change how they are intervening with the client so that they are more effective. Clients who have relapsed are provided with an individual session to determine the setting for the relapse and to explore ways of getting the client back on track immediately. The following is a description of strategies for reinstating abstinence in clients who have relapsed.

The session begins with review and reinforcement of recent abstinence success to counteract feelings of discouragement and guilt that are common after a relapse. This is followed by a reassessment of motivators and commitment to continuing abstinence through review of the cost–benefit analysis. Next, the therapist conducts a detailed functional assessment of the relapse and problem solves with the client how situations could have been handled differently to avoid drug use; additional relevant cognitive behavioral skills lessons can be planned or reviewed at this time.

The most important principle to keep in mind is that the client needs to intensify activities that will compete with drug use while working to regain abstinence. These activities can include individual sessions, attendance at Narcotics Anonymous or Alcoholics Anonymous, and engaging in social and recreational activities with family and friends. Generally, the counselor should focus on specific and concrete goals for the client to accomplish per day. Detailed day plans should be formulated and reviewed frequently. The therapist can help the client by doing the following:

- Putting the relapse into perspective. It is important to stress to the client that previous accomplishments in treatment are not lost or negated as a result of a slip and that success can be recaptured within a few days of renewed abstinence. Clients often have the perception that relapse is equivalent to starting over, when in reality the focus should be on mitigating the effects of the relapse (keeping it contained to one or two episodes of drug use). If the perception is that all is lost, the client is more likely to continue to use because the relapse indicates failure. It may be helpful to use an example of dieting with the client to illustrate this point.

  Individuals who are on diets and go off track by eating something unhealthy—even binging on unhealthy foods—are encouraged to get right back on track rather than continue unhealthy eating habits. The reason for this is that all is not lost because of a slip. You can learn from the relapse and get back on track so that you do not allow the relapse to become a reason to continue to use.

- Reviewing the cost–benefit analysis. Explore the client's feelings about the relapse. Reinstate his or her commitment to abstinence and the reasons for this commitment in the first place; implement a new abstinence sampling contract.
- Conducting a functional assessment of the relapse. It is important for both counselor and client to understand the circumstances and feelings that preceded the relapse. This knowledge forms the basis for new goal setting and day planning. Treatment planning and daily short-term goals are adjusted on the basis of the information contained in the functional assessment of the relapse (e.g., need for intensified mental health services, contract of no time with friend up the street with whom client used).
- Problem solving how this relapse could have been avoided. For example, explore what alternative behaviors and strategies could have been used that were not, such as calling a family sponsor or coming to treatment.
- Reviewing alternative housing plans. Determine whether a change in housing (even if short term) is warranted and feasible.
- Making a new day plan for the next 24 hr. Include as many distracting activities and as much contact with family or Narcotics Anonymous sponsor as possible.
- Contacting the family sponsor. Notify the family sponsor of the changed status of the client and enlist this person's aid in helping the client to remain abstinent for the next few days.
- Planning how and when the client will get to the clinic tomorrow. Offer an escort as needed.
- Escorting the client to alternative housing. If a change in housing is applicable and feasible, an escort should be provided.

The client should report to the clinic daily following a relapse to review progress and drug avoidance skills and to plan activities that will substitute for drug use. As mentioned previously, daily drug testing is ideal because it allows for early detection of relapse. Individual sessions with intensified services continue until the client once again submits a drug-negative urine sample. If daily urine testing is not feasible, there remains a need for increased intensity in individual sessions and monitoring of drug use through self-report (which can be supplemented by weekly urine test results).

DETOXIFICATION INTAKE

It may be necessary to refer clients to detoxification to resolve their physical dependence on substances and to resume drug abstinence. Often, clients who relapse stop coming to the clinic, so outreach efforts may be needed to contact them and offer the detoxification reentry option. Those who experience withdrawal or who are concerned that they will experience withdrawal should be encouraged to return to detoxification. The RBT therapist should help the client with scheduling of an intake appointment, and if feasible, transportation should be provided to ensure that the client attends the intake appointment.

Contracting for a Detoxification Appointment

Clients often want to try stopping on their own before they commit to detoxification. When attempts to encourage detoxification have failed, the client is asked to sign a written contract that indicates that the client agrees to return to a detoxification program if a negative urine sample is not provided by a specified time (usually within 1 week of signing). The client also should be informed that if withdrawal symptoms arise, the client is advised to enter detoxification immediately.

Outpatient Treatment Reentry

It is important that the client not disengage from the outpatient treatment program and that aftercare services are begun as soon as detoxification services end. Therefore, clients who attend detoxification should reenter outpatient treatment as soon as they complete the detoxification program (e.g., they leave the detoxification program and come directly to outpatient treatment). If possible, transportation or escort should be provided to avoid detours.

LACK OF TREATMENT RESPONSE

Because substance use disorders are difficult to treat, therapists should anticipate the need to use a variety of techniques to treat clients effectively. It is not unusual to modify treatment plans and implement various techniques multiple times in an attempt to "get it right." The RBT team (see the Supervision section in Chapter 9, this volume) is a valuable resource for recommending various behavioral and motivational methods and techniques. However, there are circumstances in which clients fail to respond to treatment interventions, and a referral to other treatment modalities should be made.

For example, an opioid-dependent individual who repeatedly relapses with little continuous abstinence between relapses (and who has received intensified therapy, outreach, etc.) needs to be advised on treatment alternatives that may more effectively treat opioid dependence, including medications such as suboxone or methadone. Program staff also should facilitate the client's access to alternative treatment. Detoxification is another form of treatment that will be recommended as needed; however, if may be feasible to continue to treat the client following detoxification so that this transition offers a continuum of care.

DISCHARGE PLANNING

Although discharge planning is a process that begins early in the treatment process, it remains a challenge to providers. Given the relatively short duration of treatment, it is a difficult task to solidify treatment goals and generalize treatment gains in such a manner that the client has a good prognosis for continued abstinence. Treatment elements that are provided outside of the program (in the community) are needed to sustain the successes in treatment. Clients who leave the program take with them a treatment plan that compensates for the "loss" of the formal RBT. For example, a client's treatment plan includes individual and group therapy weekly, which entails a great deal of social interaction, individual attention, and incentives. If these things are actually helping to sustain drug abstinence (i.e., if RBT is working), then one should expect removal of these interventions to place the client at high risk for relapse. Treatment programming should therefore assist clients in developing their own community networks so that they rely less on the program and more on helping networks. These elements are implemented from the start of treatment and are intensified throughout as part of the discharge planning process. For example, a client will have discharge goals such as continue Narcotics Anonymous or Alcoholics Anonymous attendance at four times per week, continue recreational activities with daughter at least two times per week, continue attendance at church with mother on Sundays, continue work of no more than 40 hr per week, and continue self-care of at least one relaxing activity just for yourself (i.e., listening to music) each week.

CONCLUSION

Substance use disorders are debilitating, and a considerable amount of behavior (attendance, group and individual participation, homework, assessments) is demanded of clients who seek and attend treatment. For this reason, treatment should be a safe and reinforcing place for clients to work on their recovery. In fact, when clients fail to engage in or benefit from treatment, one of the first places to look for deficiencies is not the client but the treatment program. After all, by their very nature, treatment programs propose to treat substance use disorders; thus, failure to do so is a failure on the part of the program. However, even the most reinforcing and equipped treatment environment is not void of challenges. Clients often miss appointments and have unmet basic needs that become the focus of treatment sessions (e.g., housing crises, domestic violence, medical issues). RBT therapists and administers must be aware of these challenges and able to deal with them.

III

SPECIAL POPULATIONS

11

PREGNANT AND CHILD-REARING WOMEN

Substance use disorders during pregnancy remain an alarming public health problem that is widespread and complex in its origins and its treatment. It is estimated that among pregnant women in the United States, approximately 423,000 used tobacco products; 310,000 drank alcohol; and 97,000 used illicit drugs in the past month (United States Department of Health and Human Services [USDHHS], Substance Abuse and Mental Health Services Administration [SAMHSA], Office of Applied Statistics, 2004–2005). The distinction between legal and illegal substances has led the public to erroneously think that there is a relationship between the legality of a substance and the severity of its negative impact on fetal and neonatal development and growth. In fact, if substances were ranked in terms of the severity of their devastating consequences to fetal and maternal health, the two legal substances alcohol and tobacco would likely trump the negative consequences associated with illicit substances like cocaine, opioids, and marijuana. A striking example of this is seen in the literature in which the effects of in utero exposure to alcohol include miscarriage; premature delivery; mental retardation; learning, emotional, and behavioral problems; and physical defects of the face and the heart and other organs (USDHHS, SAMHSA, Office of Applied Studies, 2007). In utero tobacco exposure appears to increase the risks of premature birth and low birth weight, which are risk factors for mortality, morbidity, and developmental problems later in life (Centers for Disease Control and Prevention, 2009). Although the scientific and lay communities have given an enormous amount of attention to fetal cocaine effects, the effects associated with in utero cocaine exposure appear more subtle than those of tobacco (Slotkin, 1988). Thus, the examination and treatment of women with substance use disorders during pregnancy cannot be focused on the cessation of one substance in isolation because it is the norm that these clients are using multiple substances that may have additive or even synergistic effects on the health and well-being of the mother, fetus, and neonate.

Although the potential consequences of substance use during pregnancy for the health and well-being of the mother, fetus, and neonate are concerning, substance use during pregnancy must be viewed in context and in relation to multiple other factors that can compromise healthy pregnancies. Women who use substances during pregnancy often do so in the context of intricately complex individual, social, and environmental factors, including poor nutrition, extreme stress, violence of multiple forms, poor housing conditions, exposure to environmental toxins and diseases, and depression, which can all impact postnatal outcomes ("Effects of In Utero Exposure to Street Drugs," 1993). Although the odds are often stacked against women who use substances during pregnancy, each client is unique, and each client must be viewed in the context of her own risk and protective factors to optimize her treatment and outcomes for herself and her child.

It is also important to recognize that many pregnant women are already parents of other children, and if they are pregnant for the first time they will be child-rearing women in the near future. Pooled data from the National Survey on Drug Use and Health show that alcohol, tobacco, and illicit drug use (e.g., marijuana, cocaine) was greatly reduced among pregnant women relative to child-rearing or nonpregnant women (Muhuri & Gfroerer, 2009). These data support the need for interventions for postpartum and child-rearing women. Women who use substances while child rearing are at risk of abuse and neglect of their children (Chaffin, Kelleher, & Hollenberg, 1996; for more details, see Chapter 12, this volume). Because adverse child outcomes, including child maltreatment, are not fully explained by a single risk factor of parental drug use, these data suggest that there is a complex relationship between drug use, maternal psychopathology, child-rearing practices, family environment, social support, and socioeconomic factors, including unemployment and poverty (Cicchetti & Luthar, 1999; Dawe & Harnett, 2007). Thus, these factors should be addressed in any intervention for substance-abusing pregnant and child-rearing women.

In this chapter, we outline the common clinical issues and treatment considerations that arise when working with pregnant and child-rearing women.

Additionally, we review methods for effectively applying Reinforcement-Based Treatment (RBT) principles with this population.

BARRIERS TO ACCESSING AND ENGAGING IN TREATMENT

Just as treatment for substance use disorders needs to employ a woman-centered program to address women's treatment needs, so too is this approach necessary to reduce barriers for women entering and engaging in treatment. For pregnant and child-rearing women, the stigma of being addicted, the fear of losing custody of their children and the threat of incarceration and/or being mandated to treatment often pose insurmountable barriers to their seeking treatment. Creating a treatment environment that is welcoming, nonjudgmental, and supportive is essential for overcoming such barriers. Although programs must always be clear that their responsibilities as mandated reporters will not be overlooked, they should provide the support, clinical services, and referrals necessary to eliminate or reduce the probability of the need to report the mother to child protective services (see Chapter 12).

Women who have partners with substance use disorders often face major barriers to both accessing and engaging in treatment. Their partners may not be supportive of their seeking treatment and may even threaten violence or abandonment if they do so. If a woman is successful in accessing treatment, this dynamic often continues with the partner attempting to sabotage her progress in treatment. Program and staff must be sensitive and responsive to the multiple issues of women's safety, the demands and stress of their relationships, and the impact on their ability to successfully engage in treatment.

Lack of child care and transportation are often cited as the most significant external barriers for women attempting to access services (Brady & Ashley, 2005). Transportation can be provided by vans or by giving women tokens for public transportation. Women receiving public assistance may be eligible for monthly transportation passes. Eligibility verification, enrollment, and distribution of monthly passes can be facilitated by a case manager or other program support staff.

Although there may be a critical need for child care services, the provision of services is not always a simple solution. Women may be reluctant to accept child care services for numerous reasons, such as fearing being reported to child protective services, having little experience leaving their children in a formal child care setting, and not knowing and/or not trusting child care workers (Comfort, Loverro, & Kaltenbach, 2000). Resistance may be based on experiential or clinical issues and again reiterate the complexity of treatment issues within these women's lives. Strategies to overcome resistance may include having child care staff participate in the program orientation, both to familiarize women with the child care services and to reinforce their position as members of the treatment team; inviting mothers to spend time in the child care center before bringing their children; partnering new clients with client mentors who can answer questions and alleviate anxieties; and integrating child-rearing concerns into the clinical treatment plan. It is critical that the foundation of child care services be grounded in a gentle, caring, supportive environment but one that is always clear that RBT therapists are required to report abuse and neglect to child protective services.

Offering child care services on-site while mothers attend groups, individual therapy sessions, and medical appointments; providing classes to improve child-rearing skills; including mother and child recreational activities such as trips to zoos and farms; and offering counseling support for the difficulties and stress associated with child rearing can all be helpful in reducing barriers associated with child caregiving.

For treatment to be effective with pregnant and child-rearing women, it must address multiple needs. RBT is ideal for treating pregnant and child-rearing women for substance use disorders because it is a strength-focused treatment and starts with eliciting information from the women as to the services they most need and would find most helpful. It is not unusual for them to report that the most practical concrete services, such as transportation assistance and help obtaining food, housing, and clothing, are the most useful (Hagan, Finnegan, & Nelson-Zlupko, 1994). It is important for the RBT provider to recognize that meeting the needs of everyday living go hand-in-hand with successfully engaging pregnant and child-rearing women in treatment.

The following case vignette is referred to throughout the chapter to illustrate how RBT is used to work with pregnant and child-rearing women.

FICTITIOUS CASE VIGNETTE

Penny Jacob's life story is one of survival. On her 14th birthday, her present from her stepfather was that he introduced her to heroin. After a few exposures to heroin, he began sexually molesting her. At age 15, she ran away from home and lived on the street or with friends. To make money and have food and shelter, she began prostituting and working in strip joints. She is now 30 and reports use of three Xanax pills a day (benzodiazepines), heroin (three injections totaling a $30 per day habit), and a pack of cigarettes a day. She has three living children, all of whom are in foster care. For this pregnancy, Penny enters drug treatment at 20 weeks pregnant, motivated by seeing her belly growing and the inability to deny any longer than she might be pregnant. Penny perceives this child as someone to finally "love her for her," and she wants to "do right by this baby this time." The pregnancy and expected child give Penny a reason to be "clean this time." Her drug use has only been interrupted by three prior incarcerations, two for prostitution and one for drug possession. She has an outstanding warrant for her arrest as a result of stabbing a "john." Penny is currently anemic, HIV-negative, and hepatitis C-positive. She has been afraid to seek obstetrical care because of fear the staff would report her to the authorities and possibly take away her child at delivery. Penny has three ongoing relationships with men with whom she exchanges sex for food, shelter, and other material goods. She arrives at the drug treatment clinic having taken a "small hit" of heroin to hold her over before she gets her methadone, which she has been told by other clients she will receive if she is using heroin. Penny has evidence of track marks on her arms. Her urine sample is positive for both opioids and benzodiazepines. She screens positive for depression and anxiety disorders and has neither a stable living situation—she lives off and on with her three different partners—nor an adequate supply of food and physical security. Several treatment plan elements (see Appendix K) are considered for Penny.

Functional Assessment

The RBT provider completes a functional assessment with Penny to determine the *antecedents* (what comes before) and *consequences* (what comes after) of drug use for her. With Penny, at first she is unable to articulate where she uses drugs, so the RBT therapist asks questions such as "Where do you use drugs?" and "Where do you feel most safe using drugs?" With questions such as these, the RBT therapist is able to develop a clinical picture of Penny's drug use and the typical conditions of drug use that have been practiced and repeated over the course of time. By identifying the specific features of Penny's pattern of drug use, the RBT therapist can design a treatment plan that will avoid exposure to these settings and situations. With a more complex client such as Penny, it is necessary to ask about each drug and how it is used (or not used) in combination with other drugs and where and when these drugs are used together or separately.

After determining the antecedents of Penny's drug use, the RBT therapist determines the consequences. Again, asking about the combinations and or separate use of the various drugs is important to helping to formulate the treatment plan. For example, Penny uses the Xanax to make the heroin last longer. She always uses the Xanax before bedtime to help her sleep and "get though the night without heroin." As discussed in other chapters, one important component of the functional assessment is an assessment of the individual's longest period of abstinence. Understanding what the environmental context was during this time provides the RBT therapist with valuable information about the types and frequencies of behaviors and the environmental conditions and contingencies that were in place to set the occasion for sustained drug abstinence in the past. For example, Penny's drug use has only been interrupted by three prior incarcerations. During this time, she was able to avoid drugs. She says that even though she could have bought drugs in jail, she was too scared to try it because she did not want anything worse to happen to her, like going to a higher security incarceration facility. This suggests that she might benefit from a long-term residential treatment facility and a new environment where drugs are not easily available and where the consequences for using drugs are severe.

Developing the Treatment Plan

After the initial intake information is provided, the treatment plan is developed with the client. See Appendix L for a sample initial treatment plan.

Determining Goals and Corresponding Interventions

In Penny's case, the treatment plan must address multiple issues concurrently. These issues can be categorized as follows:

- survival needs, which include safe housing free from others using drugs, adequate food, and maybe physical safety from a violent or abusing partner or family member;
- mental health treatment, including the treatment of comorbid disorders illnesses like depression and posttraumatic stress;
- medical problems, including any physical health condition such as hepatitis C and anemia;
- nutrition, which although related to the food category in the survival needs, may also be a separate category in that a client may have an abundance of food, but the foods may lack adequate nutrients (thus, Penny may need help selecting different foods for balanced nutrition);
- obstetrical treatment, including regular prenatal care;
- legal assistance, including securing a legal advocate to help Penny address her warrant for arrest;
- vocational functioning, including plans to increase education and/or obtain legal employment for financial independence from family, friends, and the government (this would also include attending and participating in the Job Club component of RBT);
- social functioning, including development of a drug-free peer network, potential termination of a relationship with a male drug user, and tools to reduce HIV risk behaviors; and

- recreational assistance, including the assessment of pleasurable activities that are drug free and the sampling and establishment of regular enjoyable drug-free activities (Penny is also expected to attend the Social Club and other program-supported recreational activities that are a part of the RBT program).

Within each of these categories, the therapist lists the specific problem areas separately and ranks them in order of urgency. After the problem has been specified, the goal for its resolution is listed.

Goals must be determined and agreed on by both the client and the RBT therapist. For example, for the problem of nicotine dependence, it may not be the client's goal to cease all cigarette use. It may be that the client will only first agree to reduce the number of cigarettes smoked daily. In such a case, the goal may be specified as reduction of cigarettes from a pack a day to 10 cigarettes a day.

Once the goal is negotiated, then the intervention that will help the client to achieve this goal is specified. For example, to address Penny's depression symptoms, the therapist (a) refers Penny to be evaluated by a psychiatrist who can then, if appropriate, place her on an antidepressant medication, and (b) provides cognitive behavioral therapy.

Once the interventions are determined, there should be methods for measuring progress toward the goals. As often as possible, these methods should be objective and quantifiable. In the case of depression, the Beck Depression Inventory (Beck, Steer, & Brown, 1996) could be used once a week to assess the presence of depressive symptoms and to determine if their frequency and severity have lessened in comparison with the previous week. It should be noted that there is not an instrument specific to a pregnant population for measuring depressive symptoms. This is important to note because there is overlap between depressive symptoms and pregnancy symptoms (e.g., sleep changes, weight and appetitive changes, fatigue), and the normal pregnancy symptoms could be misinterpreted as depressive symptoms. Thus, it is important to use the Beck Depression Inventory as a dynamic measure to talk with the client about what symptoms she is endorsing and why. In other words, the Beck Depression Inventory responses can serve as a basis for an interview with the client in regard to her endorsement of some highly relevant items, and within that interview the RBT therapist can disentangle which symptoms may be more related to pregnancy and which are related to depression.

As evidenced by the initial treatment plan, pregnant clients being treated for substance use disorders have multiple problems to be addressed concurrently and in an integrated manner. Within each problem area, the RBT therapist should determine the priority of the issues to be addressed and determine if this order matches the client's perception of the acuity of her own problems. In cases in which there is a mismatch between the RBT therapist's and client's assessment of the priority of treatment needs, the two should discuss the mismatch and negotiate on the priorities. It has been our experience that asking the client to try the RBT therapist's way first for a set period of time (e.g., 2 weeks) can be helpful, and then if some specified intermediate goals have not been attained, the order of treatment needs can be renegotiated.

Breaking Larger Goals Into Smaller, More Manageable Goals

The overall goals of abstinence from heroin and benzodiazepines can by themselves feel overwhelming to clients and need to be broken into smaller goals to provide a scaffolding to reach this overarching goal. For heroin, one way to break down this large goal is to focus first on getting a behavioral contract for 24 or 48 hr of abstinence while the client is being inducted onto an opioid agonist medication such as methadone, the medication for which most is known about its effects during pregnancy (Jones et al., 2008). Once this initial contract has been completed successfully, then a longer of period of abstinence can be negotiated in a successor contract.

Helping clients see their abstinence as a vacation from drug use can be beneficial for reducing resistance to long-term substance-use-related behavioral change. Moreover, giving clients direct advice about how to prepare their environment for their change in substance use can be beneficial. For example, the therapist may want to have each overarching treatment goal on a separate page so that there is space on the treatment plan for inclusion of the intermediate goals and plans for the intermediate goals immediately below the final goal.

It may also help to have subgoals under the overarching goal of abstinence from heroin, such as methadone induction; then, beside that subgoal can be the objective measure of verification of methadone ingestion. This goal is an "easy" one to meet, and having easy intermediate goals gives clients the opportunity to experience almost immediate accomplishment. On many little successes, one can build greater successes. Another intermediate goal under heroin abstinence could be to remove environmental cues to maximize the opportunity for sustained abstinence. In the intervention section for that goal could be the following: remove drug paraphernalia from the house, car, and other places; avoid places the client has used drugs (list places where it is safe or not safe to go); avoid hanging around people who use drugs (list people who are safe and unsafe); and avoid activities associated with drug use (list activities that the client can and cannot do—no prostitution, not less than 8 hr of sleep a night). The therapist should select behavioral items than can be verified or objectively measured in some way other than just relying on self-report.

Appendix L shows how Penny's larger treatment goals are broken down into more manageable goals. Some of these smaller goals need to be broken down even further for Penny to achieve success. For example, consider problem area 2b, Psychiatric Treatment: Comorbid Issues. Penny experiences depression, and to control her depression she needs to see a psychiatrist to prescribe an antidepressant medication. She is reluctant to see a psychiatrist, so the therapist explores the reasons for this reluctance. Penny fears that she will be placed on a medication that will hurt her child. In response to this fear, the therapist educates Penny about the risks and benefits of selective serotonin reuptake inhibitor (SSRI) medication during pregnancy and helps Penny set up an appointment with a psychiatrist who specializes in pregnancy, drug addiction, and mood disorders. Once Penny goes to the appointment and fills her prescription, she needs support in being reminded to take the medication daily, especially when she starts feeling less depressed.

Initiating the Treatment Plan

Often, looking at a long and complex list of issues that a client has in her life can seem overwhelming for both the client and RBT therapist. Thus, it is important to touch on and have a preliminary plan for addressing each issue. At the same time, it is important not to try to aggressively tackle each issue on the same day or with the same commitment of time and resources.

The RBT therapist will want first to address the client's basic survival needs to establish trust and rapport and a foundation of basic needs that can be successfully met before other, higher order issues are tackled. The plans to address housing and food are shown in the Appendix L treatment plan. For example, it may be possible to arrange for a client to enter and live in a recovery house or other shelter on the same day she enters treatment. For addressing the inadequate food supply, it may be possible to have a goal of obtaining food stamps. As a part of this process, the client may first need to obtain an identification card to apply for or reestablish eligibility for food stamps. Even this goal may need to be broken down into smaller steps, such as gathering the needed papers to provide the client's address and date of birth and citizenship.

These smaller goals of gathering papers and getting the identification card may themselves become part of the treatment plan. Often, it is not enough to ask the client for the necessary papers; instead, the RBT therapist needs a strategy to assist the client in planning what information (e.g., papers, birth certificate) she needs before she goes to the social services center, how she will get to the office, when she will go, if she needs money to pay for the identification card, how she will get this money, and how she will get home. Thinking through the barriers she may encounter and how she will overcome them is a critical step in the treatment plan. Otherwise, the client may become easily frustrated when any obstacle is encountered, and she may give up and not complete the task.

Because Penny lacks a stable living situation, an adequate supply of food, and physical security, the therapist works with her to get her to agree to enter recovery housing for the next 48 hr starting right after their meeting. The recovery house has adequate food and is well versed in dealing with victims of interpersonal violence. Penny and the therapist make an appointment for tomorrow so that they can begin the steps for securing food stamps and obtaining a restraining order on the partner.

Once initial concrete plans are made for securing housing and food, the RBT therapist can turn to quickly establishing drug abstinence. One appropriate adjunctive treatment to RBT for opioid-dependent clients is stabilizing the client on methadone. Once the client is stable on methadone, a medically assisted withdrawal from benzodiazepines can occur. As with non-pregnant clients, it is suggested that pregnant clients first be stabilized in their drug treatment before assessing for depression or anxiety. Waiting to assess the client for these disorders after a 2-week period of abstinence permits the RBT therapist to distinguish between substance-induced disorders and non-substance-induced disorders. This is important to accomplish to avoid placing a client on medication needlessly and exposing her to the medication. For pregnant women, it is especially important—for the benefit of mother and fetus—to avoid unnecessary medication exposure.

Another issue that could greatly affect drug treatment is the client's legal needs. For example, Penny has an outstanding warrant for her arrest. She should be assisted in finding legal representation to help her navigate the justice system. She may actually need to resolve her legal issues before going to the department of social services because she may risk being arrested if the department representative calls the police as a result of a search of public files for outstanding arrest warrants.

Monitoring the Treatment Plan

The treatment plan needs to be considered a dynamic process rather than a static document. As described in other chapters, the use of graphs to monitor behavior is a key component of RBT. Although attendance of treatment and drug abstinence (verified with urine samples tested for drugs) are always primary treatment goals, the order of the goals and graphs that quantify and operationalize these goals is dynamic.

Some seemingly important issues that appear on the initial treatment plan may quickly be taken off the list and replaced with other issues because of a change in the acuity of the need or the successful accomplishment of a goal or goals by the client. It is a good idea to keep a summary of all of the items that are removed from the treatment plan as a result of the client meeting her goals. Keeping a chart in the client's file and showing her all the many goals (including the small intermediate ones leading to the larger goal) can serve as a motivator for continued success or a reminder to help build motivation to get the client back on track. There are also items in the treatment plan that will need revising because the client is not successful in completing them, and therefore a smaller, more manageable intermediate goal or goals for which the client will likely show a successful outcome may be needed before placing the larger goal on the treatment plan.

The goals that are graphed for Penny at the outset of treatment include heroin-negative urine samples, days in recovery housing, days taking SSRI medication, ingestion of a prenatal vitamin and iron, obstetrical care visits, contact with a legal advocate, Narcotics Anonymous attendance, and engagement in recreational activities. As treatment progresses these goals will change, as will the order in which they are presented to Penny to show her progress.

Displaying Progress on the Treatment Plan

The treatment plan needs to be discussed with the client at every counseling session and on a daily basis when necessary. The successes of meeting the intermediate goals should be carefully tracked and displayed in a graphic format to show a snapshot of her success in meeting all goals, and then for each category, the success of meeting intermediate goals can also be shown. The treatment plan should be continually updated with new goals as the old ones are completed. Careful consideration needs to be given to whether goals are appropriate and obtainable for the client's state of recovery. Setting goals that are either too difficult or too easy may decrease motivation for drug abstinence.

Preventing and Managing Relapse

The best approach to relapse prevention is to recognize and address the client's warning signs before drug use occurs. The client's clinical presentation at each visit should be noted for changes that suggest precursors to relapse. Careful observation and probing questions about the client's behavior will often reveal what factors (e.g., environmental, personal) need to be in place to support drug abstinence. Typical warning signs of an impending relapse include but are not limited to the client missing treatment sessions; taking on too many new activities so that attending treatment is difficult; stopping or reducing the number of self-help meetings attended; wanting to use drugs again and not coping with those feelings; going to places where drugs were used in the past; hanging out with drug-using friends; and reporting feeling guilty, depressed, overtired, or angry. An example and warning signs for relapse are illustrated in a continuation of our ongoing case example.

Penny has been attending drug treatment and her prenatal care appointments for the past 2 months. On Thursday, Penny mentions that she is looking forward to the weekend because her favorite of her three boyfriends is being released following a month-long incarceration. The RBT therapist sees this as a warning sign of potential relapse because in the intake interview Penny mentioned that this was the man with whom she always used drugs. The RBT therapist talks to and role plays with Penny about the reunion with this boyfriend (e.g., if she must see him, what safe places could she meet him where she would not be tempted to use drugs, and how can she negotiate protected and drug-free sex with him?). Penny leaves her last treatment session on Friday with a concrete plan for where to meet the boyfriend and how to avoid drug use. On Monday, her RBT therapist notes that Penny is not attending treatment and calls her home in the afternoon to express concern and inquire about why she has missed treatment. Penny does not answer the phone. On Tuesday, Penny again does not show up to treatment, and the RBT therapist informs the outreach worker, who visits Penny's home that afternoon and finds her on the steps of a neighbor's house with her eyes half-closed, slumped over, and with slurred speech. The outreach worker and her safety assistant (outreach workers should always go in pairs) ask Penny to come with them in their car to admit Penny to the inpatient unit. Penny is at first resistant, saying she needs to pack clothes and can come tomorrow, but the outreach worker says there is a clothes bank at the center and emphasizes how concerned the RBT therapist is about Penny and the many benefits that treatment will provide to her. Penny returns to treatment with the outreach staff.

If the client does relapse, then it is important to understand as much about that relapse as possible so that both the RBT therapist and the client learn from the event and so that the possibility that the client might make that same mistake in the future can be minimized. A functional assessment can be used to understand what events, feelings, and circumstances came before the relapse (the antecedents) and what events, feelings, and circumstances came after the drug use behavior (the consequences). A functional assessment of drug use behavior is a close look at the circumstances surrounding each drug use episode and what skills and strengths the client has to use to avoid drug use in the future. An example of a functional assessment can be found in *A Cognitive–Behavioral*

Approach: Treating Cocaine Addiction (Carroll, 1998). As discussed previously, with the initial treatment plan, a functional assessment helps keep the focus off the *why* and onto the *who, what, how, when,* and *where* of drug use. It is important that the RBT therapist maintain a neutral tone, and body language that is neither punitive nor rewarding of the relapse provides an opportunity for the client and RBT therapist to review what went wrong and to implement changes in the treatment plan to minimize continued drug use by the client.

Although drug use of any type can be alarming, which drug a client is using may provide an important clue to determining areas for treatment plan revision. For example, a relapse to opioid use accompanied by withdrawal symptoms may indicate the need for a methadone dose increase. If withdrawal is not indicated and the medication dose is adequate, other factors that might be maintaining her behavior need to be examined (e.g., self-medication to numb the reoccurrence of intrusive thoughts about rape or other interpersonal trauma experiences). If benzodiazepines are being used, the dose of either the client's methadone or tapering benzodiazepine medication may or may not require an adjustment. First, although methadone only treats opioid dependence, it may be that the client is adding additional benzodiazepines to her benzodiazepine taper withdrawal to reduce opioid abstinence symptoms. It may also be that the benzodiazepine taper is too rapid and the speed at which it occurs needs to be reduced.

In Penny's case, while she is residing in the inpatient unit "to take a vacation from drug use," as her RBT therapist frames it for her, she has her methadone dose rechecked using both signs and symptoms of withdrawal (these are minimal and then nonexistent) and her plasma level of methadone metabolites, which is within normal limits. Her RBT therapist performs a functional assessment with her, and as the RBT therapist has suspected, the newly released boyfriend has been successful in convincing Penny to have sex with him after injecting both of them with heroin. Because it is unrealistic for Penny to leave the boyfriend—she would leave treatment before leaving him—the RBT therapist asks Penny if the boyfriend would be interested in treatment, and a plan is made to bring him in and facilitate his assessment for methadone treatment the day before Penny's release from the inpatient unit.

Completing the Treatment Plan

Unfortunately, the length of drug treatment is often not dictated by the client's progress or needs but by the ability of the third-party payer to cover the costs of treatment. From the start of the treatment plan, the RBT therapist needs to be thinking about how best to prepare and plan for the client's discharge from the program and where and how she will receive further treatment and care for her ongoing recovery from her substance use disorders as well as gynecological care and other psychiatric care.

Unique to treating substance use disorders in pregnant women, the delivery of the baby is an event that can lead to discharge after a few postpartum weeks given the need for specialized services. Having specific agencies and organizations to which clients can be referred and linked to continue treatment services without interruption is critical for their long-term recovery. Having plans in place for transition to a new treatment program and executing these plans, which should include introductions of the client to the staff at the new care facility, can be a critical ingredient for ensuring the client will follow up with the postspecialized care plan. Often, many of the overall goals found in the treatment plan are not fully met, and systems are needed to ensure that the client is referred to services that can help her continue to work toward the completion of her overarching goals.

The client should also start to be an active participant in her discharge planning and at this point in her treatment process should have the tools and skills to handle more of the active establishment of referral connections with less effort from the RBT therapist. The treatment plan completion should include a formal recognition of the client on leaving the program. This recognition could take the form of a certificate accompanied by a graphic summary of all of the goals the client met during the course of treatment. It could take the form of a handwritten note by the RBT therapist wishing the client well in her future and briefly summarizing her successes while in treatment.

Penny relapses to drugs once more after she has completed the initial relapse treatment in the inpatient unit. Her second relapse is triggered by being thrown out of the residence where she has been living as a result of her inability to pay her portion of the rent. She temporarily moves into a shelter with the help of her RBT therapist, but she uses two Xanax pills each day for a week "to deal with the stress and anxiety." This resumption of benzodiazepine use in addition to methadone is especially concerning to the RBT therapist. Again, Penny is brought inpatient to observe and monitor her closely for withdrawal. The inpatient facility also gives her a place to stay that is drug free. Her RBT therapist is successful in helping her find a long-term residential facility in which she can live for the next 2 years with her baby boy, who is born 2 weeks later. The baby's head circumference, length, and birth weight are within normal limits for the delivery at 39 weeks gestational age. The baby has some signs of withdrawal, but these are not severe enough to require medication treatment, and 2 weeks after delivery, Penny and the baby move into the long-term residential facility, where she receives her methadone and continues with her job attainment goals through specialized vocational assistance programming.

CONCLUSION

Penny's case illustrates how the initial functional assessment can be used to develop a comprehensive RBT treatment plan that addresses both survival and higher order life issues. Although there are multiple problems to address, they must be addressed in a systematic and integrated way. The treatment plan should be viewed as dynamic and should include both final goals and intermediate goals. The goals should always be set in discussion with the client to maximize her belief in herself and her enthusiasm to complete the goals. As soon as the treatment plan is completed and the client is stabilized, the client should be prepared for her eventual discharge so that she has the needed internal and external tools for long-term success.

12

PARENTS IN THE CHILD WELFARE SYSTEM

Many adults who abuse substances are parents and primary caregivers of children. Caregiver substance abuse poses significant risks to children and is associated with a range of negative child outcomes, including mental health problems, poor school performance, delinquency, and early alcohol and drug experimentation (Drucker, 2002; Schroeder, Kelley, & Fals-Stewart, 2006). These negative child outcomes are likely because it is difficult to provide consistent nurturing care to a child while abusing substances. In some cases, impairments in parenting are severe enough to be considered physically abusive toward or neglectful of the child. Parents who abuse drugs or alcohol are 3 times more likely to abuse or neglect their children than are parents who do not have substance use problems (National Center on Addiction and Substance Abuse at Columbia University, 1998). It is not surprising, then, that substance abuse by a parent is one of the leading reasons for child protective services' involvement with a family.

The child protective services system is a local (e.g., city, county, province) government-run system designed to protect children and adolescents from maltreatment. In most communities, child protective services systems are situated within a larger umbrella of welfare services for individual adults (e.g., disability subsidies), children (e.g., medical insurance for children from low-income families), and families (e.g., food stamps, housing assistance). Child protective services divisions work closely with the broader welfare system to provide a range of needed services to families in which child maltreatment is suspected or substantiated, including monitoring parent behavior and referring families to mental health or substance abuse treatment. In more severe cases, child protective services may temporarily or permanently remove children from parental care, arrange for and monitor the success of foster care placements, and arrange for permanent child adoption. Research in child protective services systems nationwide suggests that caregiver substance abuse is present in 60% to 70% of all substantiated child maltreatment cases and in 80% of cases that involve the removal of children from their homes (De Bellis et al., 2001; Osterling & Austin, 2008; Young, Boles, & Otero, 2007).

Cases involving parental substance abuse are among the most difficult for child welfare systems to address. Relative to other child welfare cases, children of parents who abuse substances are more likely to experience reabuse by the parent (Brook & McDonald, 2009; Ondersma, 2007) and out-of-home placement in foster care (U.S. Department of Health and Human Services, Administration for Children and Families, 1997). Once removed, children of substance-abusing parents spend more time in out-of-home placements (Connell, Bergeron, Katz, Saunders, & Tebes, 2007; Vanderploeg et al., 2007) and are more likely to experience a termination of parental rights (Connell et al., 2007) than are youth removed for other reasons. Out-of-home placements and long-term foster care pose their own risks to children, including attachment problems, mental health difficulties, and school failure (Harden, 2004; Stone, 2007). Given the potentially devastating effects of co-occurring substance abuse and child maltreatment, it is essential that adults within the child welfare system receive effective substance abuse treatment.

Unfortunately, parents within the child welfare system have difficulty accessing and using effective substance abuse services. A national survey of public child welfare agencies indicated that only 31% of parents in their system with an indicated need for substance abuse treatment received any substance abuse services (Child Welfare League of America, 1997). Those who do access services rarely complete them. Whereas adult substance abuse treatment completion rates in the general population are 55% to 65% (Dutra et al., 2008), it is estimated that only 20% of child welfare parents receive a full course of treatment (Child Welfare Partnership, 1998). Poor attendance and completion rates are likely due to several factors, including the competing demands of other child welfare system mandates (e.g., to attend court, parenting classes, and family therapy sessions) and structural barriers inherent in many treatment settings (e.g., lack of child care to attend sessions). Numerous researchers, advocacy groups, and federal initiatives have called for better access to substance abuse treatment for child welfare populations and better coordination between treatment and child welfare systems (e.g., Donohue, Romero, & Hill, 2006; U.S. Department of Health and Human Services, 1999).

In this chapter, we describe how Reinforcement-Based Treatment (RBT) can be used to address caregiver substance abuse in the context of a child maltreatment allegation. First, we outline some of the common clinical issues and treatment access difficulties affecting parents with child welfare system involvement and how these issues may impact substance abuse treatment. We then discuss how to apply RBT principles effectively when working with this population in a standard outpatient or intensive day treatment setting. Next, we describe a home-based version of RBT that is being used as part of two broader mental health treatment packages within a child welfare system in the state of Connecticut. One of these treatment packages, known as the Building Stronger Families model, comprehensively addresses the broad array of risk factors that contribute to both substance abuse and child maltreatment and integrates RBT components with interventions to address mental health and family functioning needs.

CLINICAL CHALLENGES

Parents who have physically abused or neglected their children often have numerous risk factors and stressors that may affect substance abuse treatment. It is common for parents involved in the child welfare system to themselves have histories of physical abuse or neglect (Kaufman & Zigler, 1987). Clinical depression and posttraumatic stress disorder also are common (Banyard, Williams, & Siegel, 2003; Kolko & Swenson, 2002). Although many households are headed by women functioning as single parents, dual-caregiver families within the child welfare system have high rates of domestic violence and verbally abusive behavior between partners (Cox, Kotch, & Everson, 2003; Slep & O'Leary, 2001).

Families in the child welfare system often are socially isolated and disengaged from extended families and other possible supports (e.g., church communities, friends who are not drug users; Rosario, Salzinger, Feldman, & Hammer, 1987). Many also face severe economic disadvantage, unstable housing, and limited connections to available community supports (e.g., food stamp or energy assistance programs; Corse, Schmid, & Trickett, 1990). Although children are never responsible for abuse or neglect by a parent, several child-level risk factors make physical abuse or neglect by a caregiver more likely to occur. Children who are aggressive, ill-tempered, or noncompliant with parental requests are more difficult for parents to manage and thus more vulnerable to maltreatment (Ammerman & Patz, 1996; Shields & Cicchetti, 1998). These problematic child behaviors often are exacerbated by the maltreatment incidents themselves and may be a significant source of ongoing stress to the parent.

SERVICE DELIVERY CHALLENGES

Clearly, the clinical needs of families in which maltreatment and parental substance abuse co-occur are complex and likely to require interventions in multiple domains (e.g., parent and child mental health, parent substance abuse, parenting skills, couples communication). Unfortunately, service systems are often ill-equipped to meet the complex needs of these families. Typically, child protection agencies refer each child affected by the maltreatment to separate therapists for individual treatment, and the parent also is referred to separate component services, such as parenting classes, substance abuse treatment, and/or mental health care. These referrals occur concurrently and often involve multiple agencies and settings, which can create significant logistical challenges (e.g., transportation to sessions, time off of work) for parents that reduce treatment attendance and compliance. Even when parents comply with all treatment components, a lack of coordination among providers can result in services that are highly fragmented and involve contradictory treatment goals (Donohue et al., 2006).

Parental substance abuse treatment has been particularly challenging to integrate with other interventions for families experiencing maltreatment. In both structure and content, many traditional adult substance abuse treatment programs do not take into consideration the client's role as a parent and the needs of the children when providing interventions (Drabble, 2007). Structurally, many substance abuse interventions require that clients remove themselves from their families to obtain services such as medical detoxification and short- or long-term residential treatment. Similarly, most day treatment and outpatient programs do not provide child care or case management services to assist clients in obtaining child care. Regarding the content of treatment, clients in traditional substance abuse treatment programs are frequently encouraged to focus on their own recovery before attending to the needs of others (Kumpfer, 1998). As a result of these factors, child protection officials often have little choice but to place children in foster care while parents receive treatment in the adult substance abuse treatment system.

REINFORCEMENT-BASED TREATMENT WITH CHILD WELFARE POPULATIONS

RBT is well suited to address the substance abuse treatment needs of parents in the child welfare system. The highly individualized nature of RBT clinical interventions, extensive case management services, and emphasis on outreach all increase the likelihood that clients' complex clinical needs will be addressed and that effective coordination with other services (e.g., mental health care) will occur. In this section, we discuss factors for outpatient treatment providers to consider when delivering RBT to this population.

Atmosphere of Reinforcement

RBT's emphasis on creating a reinforcing treatment atmosphere is particularly important when working with parents involved in the child welfare system. Such clients usually initiate treatment in a time of crisis soon after an abuse allegation has come to light, and they are under considerable pressure to make many changes in their lives quickly. They may have experienced severe condemnation from other professionals (e.g., protective services investigators, teachers at their children's school) and even friends and family members for the fact that their substance use has impacted the safety and well-being of a child. They are expected to adhere to numerous legal and treatment mandates and meet their parenting responsibilities at a time when a primary coping mechanism, substance use, is being denied them. RBT therapists should sincerely commend clients for their ability to manage these stressors and for their willingness to address their substance problems. Doing so and meeting the other demands placed on them demonstrate how much they care for their children, and their commitment is admirable. These current responsible behaviors, rather than guilt or defensiveness regarding past maltreatment incidents, should be the focus of treatment and should be continuously reinforced.

To establish an atmosphere of trust and honest disclosure, it is important for RBT clinicians to discuss and verify the client's understanding of his or her confidentiality rights and exactly what information from the treatment will be shared with the child welfare system. This discussion should occur during intake procedures and be revisited whenever necessary throughout treatment. The client's confidentiality rights also should be clearly communicated to the child welfare system caseworker. Generally, when clients are mandated for treatment, clinicians are required to provide information about the client's attendance and his or her professional opinion of the client's overall treatment progress. Thus, details regarding the client's reasons for use, relapses, or ambivalence regarding abstinence or parenting would not be disclosed. RBT clinicians should help clients understand that being honest about their drug use and relapses is one way they can demonstrate their engagement in treatment and commitment to maintaining abstinence. In other words, honesty will increase the chances that the clinician's reports to the child welfare worker will be positive and ultimately will make the treatment more successful.

Functional Assessment

Clients with child welfare system involvement are no different from other clients in terms of the functions (discussed in Chapter 2, this volume) that their drug use serves. Their use may, for example, function to meet their needs for social connection or anxiety reduction. In addition, the problems and stressors commonly experienced by child welfare families, such as trauma symptomatology, depression, domestic violence, and financial concerns, may also contribute directly to clients' use (e.g., use prevents the client from reexperiencing traumatic memories).

When conducting functional assessments with this population, RBT clinicians should be mindful that it may be difficult for clients with child welfare system involvement to admit to functions that implicate their parenting. For example, clients may fear that if they admit that one of the things they like about use is that it allows them to temporarily escape from parenting responsibilities, this information will be used against them in legal proceedings or will be judged harshly by the therapist. However, understanding this function is critical to devising an effective treatment plan. In this example, setting up appropriate sources of respite from parenting would be a priority. Fears of reprisal from child welfare may also lead clients to dispute the results of drug testing and refuse to participate in functional assessments of relapses.

Abstinence-Supporting Behavioral Goals

For many parents, in the short term, the threat of losing their children and the intense monitoring of their substance use by child welfare caseworkers is sufficient motivation to initiate abstinence. However, as with all clients, RBT therapists must help ensure that abstinence becomes genuinely reinforcing for parents if it is to be sustained after the initial crisis has passed. Parents' ability to establish recreational habits that do not involve substance use will be critical to this sustainability. The extent to which recreation will involve their children should be discussed explicitly. Parents often provide socially desirable responses to probes about recreational activities, indicating that their time with their children is always enjoyable. Although being a parent and meeting family responsibilities can be highly rewarding, the problems commonly faced by child welfare families (e.g., child noncompliance) increase the likelihood that other interventions (e.g., those addressing parenting skills) will be necessary before these tasks become consistently reinforcing for clients or before clients feel efficacious in their role as parents. In the meantime, RBT therapists can help clients set recreational goals that are truly reinforcing to them (e.g., time with sober adults without children present, self-care activities) and help clients make the distinction between time with their children that is rewarding (e.g., taking them to a playground) versus time that is not (e.g., shopping for school clothes). In addition, recreational goals that address the social isolation many child welfare families experience (e.g., to attend church or public events for children) may be particularly helpful.

It also is important that parents have an employment goal. Although many families within the child welfare system receive public assistance (e.g., housing vouchers, food stamps), such support is typically inadequate to meet family needs. In addition, many child welfare systems have explicit mandates that parents receiving assistance also work (Blank & Blum, 1997). As noted throughout this volume, maintaining consistent work directly competes with drug use, reduces isolation, and contributes to a sense of personal self-efficacy. For parents in the child welfare system, it can also provide a respite from child-rearing tasks, model responsible behavior to children, and signal to the social support network that the parent is sober. Helping parents of small children find work and arrange for child care is challenging, and considerable case management resources should be allocated for this purpose. RBT therapists can enlist the help of extended family members and child welfare caseworkers in this endeavor. RBT therapists should also inquire with caseworkers about possible work restrictions facing adults with substantiated cases of child maltreatment; they may be ineligible for human services jobs such as working with children or older people.

Anticipating Relapses

In some cases, strain in the parent–child relationship and a low sense of efficacy in the parenting role lead clients to feel ambivalent about whether they should retain or regain custody of their children. Paradoxically, when children are removed because of safety concerns related to drug use, parents often have less incentive to remain sober and their substance use increases. Child welfare systems often interpret this behavior as proof that the client does not want to regain custody of his or her children and respond with increased pressure and threats of permanent removal. This cycle can add to parents' sense of hopelessness regarding their future as effective parents and to their ambivalence about maintaining abstinence.

Clinicians should be aware of the heightened risk for relapse that a child's out-of-home placement poses to a parent and intensify their interventions at this time (e.g., increased use of behavioral contracting, day planning, recreation, and support from a family sponsor). It is particularly important to reinforce parents for their efforts (e.g., coordinating child visits with a foster parent) during periods of child removal. In addition, motivational enhancement techniques should be used to help clients reaffirm their commitment to treatment, abstinence, and parenting. The vast majority of parents truly want to have long-term positive relationships with their children. An increasing discrepancy between the positive values they hold about parenting and behaviors that are counterproductive to regaining custody of their children (e.g., spending time with drug using peers) can keep parents engaged in abstinence-supporting behaviors. Conversely, clinicians can point out that maintaining ties with children is likely to facilitate the parent's abstinence, given research suggesting that among parents receiving substance abuse treatment, involvement with children is associated with better treatment outcomes (Collins, Grella, & Hser, 2003).

Drug Testing

As suggested previously, the drug-testing component of RBT may present challenges when working with child welfare populations. When substance abuse is indicated in a child maltreatment case, regular monitoring of the parent's use is usually mandated and results factored into child placement decisions. Substance abuse treatment providers are often called on to provide drug testing and testing results. However, the purpose of drug testing within the RBT model is not to detect drug use for evidentiary purposes. Rather, RBT uses drug testing to reinforce clients for their abstinence, to monitor whether interventions are successful, and to detect relapses quickly so that treatment plans can be adjusted to be more effective.

To maintain the fidelity of the RBT, we generally recommend that clinics providing RBT reject requests to provide specific drug-testing results to child welfare system or other court officials. This policy and the reasons for it should be communicated to child welfare officials before treatment begins and explained to clients at intake. RBT clinicians should be sympathetic to the desire by child welfare case workers to have up-to-date information on the client's abstinence to protect children's safety. However, in our experience, the information obtained from drug testing that occurs as part of treatment is not well suited to meet the needs of child welfare staff (e.g., whether this particular relapse incident placed children at risk). It also rarely meets the evidentiary standards necessary for legal decision making (e.g., how samples are collected and handled in the "chain of custody" between client and lab) and is easily invalidated in the courtroom.

Under some circumstances, RBT providers may agree to contribute to the monitoring function of the child protection system by serving as the drug-testing entity. The most common reason for an exception is if failing to conduct the testing would threaten the client's ability to participate in treatment or meet treatment goals. We have seen cases in which the drug-testing burden imposed by the courts threatens the client's ability to attend treatment sessions or to maintain employment (e.g., tests occur at a court house multiple times per week at times that conflict with the client's work schedule). In such cases, and with the client's permission, RBT staff may advocate that they arrange for the testing. Ideally, testing under these circumstances would occur, for convenience, at the same time and general location as the client's RBT treatment but be conducted by staff other than the RBT providers (e.g., an affiliated clinic or unit in the same building).

REINFORCEMENT-BASED TREATMENT AS A COMPONENT OF COMPREHENSIVE HOME-BASED TREATMENT FOR CHILD MALTREATMENT: THE BUILDING STRONGER FAMILIES MODEL

As an empirically supported, individualized, and strength-based intervention that offers extensive case management services and a high degree of coordination with other treatment providers, RBT delivered in outpatient settings has the potential to meet the substance abuse treatment needs of parents within the child welfare system. An alternative approach to providing effective substance abuse treatment with this population is to integrate RBT components into existing empirically supported family-based interventions for child maltreatment (which tend to deliver treatment to clients within their homes) and to use a single provider to deliver all services to families concurrently. Relative to separate brokered services for families (even if coordinated), this approach has the potential to more efficiently and comprehensively address the interrelatedness of concurrent problems, to minimize the logistical challenge of complying with multiple services, and to eliminate inconsistency or contradictions in treatment planning.

Two programs in the state of Connecticut are using this approach to provide RBT to parents with substance abuse treatment needs within the child welfare system. In this section, we provide an overview of the first of these programs, the Building Stronger Families (BSF) model, by briefly reviewing the history and development of BSF, describing the approach, outlining how RBT is adapted and integrated with other interventions within this model, and summarizing preliminary outcome data.

History and Development of Building Stronger Families

BSF grew out of a concern by state- and local-level officials at the Connecticut Department of Children and Families (DCF; the state child welfare agency) over a rising number of complex child maltreatment cases that involved parental substance abuse and high rates of child removal. DCF officials had radically reduced the number of youth who required an out-of-home placement (as a result of criminal behavior) within the juvenile justice system by the statewide implementation of multisystemic therapy (MST; Henggeler, Schoenwald, Borduin, Rowland, & Cunningham, 2009), an empirically validated treatment for youth conduct problems. DCF leaders approached the developer of MST, Dr. Scott Henggeler, to implement a version of MST specifically designed for families with co-occurring child maltreatment and parental substance abuse. At the time, a randomized clinical trial of an adapted version of MST for child abuse and neglect (MST-CAN), developed by Dr. Cynthia Swenson, had just been completed. The trial indicated that MST-CAN was effective in reducing reabuse incidents and child out-of-home placements as well as improving parent and child mental health functioning (see Swenson, Schaeffer, Henggeler, Faldowski, & Mayhew, 2010). Ways in which MST-CAN could be expanded to also address parental substance abuse were discussed, and a search for an empirically supported and compatible substance abuse treatment model began.

Developers of RBT (i.e., Maxine Stitzer, Hendree Jones, and Michelle Tuten) were enthusiastic about a collaborative project, and the Annie E. Casey Foundation provided funding for BSF model development as part of their efforts to improve the services provided by child welfare systems. MST-CAN and RBT model developers worked extensively with DCF stakeholders and the designated treatment provider agency (Wheeler Clinic) for many months to determine how the two treatment models would be merged. In 2005, BSF services began in New Britain, Connecticut, and a pilot study to evaluate the model's efficacy was initiated. BSF has operated continuously since that time with its clinical services (including motivational incentives) fully funded by DCF. Model developers from RBT and MST and MST-CAN have provided oversight to ensure adherence to each model's treatment components. A randomized clinical trial of the model began in August 2010.

Clinical Bases of Building Stronger Families

BSF is a full integration of MST-CAN and RBT, with all interventions from both models integrated and delivered simultaneously. Figure 12.1 depicts how MST-CAN builds on standard MST and how RBT interventions extend the scope of MST-CAN still further. In the sections that follow, we describe the standard MST and MST-CAN models as a basis for understanding how interventions from these models are integrated with RBT. We next discuss how RBT is delivered within the MST and MST-CAN framework and ways in which it is modified for administration within a home-based ser-

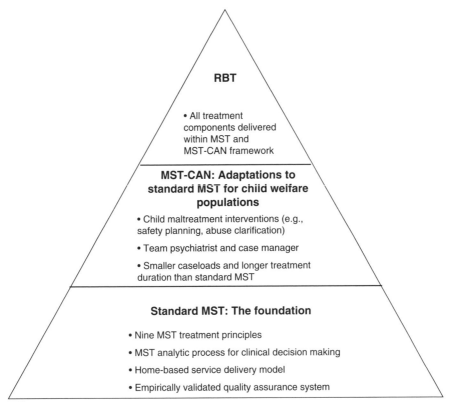

Figure 12.1. Treatment components of the Building Stronger Families model. MST = multisystemic therapy; MST-CAN = multisystemic therapy for child abuse and neglect; RBT = Reinforcement-Based Treatment.

vice delivery model. Figure 12.2 shows the overlap of these three models in terms of the populations they serve.

Standard Multisystemic Therapy

Standard MST is the core model on which BSF is based. MST was developed in the 1970s as a treatment for delinquent youth and their families, and through a rigorous 30-year program of research, MST has come to be recognized as a leading evidence-based intervention for highly complex, multineed families (Elliott, 1998; U.S. Department of Health and Human Services, Office of Public Health and Science, 2001). MST's theoretical roots are in systems theory and social ecological models of behavior (Bronfenbrenner, 1979). As such, behavior is viewed as multidetermined by characteristics of the key systems in which individuals are embedded (e.g., family, school, peer, work, neighborhood).

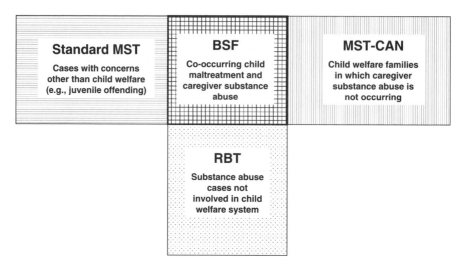

Figure 12.2. Overlap and differences between clinical populations served by standard MST, MST-CAN, RBT, and BSF. MST = multisystemic therapy; MST-CAN = multisystemic therapy for child abuse and neglect; RBT = Reinforcement-Based Treatment; BSF = Building Stronger Families.

The clinical practice of MST follows a set of nine principles that, if followed, increase the likelihood of attaining favorable clinical outcomes (Huey, Henggeler, Brondino, & Pickrel, 2000). The principles guide conceptualization (e.g., identifying the key drivers of identified problems), design (e.g., action oriented, present focused), and implementation (e.g., using family strengths as levers for change, using sustainable strategies) of interventions. Throughout all phases of treatment, the clinician follows a structured analytical process for how best to conceptualize the case, which target behaviors should be prioritized, and which specific intervention techniques should delivered. Because parents are viewed as the key to achieving favorable outcomes for their children, MST programs place great emphasis on engaging families and broader ecology members who can support the family in treatment. MST incorporates intervention techniques that are evidence based (e.g., cognitive behavior therapy, behavioral parent training, certain pharmacotherapies) within the aforementioned social ecological conceptual framework.

Structurally, MST clinicians work as a team of three or four therapists and a half-time supervisor, with each therapist carrying a caseload of four to six families for 4 to 6 months. Sessions are provided at times convenient for families, and clinicians share a round-the-clock on-call roster for after-hour crises. The treatment is intensive, and families are often seen several times per week. Finally, MST uses a quality assurance protocol that aims to enhance family outcomes by supporting therapist treatment fidelity and clinical efforts.

The quality assurance system includes a 5-day orientation training, quarterly booster training, weekly face-to-face group supervision, and weekly consultation with an MST expert. All of these quality assurance procedures are focused on optimizing family outcomes. In addition, families complete a monthly telephone interview to measure therapist model adherence.

Multisystemic Therapy for Child Abuse and Neglect

The MST-CAN model includes all of the components and characteristics noted for standard MST. In addition, several clinical, structural, and administrative adaptations have been made to meet the needs of a child welfare population. Clinically, each team has dedicated time from a psychiatrist who has the capacity to prescribe evidence-based pharmacotherapy for children and adults. A full-time crisis caseworker also provides case management support to all of the cases on the team. Moreover, several empirically based strategies for common presenting problems are used in MST-CAN as needed. These strategies include (a) protocols for child and family safety, (b) functional assessment of abusive incidents (Kolko & Swenson, 2002), (c) treatment of posttraumatic stress disorder symptomatology (Foa & Rothbaum, 1998), (d) treatment for anger management (Feindler, Ecton, Kingsley, & Dubey, 1986; Novaco, 1994), (e) family communication training (Robin, Bedway, & Gilroy, 1994), and (f) clarification of the abuse (Lipovsky, Swenson, Ralston, & Saunders, 1998).

Regarding structural and administrative adaptations, because the cases are generally more severe than delinquency cases, MST-CAN therapists carry a lower caseload (no more than four families) than MST therapists for a longer treatment period of 6 to 9 months. Administratively, considerable attention is given to the relationships among the family, child welfare staff, and the MST-CAN team. Child welfare caseworkers participate with the team in the 5-day MST training and the 2-day MST-CAN training, attend key sessions with families, and are in regular ongoing contact with the team to facilitate clinical outcomes for families.

Reinforcement-Based Treatment Within Building Stronger Families

All RBT treatment components described in this volume are implemented within BSF, including a motivational incentive (monetary vouchers) for negative urine drug screens and breathalyzer tests. The most significant difference from clinic-based versions is that RBT within BSF has only one group-based component, the weekly Social Club meeting, whereas outpatient RBT uses group-based interventions for several treatment components (i.e., recreation, Job Club for employment goal attainment, and adjunctive psychoeducational interventions). All parents receiving substance abuse treatment within the BSF model attend Social Club every Friday, and former clients are welcome to return to Social Club at any time. Although in BSF the members of Social Club do not know each other as well as RBT outpatient clients (who interact in treatment several times a week) do, we have found that a festive, supportive atmosphere can be achieved nonetheless. Interventions related to job and recreational goal attainment are delivered primarily by the team's crisis caseworker and are achieved through in-home interactions with the client.

BSF therapists use an in-home client charting system to administer RBT clinical tools and keep them active with clients. Copies of behavioral contracts, functional behavioral assessment interviews, feedback reports, and client behavioral graphs are maintained within this chart and are updated and reviewed with clients multiple times each week. All BSF staff members (therapists, supervisors, crisis caseworkers) are prepared to administer functional assessments with clients at any time they discover a relapse has occurred. Therapists also carry stockpiles of congratulation vouchers, colored pens and markers, and stickers with them at all times to immediately positively reinforce a negative drug-testing result or progress on a behavioral goal graph. Although BSF clients have many goals in addition to abstinence, behavioral graphs are used only to depict and reinforce behaviors that directly compete with drug use. This way, the intense focus of standard RBT on the reinforcement of daily behaviors that support abstinence can be maintained and is not lost in the sometimes overwhelming array of tasks clients in the child welfare system must accomplish. Other treatment goals (e.g., to improve parenting skills) are monitored and reinforced primarily through techniques within the MST model (e.g., family therapy sessions in which spouses and children praise the parent for gains in parenting skills).

Components of the Building Stronger Families Model

BSF provides services for youth ages 6 to 17 and their families who are under the guidance of DCF as a result of physical abuse and/or neglect and parental substance abuse. As with MST-CAN, a single BSF therapist administers all intervention components to a particular family. Therapists have a caseload of no more than four families and are supported within their team by two additional therapists, a full-time supervisor, a crisis case manager, expert consultants, and a part-time child and adult psychiatrist. Interventions are provided in individual sessions with parents in much the same way that other caregiver interventions (e.g., exposure sessions for trauma) are delivered in MST-CAN programs. However, unlike other individual treatment components that may reach completion points, RBT components are provided continuously and intensively throughout the course of treatment to ensure that abstinence and supporting activities become generalized and sustainable. The crisis case manager provides supportive services for all families (e.g., finding better housing, applying for health care benefits) and helps deliver many of the RBT vocational and recreational components (e.g., helping clients find jobs and recreational opportunities). Like MST-CAN, treatment duration in BSF usually ranges from 6 to 9 months, though some families may be served longer, depending on severity and need.

Safety Planning

A central focus of BSF is extensive planning for child safety in the event the parent relapses. All BSF team members work closely with child welfare caseworkers to monitor child safety and gauge parent progress in obtaining abstinence and other goals. Substance use monitoring for safety involves urine and breathalyzer testing conducted randomly within the home a minimum of three times a week for the duration of treatment. Ideally, child safety plans involve collaboration with members of the family's natural ecology and contingencies that require parental, not child, removal from the home until abstinence can be reestablished. This arrangement helps to ensure that parents are not unintentionally reinforced (i.e., are able to remain living in their homes without parenting demands) during relapses. BSF and DCF staff convey jointly to parents their understanding that relapses often are a part of the recovery process and that the child's formal removal from the home will depend ultimately more on the parent's adherence to safety plans and use of substance abuse treatment than on the results of any particular drug test.

Flow of Treatment

The sequence of interventions and the integration of model components provided within BSF are depicted in Figure 12.3. Before parents consent to participate in BSF, they are provided with a careful explanation of the purpose and implications of drug-testing results during treatment. Specifically, drug testing is for the purpose of clinical monitoring to aid the development of interventions that help maintain abstinence. However, clients are informed that child welfare caseworkers will be aware of clinical progress, including drug-testing results, on an ongoing basis. Immediately after parents consent to BSF treatment, urine and breathalyzer testing is conducted; initial safety plans are developed (and if the client tests positive, implemented); and a baseline assessment of drug use is obtained. For clients who have (or are suspected of having) a physical dependency on a drug (e.g., alcohol, opiates), a 5- to 7-day stay in an inpatient detoxification facility is facilitated, and care arrangements are made for the children using family supports, if possible.

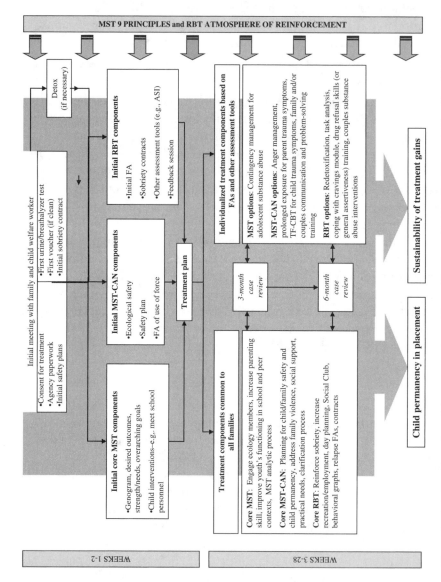

Figure 12.3. Integration of model components and flow of treatment in Building Stronger Families. MST = multisystemic therapy; MST-CAN = multisystemic therapy for child abuse and neglect; RBT = Reinforcement-Based Treatment; BSF = Building Stronger Families; FA = functional assessment; ASI = Addiction Severity Index; TF-CBT = trauma-focused cognitive–behavioral therapy.

Family strengths and needs are assessed next, and desired outcomes for treatment are obtained from multiple ecology members and stakeholders (e.g., caseworkers, probation officers). Desired outcomes are translated into overarching treatment goals. Detailed functional assessments are conducted for all drugs used by the parent and for any physical abuse that has occurred. Using the structured analytical process noted earlier, BSF team members identify fit factors or drivers of the problem for each target behavior. Interventions are then planned and delivered to address the key drivers of the substance abuse, maltreatment, and other desired outcomes (e.g., a teenager reenrolling in school). For example, if it is determined that posttraumatic stress disorder is a primary driver of parental substance abuse (i.e., that use functions to help the client avoid trauma memories), empirically supported treatment for posttraumatic stress disorder is begun to reduce those symptoms while simultaneously conducting RBT interventions and strategies to assist with child behavior problems.

Once a week, all BSF clients who are able (i.e., not yet working, no child care responsibilities) attend a 2-hr Social Club held at the provider agency. Throughout treatment, clients provide urine and breathalyzer tests using a testing frequency that matches the drug detection windows of targeted substances (at a minimum, three times each week). During the first 14 weeks of treatment, the motivational incentive of a $10 voucher for each negative drug and alcohol screen is provided to clients. Clients can earn up to $420 to spend at retail stores (by exchanging vouchers for store gift cards) or to use for other purposes of their choosing (e.g., as a security deposit or to pay off a debt). BSF therapists also reinforce negative drug and alcohol screens using behavioral graphs. Progress toward achieving job and recreational goals is graphed, discussed, and reinforced continuously, and techniques from the motivational-interviewing approach are used to enhance client engagement in particular treatment components. A clarification process that addresses both maltreatment and parental substance abuse is conducted when the parent has sustained abstinence and abstinence-supporting lifestyle changes for multiple weeks. Treatment is considered successfully completed when clients have met their overarching goals, child permanence in placement has been obtained, parents have sustained abstinence, and changes in target behaviors have been maintained for at least 2 months.

Preliminary Outcomes for Building Stronger Families

In the first 4 years of implementation, 87% of parents offered BSF agreed to participate, and 93% of those completed treatment (Swenson et al., 2009). This completion rate far surpasses that of other treatments for children who have experienced intrafamilial violence (64%; Koverola, Murtaugh, Connors,

Reeves, & Papas, 2007) and adults in substance abuse treatment (55% to 65%; Dutra et al., 2008). Moreover, over 4 years, the average number of individuals treated per family was six. Thus, the capacity of BSF to effect wide-sweeping change in the family system in these cases is great.

A pilot study was conducted to examine outcomes following BSF for the first 26 families who initiated treatment (Schaeffer, Swenson, Tuerk, & Henggeler, 2010). Parents experienced significant reductions from pre- to posttreatment in self-reported alcohol and drug use, and 85% had negative urine toxicology screens and breathalyzer tests for at least 30 days before discharge. Parents also reported significant reductions in symptoms of depression and significantly reduced their use of psychological aggression toward their child. Children reported significant decreases in anxiety symptoms.

A comparison sample of 26 families who did not receive BSF was obtained from a DCF record review. These families all met the same criteria for referral to BSF (i.e., recent maltreatment report, child ages 6 to 17 years, and indicated parental substance abuse) and were matched to the BSF cases on child age and date range of DCF involvement. The groups did not differ on key demographic or abuse variables at baseline, although BSF parents were more likely to be female. Reabuse incidents and child out-of-home placement data were obtained from the DCF reporting system for both groups over a follow-up period of 24 months post baseline (i.e., from the onset of BSF or the anchoring date for comparison families). During this time frame, parents who received BSF had 64% fewer new reabuse reports than comparison parents (0.26 and 1.06, respectively), and children who received BSF were 65% less likely than comparison children to have experienced a placement outside of the home (13% vs. 39%, respectively; see Schaeffer et al., 2010).

BSF's successful outcomes with families in the child welfare system can be attributed to several factors. First, by delivering treatment in families' homes and other community locations at times convenient to parents, BSF overcomes many of the barriers to service access for child welfare families described in the substance abuse treatment literature (Donohue et al., 2006). In addition, BSF incorporates evidence-based treatments for adult substance abuse, child maltreatment, and parent and child mental health problems and integrates them coherently to comprehensively address family needs. Moreover, the high degree of coordination of BSF staff with the child welfare system allows for the effective management of the risk to children's safety posed by caregiver substance use while also acknowledging that relapses often are a part of recovery and do not always necessitate child removal from the home. This coordination ensures that the contingencies placed on parents by the child welfare system are constructive and allows families to safely stay together during the time that it takes for the positive effects of the parents' substance abuse treatment to emerge.

Building Stronger Families Case Example

Angelica and her husband, Tony, were referred to the BSF team by child protective services because of substance-abuse-related child neglect. Neighbors had reported that their four children (ranging in age from 4 to 17) were frequently left unattended, with the 4-year-old recently found roaming the neighborhood several blocks away from the couple's home. The couple had numerous previous reports of maltreatment and had resisted child protective services' interventions in the past. At the initial assessment, both parents tested positive for cocaine, and Angelica also reported heavy alcohol use. An initial safety plan was developed and implemented, with the children staying with a neighbor for 2 days until both parents tested negative for drugs. The BSF therapist met with the couple multiple times during the first week of treatment to assess their strengths and needs, their patterns of drug use, and their desired outcomes of treatment for themselves and their children. She also met with the children, whose main request was that their parents stay together and stop fighting.

Initial conversations revealed many systemic strengths but also numerous needs. Angelica and Tony both loved their children, frequently engaged in family activities with them, and expressed a strong desire to retain custody of them. Both parents also were interested in seeking employment and wanted to see their oldest daughter attend college following her graduation from high school in a few months. The children themselves were polite and well behaved at home and well liked at school by teachers and peers. The family had reliable transportation and one extended family member (Tony's sister) with whom they were close. In terms of needs, the couple had massive debt and were likely to lose their home to foreclosure in a few months. Neither parent had a strong employment history, and a previous felony offense on Tony's record impeded his ability to find work. The marital relationship was characterized by a great deal of conflict regarding who was to blame for their debt problem and anger over an affair that Angelica had several years prior. The couple was socially isolated, cut off from their extended families and with few friends other than neighbors with whom they tended to use drugs and alcohol. With the BSF therapist, the couple set mutual goals for abstinence, providing a safe environment for the children, improving their marital relationship, and finding employment. In addition, Angelica set an individual goal to address her severe anxiety symptoms, and Tony agreed to work on his explosive anger during arguments.

A functional assessment revealed that Angelica's drug of choice was alcohol, which she used to avoid withdrawal symptoms and to reduce both generalized and social anxiety. Angelica drank throughout the day every day, primarily at home while the children were at school or after they went to bed.

Her cocaine use, which occurred more sporadically, functioned primarily as a way of connecting to Tony, although she reported also enjoying its energizing effects. Tony's functional assessment indicated that he used cocaine four to five times a week, primarily at home in the evening or with neighbors socially. For him, cocaine functioned as a means of connecting to others, escaping his financial worries, and having fun. Given Angelica's likely physical dependence on alcohol and multiple cues for drinking at home, the BSF therapist's first intervention was to recommend detox followed by a stay in a recovery house. Initially, Tony was strongly opposed to Angelica living away from home, viewing it as a "holiday" from household responsibilities; much of their marital conflict centered on the fact that Tony did most of the family's cooking, cleaning, and child care.

The BSF therapist helped Tony to see that Angelica would never be able to contribute to the household until she achieved stable abstinence and that several weeks away from home would increase the chances that she would be successful. With Tony's support, Angelica completed a 5-day detox and moved into a women's recovery house, where she stayed for 6 weeks. During this time the BSF therapist held frequent individual sessions with Tony and Angelica as well as couples and family therapy sessions during Angelica's visits home. The therapist reinforced Tony for his own abstinence and responsible behavior in caring for his children. He agreed to stop contact with his friends who used cocaine and to sample new recreational activities such as attending church services with his children. In addition to providing frequent reinforcement for abstinence, individual sessions with Angelica focused on coping with anxiety symptoms (using cognitive behavioral techniques), engaging in recreation and self-care, and establishing new friendships with women at her recovery house and Alcoholics Anonymous meeting.

In marital therapy sessions, Tony and Angelica negotiated a workable division of labor in their home, and Angelica began taking on more household responsibilities while still living at the recovery house. They also discussed rules and structure for the children, and Angelica learned how to be more effective in her discipline and monitoring. They engaged in problem-solving sessions to find solutions for their immediate financial and housing crises. Because the couple had difficulty talking with each other without yelling and insults, the therapist trained them in couples communication techniques and reinforced them for staying calm and using new interaction skills. She also reinforced Tony for using anger management techniques he learned in their individual sessions. Tony and Angelica agreed to postpone discussions of the emotional issues in their marriage (i.e., Tony's anger over her affair, Angelica's feeling that she would always be punished for it) until they felt more stable in their housing, parenting, and abstinence.

After several weeks of sobriety and improved relations, Angelica moved back home, and both she and Tony began pursuing work. Angelica began by volunteering at her son's elementary school, and Tony enrolled in a vocational program designed to help people with felonies obtain work. The therapist used case management interventions to help the couple secure financial aid for their oldest daughter to attend community college and to address the impending foreclosure. Because social isolation continued to be a serious concern for the family, the therapist helped the couple to identify more extended family members with whom they could reconnect. Tony overcame his feeling that Angelica's family had facilitated her affair, and Angelica agreed to make amends with Tony's parents. These interventions helped the couple to resolve the emotional fallout from Angelica's affair and to recommit to their marriage. In addition, Angelica continued to attend the Alcoholics Anonymous group she had started while at the recovery house and engaged in recreation with some of the women she had met there.

At the end of 6 months of treatment, both Angelica and Tony were abstinent, and there were no further reports to child protective services. Angelica's anxiety symptoms decreased, and Tony demonstrated better anger management in their interactions. Their daughter started college; Angelica began working full time at an assisted living facility; and Tony continued in his vocational program. The family relocated to an apartment, began attending church regularly, and were becoming more involved with extended family. The couple decided to pursue marital therapy with a pastoral counselor at their church after BSF ended to maintain the progress they had made and to continue to resolve the issues of their past.

Recent Developments: The Family-Based Recovery Model

The initial success of BSF has led DCF leaders to develop and implement a similar model, Family-Based Recovery (FBR), to comprehensively address the needs of substance-abusing parents of children ages 0 to 3 involved with the child welfare system. FBR combines RBT with an attachment-based parent–child therapy, Coordinated Intervention for Women and Infants (National Abandoned Infants Assistance Resource Center, 2003), which also is delivered in the home. Ongoing evaluations of both FBR and BSF continue, and dissemination to other states is a goal. BSF and FBR have the potential to improve the way child welfare staff intervene with parents with addictions. Feedback from DCF supervisors and administrators indicate that caseworkers who partner with these clinical teams are more supportive of parents with substance abuse difficulties and more tolerant of relapses. In addition, improved morale of caseworkers working with these programs has been reported.

CONCLUSION

Parents with substance abuse problems in the child welfare system tra-ditionally have been poorly served by substance abuse treatment systems. The many individual, child, family, and legal challenges these parents often face present barriers to successful engagement in and completion of substance abuse services. Moreover, substance abuse treatment is likely to be unsuccess-ful if not highly coordinated with other needed services, such as mental health treatment and parenting skill development. Outpatient and home-based versions of RBT have the potential to effectively treat parents' sub-stance abuse and greatly reduce the need to remove children from the home. Ultimately, investment by child welfare agencies in evidence-based substance abuse treatment models such as RBT and BSF will lower costs associated with nonfamilial child placements and reduce suffering among children and fam-ilies affected by substance abuse.

AFTERWORD: FUTURE DIRECTIONS FOR PRACTICE AND RESEARCH

Reinforcement-Based Treatment (RBT) is a well-studied treatment model with much promise for improving drug abstinence rates among individuals with substance use disorders. However, much remains to be learned about the applicability of the approach with various populations in different settings. In particular, what modifications can be made to RBT to suit the resource-scarce environment of fee-for-service community practice? And how can RBT therapists and administrators ensure that modifications do not compromise fidelity to the RBT model? Two real-world applications of RBT—the Cornerstone program in Baltimore, Maryland, and the Building Stronger Families model in the Connecticut child welfare program—have yielded insights into these issues. (For an overview of these programs, see the Introduction and Chapter 12, this volume.)

MODIFICATIONS TO REINFORCEMENT-BASED TREATMENT

The ongoing translation of RBT from science (i.e., large-scale research studies) to real-world community practice (i.e., fee-for-service non-grant-funded community practice) has taught us a considerable amount about the difficult context in which substance abuse treatment agencies operate and the challenges involved in implementing an evidence-based model in the resource-scarce context . For example, the Cornerstone program in Baltimore (described in the Introduction) has modified the RBT model in significant ways to accommodate the demands of a fee-for-service environment. The major changes are related to reducing program costs and include the following:

- the use of the fishbowl technique (i.e., a lottery-style incentive schedule designed to reinforce target behaviors while reducing program costs; see Chapter 6 for more information on the fishbowl technique),
- testing of urine samples on a random weekly basis rather than 3 times weekly (although this schedule is less intensive than the schedule used in RBT research, studies have shown that even once weekly urine selection schedules produce similar outcomes to once monthly urine selection conditions [Chutuape, Jasinski, Fingerhood, & Stitzer, 2001; Saxon, Calsyn, & Haver, 1990], and these data suggest that current urine-monitoring practices may be sufficient for assessing the clinical benefits of an RBT program),
- twice-per-week on-site recreational activities rather than daily off-site activities, and
- caseloads of approximately 15 per counselor compared with five to 12 in the randomized trials.

Among these modifications, the most clinically significant is the increase in therapist caseloads. The intensity of the model requires considerable time and dedication on the part of the RBT therapist to avoid a reduction in the intensity of the intervention. Higher caseloads require greater time management skills, more supervisory oversight, and continued diligence on the part of all staff to ensure that the essential elements of the model are not compromised.

Perhaps the most significant challenge to the model relates to insurance reimbursement. Insurance carriers cap the number of sessions that a client can receive (both within a 12-month period and also sessions per day or per week), which significantly impairs the model's ability to remain individualized and to respond to the client's progress in treatment. For example, an increase in treatment intensity (more sessions per week) may be behaviorally indicated during a high-risk period (e.g., when a client has recently lost housing); however, such increases in treatment intensity are not reimbursable. The same dilemma occurs with the overall length of treatment, which also is often capped by insurance providers, depending on the level of care being provided. Thus, it is important that providers advocate with insurance carriers to seek as much service as is needed for clients and to educate and collaborate with them on the necessity of intensive services that can adequately compete with the challenge of substance use disorders. That being stated, the issues with insurance reimbursement will continue to affect the implementation of RBT—and it should be noted, any evidence-based model—in community practice.

The challenges facing the model notwithstanding, the benefits of successfully implementing an evidence-based model in a community setting should not be overlooked. To the extent that RBT can be successfully translated, clients may benefit in terms of higher abstinence rates and other improved psychosocial outcomes (i.e., more employment, stable drug-free housing, less involvement in illegal activities). To that end, research is needed to compare the real world RBT intervention with standard practice so that the effectiveness of the modified RBT model can be scientifically evaluated.

TREATMENT FIDELITY

As with other treatment models (i.e., cognitive behavioral therapy, motivational interviewing), adaptation of the RBT treatment model is both expected and necessary. However, as the model is implemented in a diversity of settings by various practitioners, fidelity to the core elements of the approach becomes an increasing concern. It is overly simplistic to think that if a program is providing the 10 basic elements of RBT (see the Introduction, this volume), the treatment is being implemented with fidelity. The degree to which the elements are implemented and the manner in which they are implemented are of critical importance. For example, a program may indicate that it conducts outreach with clients who miss treatment but does so using the last available number left by the client (which may be an out-of-order cell phone) and when schedules permit (sometimes days after the no-show or just prior to the time the client is scheduled to be discharged). Clearly, this level of outreach does not meet the outreach element of RBT in manner or intensity. Measures of the fidelity to the manner and intensity of the treatment elements are important because these signify a significant departure from standard treatment and may well be active ingredients in the model's success. In a similar vein, the way the function of drug use is conceptualized (and thus how competing goals are determined) can radically alter a treatment approach and thus the treatment outcome. If treatment goals do not match the functions of drug use behavior (as the result of a poorly conducted functional assessment), the model is compromised at the onset. The measure of whether a program is using RBT as intended, then, is based on (a) proper application of behavioral principles (e.g., ability to understand drug use and how it functions for the individual), (b) implementation of the treatment elements, and (c) adequate intensity of the element. Clearly, measuring such domains is a challenge.

Because the number of sites providing RBT is still relatively small, quality assurance has been maintained through direct clinical oversight of each site by one of the model developers (Hendree Jones or Michelle Tuten) or by a first-generation trainee in the model who, in the opinion of a model developer, has achieved a sufficient level of expertise. For example, the fidelity and quality of RBT interventions within BSF (the substance abuse treatment program in the Connecticut child welfare system; see Chapter 12) is maintained through the use of a first-generation RBT expert consultant who works closely with the BSF team supervisor and therapists. On a weekly basis, the expert consults with the supervisor and therapists about the progress of and strategies for each case and provides team members with feedback regarding the clinical tools used in each case (e.g., client feedback reports, graphs, contracts, functional assessments). The consultant also provides initial (for new team members) and quarterly booster (for existing staff) trainings and is available for emergency consultation as needed. As another safeguard against model drift, a model developer periodically listens to the consultant's weekly case review meetings with the team and provides the consultant with feedback regarding issues of fidelity. This approach is similar to the extensive and well-specified quality assurance procedures used in MST, a widely disseminated intensive family-based intervention for serious clinical problems, such as juvenile offending and adolescent psychiatric emergencies (for more details about quality assurance protocols within MST, see Henggeler, Schoenwald, Borduin, Rowland, & Cunningham, 2009).

Other options for monitoring adherence to RBT also are being considered. For example, in the BSF pilot study, clients completed a monthly phone survey (the Adherence Rating of Therapists; Saldana, Tuten, & Jones, 2007) during their time in treatment and answered questions regarding the extent to which they experienced various aspects of RBT (e.g., "My therapist reviewed my graphs with me at least every week"; "My therapist praised me when I accomplished my goals"). Our goal is to analyze these client self-report data to see if higher endorsement of RBT items is correlated with positive posttreatment outcomes (i.e., abstinence, employment). If the self-report instrument predicts outcomes, it could be implemented as a low-cost way of monitoring therapist behavior and providing corrective feedback to therapists. Another option for monitoring and maintaining the fidelity of RBT going forward is to use a "train the trainers" approach similar to that used to disseminate motivational interviewing (MI; Miller & Rollnick, 2002). In this approach, therapists who have been trained and who have provided MI to clients can have their skills reviewed by an MI expert and become certified trainers themselves. This approach creates a community of MI providers who collectively preserve the fidelity of MI and who can provide consultation and training in the model in a variety of contexts.

RESEARCH DIRECTIONS FOR REINFORCEMENT-BASED TREATMENT

In addition to the previously stated practice issues, research is important for maintaining and increasing the effectiveness of the RBT model. For example, which of the many elements of RBT are most effective overall and for subgroups of clients with specific issues and/or pretreatment characteristics, and what "dose" of RBT is necessary for improved outcomes in the individuals? Which training methods are best for different types of therapists, and what level and types of efforts are needed to ensure fidelity to the treatment? Currently, two studies of RBT are underway that will answer some of these and other important questions.

Reinforcement-Based Treatment Intensity Study Among Pregnant Drug-Dependent Women

Extant research results suggest that RBT is an effective intervention. However, it is unclear which of the model's treatment elements are most effective or what dose of RBT is necessary for whom. Given the brief window of opportunity often afforded treatment programs, an intervention that can be tailored to the unique needs of the individual on the basis of early treatment response has considerable advantages in terms of efficiently using resources to accelerate clinical progress. Currently, we are conducting a 5-year research study, funded by the National Institute on Drug Abuse, which uses a dynamic treatment regime that adjusts RBT on the basis of patients' initial treatment response. The sample used in the study is treatment-seeking pregnant women who have current substance use disorder diagnoses. It is expected that providing RBT in stepped care forms (i.e., providing the lowest appropriate treatment and then either stepping up to more intensive specialist services if there is a nontreatment response or stepping down if there is a positive treatment response and the initial intensity of treatment is not needed) will optimize maternal treatment benefits and birth outcomes. In the study, clients are classified as either early responders or early nonresponders, and RBT treatment services are matched to patient needs using a decision-tree approach to guide changes in treatment intensity (e.g., a client demonstrates 2 weeks of consistent drug abstinence and treatment intensity is lowered so that she attends treatment 5 days rather than 7 days a week) and/or scope (e.g., a client demonstrates continued drug abstinence and obtains employment, and the scope of treatment is reduced so that Job Club is no longer provided). The study is one of the first to examine the utility of a using a decision-tree approach for treatment decision making. If the use of this method is equally or more effective than RBT implemented under standard conditions (i.e., individualized to client needs but without formal assessment of initial treatment response), it is possible that new versions of RBT that are more cost-effective can be developed. This study is also considering which RBT variant is most cost-effective for which type of client.

As each client presents to treatment with a unique set of issues, needs, and characteristics, this study also will help us answer important clinical questions about the client factors that might mediate and moderate RBT treatment response. Regarding potential mediators, with the final data we will be able to determine (a) why RBT works by examining the therapeutic processes potentially mediating between treatment participation and behavioral outcome, (b) whether these therapeutic mechanisms are common to all or unique to certain types of RBT, (c) whether severity of drug withdrawal and amount of illegal activity (i.e., prostitution) predict treatment response, and (d) whether these two factors moderate the treatment efficacy of RBT such that they are differentially important in determining treatment outcome in the different RBT conditions.

In summary, this current project is aimed at answering important questions related to helping community settings decide whether RBT is right for them and, if so, what elements of RBT will be most helpful to their patients. Although this study is being conducted with pregnant patients, its results are anticipated to have wide-reaching implications and applicability for other individuals in need of or being treated for substance use disorders.

Evaluation of Home-Based Reinforcement-Based Treatment: The Building Stronger Families Study

As discussed in Chapter 12, the Building Stronger Families (BSF) model (in Connecticut child protective services) is a home-based version of RBT that is incorporated into a comprehensive family treatment for adults involved in the child welfare system as a result of physical abuse or neglect of a child. BSF has demonstrated success in reducing parental substance use, retaining children in their homes, and preventing reabuse incidents in a pilot study (see Chapter 12, this volume, for a description of outcome data; Schaeffer et al., 2010; Swenson et al., 2009).

Although the results of the pilot study of BSF are impressive, the intervention has yet to be tested in a randomized trial. Recently, the National Institute on Drug Abuse provided funds for model developers to conduct a randomized clinical trial of BSF. In the 5-year study, parents who have a recent incident of child maltreatment and who meet criteria for a substance abuse problem will be randomly assigned to receive either BSF or standard community treatment as a condition of their involvement with child protective services (i.e., the Department of Children and Families) in New Britain, Connecticut. Data regarding parental substance use, parent and child mental health symptomatology, and family interaction patterns as well as child welfare service system data (e.g., reabuse incidents, child days in out-of-home placement) will be collected at five time points over a period of 18 months.

This large-scale evaluation of BSF will help to establish whether RBT can be successfully implemented using a home-based model of service delivery and within the context of other intensive interventions addressing family interactions and individual mental health needs. Although RBT is only one of the interventions used in the comprehensive model of BSF, the randomized trial will reveal information about the feasibility of home-based implementation of the RBT elements, the contribution of the RBT model to reductions in substance abuse and related outcomes (e.g., employment), and the applicability of the model in a child welfare context.

More broadly, the study will help to address key questions regarding service utilization patterns (e.g., whether parents receiving BSF experience more hours of substance abuse treatment and fewer missed sessions) and cost-effectiveness issues in treating this population. These questions are being examined in the context of one of the most innovative systems of care for substance abuse treatment in the country. The use of a high-quality and well-coordinated substance abuse treatment system as the comparison condition helps to ensure a rigorous test of BSF's effectiveness. Indeed, standard substance abuse treatment in Connecticut has a number of state-of-the-art components, such as comprehensive evaluations of client use, mental health, and practical needs; a continuum of treatment options (e.g., outpatient, intensive outpatient, and residential treatment); gender-specific treatment groups; psychiatric care; case management services; and trauma-informed care. Moreover, the Connecticut substance abuse treatment system works closely with the Department of Children and Families to coordinate care between substance abuse providers, other providers (e.g., for children's mental health treatment), and child welfare personnel through its Project Safe program. The coordination between the Department of Children and Families and substance abuse treatment providers is among the best of any child welfare system in the nation, according to a recent Child and Family Services Review by the U.S. Department of Health and Human Services, Administration for Children and Families (2009).

We hope that this volume has conveyed the importance of a positive, comprehensive approach to treating substance use disorders. RBT model developers will more fully specify training, supervision, and consultation protocols in the coming years. Our experience working with RBT therapists and other stakeholders in sites around the country has been invaluable for understanding what techniques are most helpful for allowing new sites to learn and uphold the model in clinical practice. Substance abuse providers or agencies that are interested in bringing RBT to their community should contact L. Michelle Tuten (mtuten@jhmi.edu) to devise an implementation strategy that would work best within their particular local context.

APPENDIX A: NEW CLIENT WELCOME CERTIFICATE

APPENDIX B: FUNCTIONAL ASSESSMENT OF DRUG USE

I want to start by asking you about a time after you started using when you were abstinent from drugs completely.

Can you tell me about your longest period of abstinence?

Probes: Where were you living during that period if time? What was going on with you socially? With your family? Employment? Recreational activities? Other activities, such as church?

You have likely heard that in recovery there is a need to examine people, places, and things. I am going to talk with you about each of these areas so that we can determine the best treatment goals for you.

PEOPLE

Who are you typically with when you use (insert drug name)?

What do you like about using with these individuals (as opposed to others)?

Who else do you use with occasionally?

Whom do you know well that you never use with or around?

Whom do you think you might have a relationship with if you were not using?

Besides yourself, who cares most about your getting assistance with your drug use?

PLACES

Where are you typically when you use?

Where else do you use on a regular basis?

What do you like about using in these locations (as opposed to other places)?

Where do you go where you don't use (e.g., relative's or friend's house)?

Where would you visit or go if you were not using (e.g., any places you used to go on a regular basis that you stopped going to because of your use)?

THINGS

How do you typically use (insert drug name), by what route?

What do you like about using this route?

How much (insert drug name) do you typically use in dollar amount in a day?

Emotional

How would you describe your mood or what you are feeling typically before you use (insert drug name)?

Describe your mood after you use (what happens after you take the drug).

What are some of the pleasant feelings you have after you use (insert drug name)?

Physical

How are you feeling physically before you use?

How about how you are feeling physically after you use?

Other

Please describe a typical day of drug use from the time you get up until you go to bed.

What is your motivation for treatment—why did you come to treatment now?

APPENDIX C: FUNCTIONAL ASSESSMENT FOR RELAPSE

Drug(s) or alcohol used: _____

Please describe the day of your relapse from the time you woke up in the morning until you went to bed. This will help us to examine the details leading up to and following your drug use.

PEOPLE

Who were you with when you last used (insert drug name)?

PLACES

Where were you when you last used (insert drug name)?

THINGS

Describe your mood right before you last used (insert drug name).

Describe your mood after you used (what happened after you took the drug).

What were you feeling physically right before you last used?

What physical changes did you notice after you used?

APPENDIX D: CLIENT FEEDBACK FORM

Cornerstone   Confidential Feedback Form for: _____

Date: _____

1. Healthy Behaviors (Check all that apply)

☐ Participating in Cornerstone treatment   ☐ _____
☐ Agreed to sample sobriety   ☐ _____
☐ _____   ☐ _____

Other healthy behaviors to consider:
☐ _____   ☐ _____
☐ _____   ☐ _____
☐ _____   ☐ _____

2. Your Drug Use: A Description

Age you first used _____ regularly: _____
Age you first used _____ regularly: _____

Number of months you have used _____ regularly: _____
Number of months you have used _____ regularly: _____

_____
_____

___ % of Americans in your age group who have used _____ in the past year.
___ % of Americans in your age group who have used _____ in the past month.

___ % of Americans in your age group who have used _____ in the past year.
___ % of Americans in your age group who have used _____ in the past month.

Average amount of money spent on drugs in the 30 days before treatment: _____
Average amount of money spent on drugs in your lifetime: _____

3. Risk Factors

☐ Yes ☐ No	Living with another drug user
☐ Yes ☐ No	Friends or associates who are drug users
☐ Yes ☐ No	Easy access to drugs
☐ Yes ☐ No	IV drug use
☐ Yes ☐ No	Family history of drug and/or alcohol problems

4. Life Areas Impacted by Drug Use

How important is treatment for the following?

Alcohol Use

Not at all	Slightly	Moderately	Considerably	Extremely

Drug Use

Not at all	Slightly	Moderately	Considerably	Extremely

Employment/Education

Not at all	Slightly	Moderately	Considerably	Extremely

Family/Social

Not at all	Slightly	Moderately	Considerably	Extremely

Legal Status

Not at all	Slightly	Moderately	Considerably	Extremely

Psychiatric/Emotional Well Being

Not at all	Slightly	Moderately	Considerably	Extremely

5. Functional Assessment of Drug Use

When, Where, and Why you use?

When: _____

_____

Where: _____

_____

Why: _____

_____

6. Good Things About Drug Use

Bad Things About Drug Use

_____

_____

_____

_____

_____

_____

7. Confidence and Importance

| Extremely |
| Considerably |
| Moderately |
| Slightly |

How important is it to you to get treatment for your drug problem now?

| Extremely |
| Considerably |
| Moderately |
| Slightly |

How confident are you that you will be successful in your treatment?

APPENDIX E: CLIENT FEEDBACK PAMPHLET

Confidential
Feedback Report
for:
Name

REPORT

Your Healthy Behaviors

- Coming to treatment at CAP
- Eating regular meals
- Keeping stress levels down
- Drinking water and Juice
- Getting enough sleep
- Getting some exercise

Other Healthy Behaviors to Consider

➡Take prenatal vitamin each day
➡Reducing smoking (especially when stressed)
➡Avoiding all drug and alcohol

Your Tobacco Use

Months of regular smoking:___180___

Amount spent on cigarettes:___$17,500___

Number of cigarettes each month:___600___

Fagerstrom score: 4

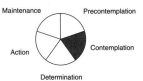

| | | 6 | 7-10 |

4+ = dependence

Carbon Monoxide level: 6 (ALU)/ 13 (outpatient)

Previous quit attempts:___1___

Stages of Change

Maintenance

Precontemplation

Action

Contemplation

Determination

What does this report mean?

Healthy Behaviors

Many women begin to increase positive health behaviors when they find out they are pregnant. We have listed a number of healthy behaviors that you reported. We congratulate you on making these healthy choices.

The "behaviors to consider" are simply other changes that you could consider making for your own health and the health of your pregnancy. We have listed some behaviors that may increase a woman's chance for a healthier pregnancy. Reducing or quitting smoking is one of the healthiest changes you can make for yourself and your baby.

Tobacco use/Smoking

General Information:
80% of women do *not* smoke during pregnancy. Furthermore, approximately 20% of women quit smoking completely upon learning that they are pregnant. Many more women reduce smoking levels during pregnancy. Some women begin by making reductions in their smoking and then quit later.

Fagerstrom Score:
The Fagerstrom is a scale that looks at several factors related to cigarette smoking. Research has shown that people who score high on this scale (4 or more) have more difficulty refraining from smoking than those with lower scores.

Carbon Monoxide (CO) Level:
The number on your feedback report indicates the level of the carbon monoxide you have inhaled from cigarette smoking. Carbon monoxide is a gas that interferes with how oxygen is delivered from your blood system throughout your body. It is the same gas that is released from automobile exhaust fumes. A CO level above 8 ppm means that you are being exposed to unhealthy levels of CO from cigarette smoking.

This section summarizes the information you gave us about your smoking, including how long you have been smoking, how much you have spent on cigarettes, and approximately how many cigarettes you smoke per month.

Number of Quit Attempts:
This number is simply the number of times you report that you have tried to quit smoking.

Who Wants to Quit Smoking?
According the U.S. Centers for Disease Control and Prevention, about 70% of adult smokers report that they want to quit. Based on a survey at CAP, 60% of patients report that they would like to quit smoking.

Unfortunately, it is often difficult to make such a big change. The good news is that efforts to quit smoking bring you one step closer to getting it right. In other words, even if you are not successful in quitting, you are practicing ways to reduce or stop smoking one day. Any changes that you make are positive. There are many things you can do to reduce smoke exposure. Of course it is best for you and your pregnancy if you quit smoking altogether. But you can also choose other options: not smoking inside your house, cutting down on the number of cigarettes you smoke, smoking only one cigarette on your smoke breaks, talking to other smokers about the difficulties of quitting smoking, talking to your doctor about your smoking, keeping a journal of number of cigarettes smoked per day, delaying when you smoke (not until after a certain time of day), etc.

Any change you can make to reduce smoke exposure is good for you and your family. You have many options. The choice to make a change (or not to change) in your cigarette smoking is up to you.

Stage of Change

In the assessment we asked you a number of questions about how you felt about your smoking. Your particular "stage" describes where you are right now in the process of change. You may even be "between stages" which means you scored the same in two stages.

STAGE 1: PRECONTEMPLATION
A person in this stage hasn't really thought much about changing her smoking and hasn't taken any action to make any changes.

STAGE 2: CONTEMPLATION
A person in this stage has begun to think about making changes in her smoking and is also weighing the pros and cons of making changes.

STAGE 3: DETERMINATION
A person in this stage has thought seriously about her smoking and has decided that she wants to reduce or quit but hasn't yet done so.

STAGE 4: ACTION
A person in this stage has taken action to change her behavior, which means she has either reduced or quit smoking.

STAGE 5: MAINTENANCE
A person in this stage has been able to reduce smoking or has quit altogether for six months or longer.

Note: The "behaviors to consider" listed on your feedback report are not intended to take the place of physician advice regarding your own unique nutritional, medical, and fitness needs during pregnancy.

**Johns Hopkins University
School of Medicine
Mason F. Lord Building
4940 Eastern Avenue
Baltimore, MD 21224**

APPENDIX F: DAY PLAN

Name:_____   Date:_____

My Day Plan

Time	Plan
9:00 a.m.	
10:00 a.m.	
11:00 a.m.	
12:00 noon	
1:00 p.m.	
2:00 p.m.	
3:00 p.m.	
4:00 p.m.	
5:00 p.m.	
6:00 p.m.	
7:00 p.m.	
8:00 p.m.	
9:00 p.m.	
10:00 p.m.	

APPENDIX G: ABSTINENCE SAMPLING CONTRACT

I _____ (Client) agree to sample sobriety and follow treatment recommendations given to me by my counselor for a period of 24 hours.

This means that I commit to abstinence for the week period of _____ through _____ and that I will do anything and everything I can to remain free from drugs so that I give my recovery a chance (some things I can do: talk to my counselor at Cornerstone and CAP, talk to recovery house personnel, go to NA, or call a supportive person).

Client:_____   Date:_____
Counselor:_____   Date:_____

APPENDIX H: ALTERNATIVE HOUSING PLAN

This is the address where I will reside while in treatment at Cornerstone:

_____
_____
_____

Who lives here?
1. _____
2. _____
3. _____
4. _____

Please list safe alternative addresses where you could potentially reside (identify places that are safest for your recovery):

_____
_____
_____
_____
_____
_____

Would you be willing to move to a shelter if you need to get away from where you used drugs? (Please circle one)

Yes   No

Patient's Statement:
I understand that where I live is an essential factor in my ability to remain abstinent. People who are successful in living drug-free lives learn to overcome the easy access they have to drugs. If I decide that I am in danger of relapsing due to where I live, I understand that Cornerstone staff will assist me in moving to safer alternative housing.

Patient's Signature _____   Date _____

Staff Signature _____   Date _____

APPENDIX I: TRACKING LOCATOR FORM

Cornerstone Client Tracking Locator Form

First Name: _____ Last: _____ Maiden:_____

What is your nickname? _____

Today's date: ____/_____/____

Cornerstone intake date: ____/_____/____

DOB: _____

What is your current address?

Street: _____

City, State, Zip: _____

Telephone: ____-____-____ Pager/Cell: ____-____-_____

First contact name: _____

Street: _____

City, State, Zip: _____

Telephone: ____-____-____ Relationship to you: _____

May we contact this person by phone? Yes ☐ No ☐

letter? Yes ☐ No ☐

in person? Yes ☐ No ☐

Second contact name: _____

Street: _____

City, State, Zip: _____

Telephone: ____-____-____ Relationship to you: _____

May we contact this person by phone? Yes ☐ No ☐

letter? Yes ☐ No ☐

in person? Yes ☐ No ☐

Third contact name: _____

Street: _____

City, State, Zip: _____

Telephone: ____-____-____ Relationship to you: _____

May we contact this person by phone? Yes ☐ No ☐

letter? Yes ☐ No ☐

in person? Yes ☐ No ☐

Signature: _____

Date: ____/____/____

Where do you usually hang out during the day? _____
Where do you usually hang out at night? _____
In what other states or cities have you lived? _____

**If we have trouble getting in touch with your other contacts,
may we contact your:**

Mother?   Yes ☐ No ☐   Name: _____
Street: _____
City, State, Zip: _____
Telephone: _____-_____-_____

Other Relative/Friend?   Yes ☐ No ☐   Name: _____
Street: _____
City, State, Zip: _____
Telephone: _____-_____-_____

Spouse/Partner?   Yes ☐ No ☐   Name: _____
Street: _____
City, State, Zip: _____
Telephone: _____-_____-_____

Social Worker?   Yes ☐ No ☐   Name: _____
Street: _____
City, State, Zip: _____
Telephone: _____-_____-_____

Probation Officer?   Yes ☐ No ☐   Name: _____
Street: _____
City, State, Zip: _____
Telephone: _____-_____-_____

Signature: _____
Date: _____/_____/_____

APPENDIX J: COST–BENEFIT ANALYSIS

Which positive or negative drug consequences would apply to you if you stopped your drug use?

Negative consequences	Positive consequences

☐ I will have difficulty relaxing.
☐ I will lose a lifestyle I enjoy.
☐ I will feel frustrated and anxious.
☐ I will get depressed.
☐ I will have difficulty coping
    with problems.
☐ I will feel withdrawal or cravings.
☐ I will have too much time
    on my hands.
☐ I will have difficulty not using drugs.
☐ I will feel lonely.
☐ I will feel bored.
☐ I will be irritable.
☐ I will miss the taste/feeling.
☐ I will have difficulty having a good time.
☐ I will feel stressed out.
☐ I will miss the feeling of being high.
☐ I will be harassed by people I used
    to get drugs from.
	☐ I will feel better physically.
	☐ I will have fewer problems
	    with my family.
	☐ I will have more money to do
	    other things with.
	☐ I will be more active and alert.
	☐ I will have fewer problems with friends.
	☐ I will feel better about myself.
	☐ I will regain some self-respect.
	☐ I will accomplish more of the things
	    I want to get done.
	☐ I will have better relationships
	    with my family.
	☐ My health will improve.
	☐ I will live longer.
	☐ I will be more in control of life.
	☐ I will be more financially stable.
	☐ I will have better relationships
	    with my friends.
	☐ I will save more money.
	☐ I will have fewer legal problems.

APPENDIX K: TREATMENT TEAM, TREATMENT PLAN ELEMENTS, AND KEY DECISIONS

Adapted from "Treatment of Opioid-Dependent Pregnant Women: Clinical and Research Issues," by H. E. Jones, P. R. Martin, S. H. Heil, K. Kaltenbach, P. Selby, M. G. Coyle, S. M. Stine, K. E. O'Grady, A. M. Arria, and G. Fischer, 2008, *Journal of Substance Abuse Treatment, 35*, p. 246. Copyright 2008 by Elsevier. Adapted with permission.

Treatment Team

Counselor   Psychiatrist   Social worker   Obstetrician   Lactation consultant
Pediatrician   Child Protective Services worker

Treatment Plan Elements Based on Initial Assessment

❑ **1 Survival**
   ❑ Housing
   ❑ Food
❑ **2a Psychiatric treatment for addiction**
   ❑ Methadone for heroin dependence
   ❑ Medically assisted withdrawal
      from benzos
   ❑ Start nicotine cessation program
❑ **2b Psychiatric treatment of comorbid conditions**
   ❑ Depression (medication and
      behavioral therapy)
   ❑ Refer to PTSD and addictions
      therapy
   ❑ Select agonist medication for
      heroin dependence
   ❑ Start individual and group
      counseling to address drug use
❑ **3 Medical treatment**
   ❑ Hepatitis C medication
   ❑ Iron for anemia
   ❑ Regular prenatal laboratory testing
❑ **4 Nutrition**
   ❑ Initiate a food diary
   ❑ Prenatal vitamin prescription and
      track adherence to ingestion
   ❑ Nutrition education group

❑ **5 Obstetrical treatment**
   ❑ Referral to OB addiction expert
   ❑ Track OB appointment
      attendance
   ❑ Refer to OB education group
❑ **6 Legal assistance**
   ❑ Help with outstanding warrant
❑ **7 Vocational assistance**
   ❑ Determine education or job
      goals
❑ **8 Social functioning**
   ❑ Obtain NA sponsor
   ❑ Track NA attendance
   ❑ Couples therapy
   ❑ HIV risk-reduction skills
   ❑ Stable drug-free housing
      (if she stays in relationship)
❑ **9 Recreation**
   ❑ Identify and practice drug free
      fun activities

Key Decisions During Treatment

❑ Opioid medication induction regimen
❑ Medication-assisted withdrawal from benzos
❑ Selection of an antidepression medication
❑ Selection of treatment regimen for PTSD
❑ Selection of vocational/educational goal
❑ Decision about remaining in current relationships
❑ How to build a drug-free peer network
❑ Selection of NA sponsor
❑ Decision to breast-feed
❑ Decision regarding postpartum medication

Decisions to Prepare for Discharge

❑ Opioid medication program transfer
❑ Physician to transfer depression and anxiety management
❑ Plan for continuing job maintenance behaviors
❑ Plan to continue in parenting skills training

APPENDIX L: SAMPLE INITIAL TREATMENT PLAN ELEMENTS FOR PREGNANT AND CHILD-REARING WOMEN

Problem area (priority ranking)	Goal	Intervention	Objective measure
1. Survival needs			
1. Lack of safe housing	1. Recovery house	1. Live in recovery house	1. Verify with house manager
2. Food	2. Food assistance	2. Go to Department of Social Services	2. Self-report and bring in Department of Social Services card
2a. Psychiatric treatment: Substance dependence			
1. Heroin	1. Abstinence	1. Comprehensive treatment	1. Urine sample negative
1a. Benzodiazepine	1a. Abstinence	1a. Medication-assisted withdrawal	1a. Ingestion of less medication 1a. Low benzodiazepine withdrawal scores
2. Nicotine	2. Abstinence	2. Nicotine replacement	2. Carbon monoxide less than 8 parts per million
2b. Psychiatric treatment: Comorbid issues			
1. Depression (medication and behavioral therapy)	1. Controlled depression	1. SSRI 1. Individual cognitive–behavioral therapy	1. Low Beck Depression Inventory scores
2. Posttraumatic stress disorder (PTSD)	2. Controlled PTSD	2. PTSD and addiction group	2. Low scores on Symptom Checklist-90
3. Medical			
1. Hepatitis C	1. Manage effects	1. Medication 1. Liver function testing	1. Self-report and verify 1. Prescription given and filled
2. Anemia	2. Adequate iron	2. Daily iron ingestion 2. Prenatal blood testing	2. Self-report and verify and prescription given and filled
4. Nutrition			
1. Lack of information	1. Balanced diet	1. Initiate a food diary 1. Prenatal vitamin prescription and taking prenatal vitamin 1. Nutrition education group	1. Track adherence to diary and ingestion

Problem	Goal	Intervention	Measurement
5. Obstetrical treatment			
1. No prenatal care	1. Regular prenatal care	1. Referral to obstetrics addiction expert 1. Referral to obstetrics education group	1. Track obstetrics appointment attendance 1. Track obstetrics education group attendance
6. Legal assistance			
1. Warrant for arrest	1. No legal issues	1. Legal advocate	1. Document from legal advocate
7. Vocational functioning			
1. Education	1. Obtain general education diploma	1. Contact community agency	1. Bring attendance record
2. Employment	2. Part-time work	2. Job Club once per week 2. Identify five job ads each week	2. Attendance 2. Show ads and self-report
8. Social functioning (e.g., social support)			
1. Lack of drug-free peer social interaction	1. Develop social support network	1. Attend Narcotics Anonymous once a day 1. Obtain Narcotics Anonymous sponsor	1. Self-report and house manager 1. Phone verification 1. Track Narcotics Anonymous attendance
2. Drug-using partners	2. Drug-free relationship	2. Couples therapy	2. Track attendance
3. HIV drug risk and sex risk behaviors	3. No risk behaviors	3. HIV risk reduction skills	3. Track attendance 3. Behavior quiz
9. Recreational			
1. Lack of recreational activities	1. Engage in regular drug-free activities	1. Attend three recreation activities per week	1. Self-report

Client's signature   Date

Counselor's signature   Date

REFERENCES

Adamson, S. J., Sellman, J. D., & Frampton, C. M. A. (2009). Patient predictors of alcohol treatment outcome: A systematic review. *Journal of Substance Abuse Treatment, 36,* 75–86. doi:10.1016/j.jsat.2008.05.007

Ammerman, R. T., & Patz, R. J. (1996). Determinants of child abuse potential: Contribution of parent and child factors. *Journal of Clinical Child Psychology, 25,* 300–307. doi:10.1207/s15374424jccp2503_6

Banyard, V. L., Williams, L. M., & Siegel, J. A. (2003). The impact of complex trauma and depression on parenting: An exploration of mediating risk and protective factors. *Child Maltreatment, 8,* 334–349. doi:10.1177/1077559503257106

Beck, A. T., Steer, R. A., & Brown, G. (1996). *Beck Depression Inventory—II manual.* San Antonio, TX: The Psychological Corporation.

Bickel, W. K., Amass, L., Higgins, S. T., Bager, G. L., & Esch, R. A. (1997). Effects of adding behavioral treatment to opioid detoxification with buprenorphine. *Journal of Consulting and Clinical Psychology, 65,* 803–810. doi:10.1037/0022-006X.65.5.803

Bickel, W. K., & Vuchinich, R. E. (2000). *Reframing health behavior change with behavioral economics.* Mahwah, NJ: Erlbaum.

Bien, T. H., Miller, W. R., & Boroughs, J. M. (1993). Motivational interviewing with alcohol outpatients. *Behavioural and Cognitive Psychotherapy, 21,* 347–356.

Blank, S. W., & Blum, B. B. (1997). A brief history of work expectations for welfare mothers. *The Future of Children, 7,* 28–38. doi:10.2307/1602575

Booth, B. M., Curran, G. M., & Han, X. (2004). Predictors of short-term course of drinking in untreated rural and urban at-risk drinkers: Effects of gender, illegal drug use and psychiatric comorbidity. *Journal of Studies on Alcohol and Drugs, 65,* 63–73.

Borsari, B., & Cari, K. B. (2000). Effects of a brief motivational intervention with college student drinkers. *Journal of Consulting and Clinical Psychology, 68,* 728–733. doi:10.1037/0022-006X.68.4.728

Brady, T. M., & Ashley, O. S. (Eds.). (2005). *Women in substance abuse treatment: Results from the alcohol and drug services study (ADSS)* (DHHS Publication No. SMA 04-3968, Analytic Series A-26). Rockville, MD: U.S. Department of Health and Human Services, Substance Abuse and Mental Health Services Administration, Office of Applied Studies.

Bronfenbrenner, U. (1979). *The ecology of human development: Experiments by design and nature.* Cambridge, MA: Harvard University Press.

Brook, J., & McDonald, T. (2009). The impact of parental substance abuse on the stability of family reunifications from foster care. *Children and Youth Services Review, 31,* 193–198.

Brown, J. M., & Miller, W. R. (1993). Impact of motivational interviewing on participation and outcome in residential alcoholism treatment. *Psychology of Addictive Behaviors, 7*, 211–218. doi:10.1037/0893-164X.7.4.211

Brown, R. L., & Rounds, L. A. (1995). Conjoint screening questionnaires for alcohol and other drug abuse: Criterion validity in a primary care practice. *Wisconsin Medical Journal, 94*, 135–140.

Budney, A. J., & Higgins, S. T. (1998.) *A community reinforcement plus vouchers approach: Treating cocaine addiction. Therapy manuals for drug addiction* (NIH Publication No. 98-4309). Washington, DC: U.S. Department of Health and Human Services.

Budney, A. J., Higgins, S. T., Delaney, D. D., Kent, L., & Bickel, W. K. (1991). Contingent reinforcement of abstinence with individuals abusing cocaine and marijuana. *Journal of Applied Behavior Analysis, 24*, 657–665. doi:10.1901/jaba.1991.24-657

Burke, B. L., Arkowitz, H., & Dunn, C. (2002). The efficacy of motivational interviewing. In W. R. Miller & S. Rollnick (Eds.), *Motivational interviewing: Preparing people for change* (2nd ed., pp. 217–250). New York, NY: Guilford Press.

Burke, B. L., Arkowitz, H., & Menchola, M. (2003). The efficacy of motivational interviewing: A meta-analysis of controlled clinical trials. *Journal of Consulting and Clinical Psychology, 71*, 843–861. doi:10.1037/0022-006X.71.5.843

Carlson, M. J., & Gabriel, R. M. (2001). Patient satisfaction, use of services, and one-year outcomes in publicly funded substance abuse treatment. *Psychiatric Services, 52*, 1230–1236. doi:10.1176/appi.ps.52.9.1230

Carroll, K. M. (1996). Relapse prevention as a psychosocial treatment: A review of controlled clinical trials. *Experimental and Clinical Psychopharmacology, 4*, 46–54. doi:10.1037/1064-1297.4.1.46

Carroll, K. M. (1998). *A cognitive behavioral approach: Treating cocaine addiction* (NIH Publication No. 98-4308). Rockville, MD: U.S. Department of Health and Human Services.

Carroll, K. M. (2001). Combined treatments for substance dependence. In M. T. Simmons & N. B. Schmidt (Eds.), *Combined treatment for mental disorders: A guide to psychological and pharmacological interventions* (pp. 215–237). Washington, DC: American Psychological Association. doi:10.1037/10415-009

Carroll, K. M., Sinha, R., Nich, C., Babuscio, T., & Rounsaville, B. J. (2002). Contingency management to enhance naltrexone treatment of opioid dependence: A randomized clinical trial of reinforcement magnitude. *Experimental and Clinical Psychopharmacology, 10*, 54–63. doi:10.1037/1064-1297.10.1.54

Carter, D. R., & Horner, R. H. (2009). Adding function-based behavioral support to first step to success: Integrating individualized and manualized practices. *Journal of Positive Behavior Interventions, 11*, 22–34. doi:10.1177/1098300708319125

Centers for Disease Control and Prevention. (2009). *Smoking and tobacco use: Women and tobacco.* Retrieved from http://www.cdc.gov/tobacco/data_statistics/fact_sheets/populations/women/

Central East Addiction Technology Transfer Center. (2007). *Outreach competencies: Minimum standards for conducting street outreach for hard-to-reach populations.* Retrieved from http://www.attcnetwork.org/REGCENTERS/productdetails.asp?prodID=438&rcID=2

Chaffin, M., Kelleher, K., & Hollenberg, J. (1996). Onset of physical abuse and neglect: Psychiatric substance abuse and social risk factors from prospective community data. *Child Abuse & Neglect, 20,* 191–203. doi:10.1016/S0145-2134(95)00144-1

Child Welfare League of America. (1997). *Alcohol and other drug survey of state child welfare agencies.* Retrieved from http://www.cwla.org/programs/bhd/1997stateaodsurvey.htm

Child Welfare Partnership. (1998). *A study of families with children entering foster care in Oregon between 1992 and 1995, Cohort III.* Portland, OR: Portland State University.

Chutuape, M. A., Jasinski, D. R., Fingerhood, M. I., & Stitzer, M. L. (2001). One-three- and six-month outcomes after brief inpatient opioid detoxification. *The American Journal of Drug and Alcohol Abuse, 27,* 19–44. doi:10.1081/ADA-100103117

Cicchetti, D., & Luthar, S. S. (1999). Developmental approaches to substance use and abuse. *Development and Psychopathology, 11,* 655–656. doi:10.1017/S0954579499002254

Cohen, M., Liebson, I. A., & Faillace, L. A. (1972). A technique for establishing controlled drinking in chronic alcoholics. *Diseases of the Nervous System, 33,* 46–49.

Collins, C. C., Grella, C. E., & Hser, Y. (2003). Effects of gender and level of parental involvement among parents in drug treatment. *The American Journal of Drug and Alcohol Abuse, 29,* 237–261. doi:10.1081/ADA-120020510

Comfort, M., Loverro, J., & Kaltenbach, K. (2000). A search for strategies to engage women in substance abuse treatment. *Social Work in Health Care, 31,* 59–70. doi:10.1300/J010v31n04_04

Connell, C. M., Bergeron, N., Katz, K. H., Saunders, L., & Tebes, J. K. (2007). Re-referral to child protective services: The influence of child, family, and case characteristics on risk status. *Child Abuse & Neglect, 31,* 573–588.

Corse, S. J., Schmid, K., & Trickett, P. K. (1990). Social network characteristics of mothers in abusing and nonabusing families and their relationships to parenting beliefs. *Journal of Community Psychology, 18,* 44–59. doi:10.1002/1520-6629(199001)18:1<44::AID-JCOP2290180107>3.0.CO;2-F

Cox, C. E., Kotch, J. B., & Everson, M. D. (2003). A longitudinal study of modifying influences in the relationship between domestic violence and child maltreatment. *Journal of Family Violence, 18,* 5–17. doi:10.1023/A:1021497213505

Dawe, S., & Harnett, P. (2007). Reducing potential for child abuse among methadone-maintained parents: results from a randomized controlled trial. *Journal of Substance Abuse Treatment, 32,* 381–390. doi:10.1016/j.jsat.2006.10.003

De Bellis, M. D., Broussard, E. R., Herring, D. J., Wexler, S., Moritz, G., & Benitez, J. G. (2001). Psychiatric co-morbidity in caregivers and children involved in maltreatment: A pilot research study with policy implications. *Child Abuse & Neglect, 25*, 923–944. doi:10.1016/S0145-2134(01)00247-2

Donohue, B., Romero, V., & Hill, H. H. (2006). Treatment of co-occurring child maltreatment and substance abuse. *Aggression and Violent Behavior, 11*, 626–640. doi:10.1016/j.avb.2005.08.007

Donovan, D. M., & Wells, E. A. (2007). "Tweaking 12-step": The potential role of 12-step self-help group involvement in methamphetamine recovery. *Addiction, 102*(Suppl. 1), 121–129.

Downey, K. K., Helmus, T. C., & Schuster, C. R. (2000). Treatment of heroin-dependant poly-drug abusers with contingency management and buprenorphine maintenance. *Experimental and Clinical Psychopharmacology, 8*, 176–184. doi:10.1037/1064-1297.8.2.176

Drabble, L. (2007). Pathways to collaboration: Exploring values and collaborative practice between child welfare and substance abuse treatment fields. *Child Maltreatment, 12*, 31–42. doi:10.1177/1077559506296721

Drucker, P. M. (2002). An exploratory factor analysis of children's inventory scores in young children of substance abusers. *Psychological Reports, 91*, 131–141. doi:10.2466/PR0.91.5.131-141

Dutra, L., Stathopoulou, G., Basden, S. L., Leyro, T. M., Powers, M. B., & Otto, M. W. (2008). A meta-analytic review of psychosocial interventions for substance use disorders. *The American Journal of Psychiatry, 165*, 179–187. doi: 10.1176/appi.ajp.2007.06111851

Effects of in utero exposure to street drugs. (1993). *American Journal of Public Health, 83*(Suppl. 1), 1–32. doi:10.2105/AJPH.83.

Ellingson, S. A., Miltenberger, R. G., Stricker, J., Galensky, T. L., & Garlinghouse, M. (2000). Functional assessment and intervention for challenging behaviors in the classroom by general classroom teachers. *Journal of Positive Behavior Interventions, 2*, 85–97.

Elliott, D. S. (Series Ed.). (1998). *Blueprints for violence prevention.* Boulder: University of Colorado, Center for the Study and Prevention of Violence.

Epstein, D. H., Hawkins, W. E., Covi, L., Umbricht, A., & Preston, K. L. (2003). Cognitive-behavioral therapy plus contingency management for cocaine use: Findings during treatment and across 12-month follow-ups. *Psychology of Addictive Behaviors, 17*, 73–82. doi:10.1037/0893-164X.17.1.73

Epstein, E. E., & McCrady, B. S. (1998). Behavioral couples treatment of alcohol and drug use disorders: Current status and innovations. *Clinical Psychology Review, 18*, 689–711. doi:10.1016/S0272-7358(98)00025-7

Epstein, L. H., & Wing, R. R. (1984). Behavioral contracting: Health behaviors. In C. Franks (Ed.), *New developments in behavioral therapy from research to clinical application* (pp. 409–449). New York, NY: Haworth Press.

Feindler, E. L., Ecton, R. B., Kingsley, D., & Dubey, D. R. (1986). Group anger-control training for institutionalized psychiatric male adolescents. *Behavior Therapy, 17*, 109–123. doi:10.1016/S0005-7894(86)80079-X

Fiorentine, R. (2001). Counseling frequency and the effectiveness of outpatient drug treatment: Revisiting the conclusion that "more is better." *The American Journal of Drug and Alcohol Abuse, 27*, 617–631. doi:10.1081/ADA-100107659

Foa, E. B., & Rothbaum, B. O. (1998). *Treating the trauma of rape: Cognitive-behavioral therapy for PTSD.* New York, NY: Guilford Press.

French, M. T., McCollister, K. E., J. Cacciola, J., Durell, J., & Stephens, R. L. (2002). Benefit–cost analysis of addiction treatment in Arkansas: Specialty and standard residential programs for pregnant and parenting women. *Substance Abuse, 23*, 31–51.

Gavin, D. R., Ross, H. E., & Skinner, H. A. (1989). Diagnostic validity of the drug abuse screening test in the assessment of *DSM–III* drug disorders. *British Journal of Addiction, 84*, 301–307. doi:10.1111/j.1360-0443.1989.tb03463.x

Grabowski, J., O'Brien, C. P., Greenstein, R., Ternes, J., Long, M., & Steinberg-Donato, S. (1979). Effects of contingent payment on compliance with a naltrexone regimen. *American Journal of Drug Abuse, 6*, 355–365. doi:10.3109/00952997909001724

Gruber, K., Chutuape, M. A., & Stitzer, M. L. (2000). Reinforcement-based intensive outpatient treatment for inner city opiate abusers: A short-term evaluation. *Drug and Alcohol Dependence, 57*, 211–223. doi:10.1016/S0376-8716(99)00054-X

Hagan, T. A., Finnegan, L. P., & Nelson-Zlupko, L. (1994). Impediments to comprehensive models for substance dependent women: Treatment and research questions. *Journal of Psychoactive Drugs, 26*, 163–171.

Harden, B. J. (2004). Safety and stability for foster children: A developmental perspective. *The Future of Children, 14*, 30–47. doi:10.2307/1602753

Heather, N., Rollnick, S., Bell, A., & Richmond, R. (1996). Effects of brief counseling among heavy drinkers identified on general hospital wards. *Drug and Alcohol Review, 15*, 29–38. doi:10.1080/09595239600185641

Heil, S. H., Tidey, J. W., Holmes, H. W., Badger, G. J., & Higgins, S. T. (2003). A contingent payment model of smoking cessation: Effects on abstinence and withdrawal. *Nicotine & Tobacco Research, 5*, 205–213. doi:10.1080/1462220031000074864

Henggeler, S. W., Schoenwald, S. K., Borduin, C. M., Rowland, M. D., & Cunningham, P. B. (2009). *Multisystemic treatment for antisocial behavior in children and adolescents* (2nd ed.). New York, NY: Guilford Press.

Higgins, S. T., Budney, A. J., Bickel, W. K., Foerg, F. E., Donham, R., & Badger, G. J. (1994). Incentives improve treatment retention and cocaine abstinence in ambulatory cocaine-dependent patients. *Archives of General Psychiatry, 51*, 568–576.

Higgins, S. T., Budney, A. J., Bickel, W. K., Hughes, J. R., Foerg, F., & Badger, G. (1993). Achieving cocaine abstinence with a behavioral approach. *The American Journal of Psychiatry, 150*, 763–769.

Higgins, S. T., Heil, S. H., & Lussier, J. P. (2004). Clinical implications of reinforcement as a determinant of substance use disorders. *Annual Review of Psychology, 55*, 431–461. doi:10.1146/annurev.psych.55.090902.142033

Higgins, S. T., Wong, C. J., Badger, G. J., Haug Ogden, D. E., & Dantona, R. L. (2000). Contingent reinforcement increases cocaine abstinence during outpatient treatment and 1 year of follow-up. *Journal of Consulting and Clinical Psychology, 68*, 64–72.

Horner, R. H., & Carr, E. G. (1997). Behavioral support for student with severe disabilities: Functional assessment and comprehensive intervention. *The Journal of Special Education, 31*, 84–109. doi:10.1177/002246699703100108

Hser, Y. I., Evans, E., Huang, D., & Anglin, D. M. (2004). Relationship between drug treatment services, retention, and outcomes. *Psychiatric Services, 55*, 767–774. doi:10.1176/appi.ps.55.7.767.

Hubbard, R. L., Craddock, S. G., & Anderson, J. (2003). Overview of 5-year follow-up outcomes in the drug abuse treatment outcome studies (DATOS). *Journal of Substance Abuse Treatment, 25*, 125–134. doi:10.1016/S0740-5472(03)00130-2

Huey, S. J., Jr., Henggeler, S. W., Brondino, M. J., & Pickrel, S. G. (2000). Mechanisms of change in multisystemic therapy: Reducing delinquent behavior through therapist adherence and improved family and peer functioning. *Journal of Consulting and Clinical Psychology, 68*, 451–467. doi:10.1037/0022-006X.68.3.451

Ingram, K., Lewis-Palmer, T., & Sugai, G. (2005). Function-based intervention planning: Comparing the effectiveness of FBA function-based and non-function-based intervention plans. *Journal of Positive Behavior Interventions, 7*, 224–236.

Irvin, J. E., Bowers, C. A., Dunn, M. E., & Wang, M. C. (1999). Efficacy of relapse prevention: A meta-analytic review. *Journal of Consulting and Clinical Psychology, 67*, 563–570. doi:10.1037/0022-006X.67.4.563

Iwata, B. A., Vollmer, T. R., & Zarcone, J. R. (1990). The experimental (functional) analysis of behavior disorders: Methodology, applications, and limitations. In A. C. Repp & N. N. Singh (Eds.), *Perspectives on the used of non-aversive and aversive interventions for persons with developmental disabilities* (pp. 301–330). Sycamore, IL: Sycamore Publishing.

Johnson, J. E., Finney, J. W., & Moos, R. H. (2006). End-of-treatment outcomes in cognitive-behavioral treatment and 12-step substance use treatment programs: Do they differ and do they predict 1-year outcomes? *Journal of Substance Abuse Treatment, 31*, 41–50. doi:10.1016/j.jsat.2006.03.008

Jones, H. E., Martin, P. R., Heil, S. H., Kaltenbach, K., Selby, P., Coyle, M. G., . . . Fischer, G. (2008). Treatment of opioid dependent pregnant women: Clinical and research issues. *Journal of Substance Abuse Treatment, 35*, 245–259. doi:10.1016/j.jsat.2007.10.007

Jones, H. E., Tuten, M., & O'Grady K. E. (2011). Treating the partners of opioid-dependent pregnant patients: Feasibility and efficacy. *American Journal of Drug and Alcohol Abuse, 37*, 170–178.

Jones, H. E., Wong, C. J., Tuten, M., & Stitzer, M. L. (2005). Reinforcement-based therapy: 12-month evaluation of an outpatient drug-free treatment for heroin abusers. *Drug and Alcohol Dependence, 79*, 119–128. doi:10.1016/j.drugalcdep.2005.01.006

Kadden, R. M., & Mauriello, I. J. (1991). Enhancing participation in substance abuse treatment using an incentive system. *Journal of Substance Abuse Treatment, 8*, 113–124. doi:10.1016/0740-5472(91)90002-R

Katz, E. C., Gruber, K., Chutuape, M. A., & Stitzer, M. L. (2001). Reinforcement-based outpatient treatment for opiate and cocaine abusers. *Journal of Substance Abuse Treatment, 20*, 93–98.

Kaufman, J., & Zigler, E. (1987). Do abused children become abusive parents? *American Journal of Orthopsychiatry, 57*, 186–192. doi:10.1111/j.1939-0025.1987.tb03528.x

Kazdin, A. E. (1994). *Behavior modification in applied settings* (5th ed,). Pacific Grove, CA: Brooks/Cole.

Kellogg, S. H., Stitzer, M. L., Petry, N. M., & Kreek, M. J. (n.d.). *Contingency management: Foundations and principles* [Unpublished chapter]. Retrieved from http://www.nattc.org/pami/PDF/Contingency_Mgt_F_P.pdf

Kolko, D. J., & Swenson, C. C. (2002). *Assessing and treating physically abused children and their families: A cognitive-behavioral approach*. Thousand Oaks, CA: Sage.

Koverola, C., Murtaugh, C. A., Connors, K. M., Reeves, G., & Papas, M. A. (2007). Children exposed to intra-familial violence: Predictors of attrition and retention in treatment. *Journal of Aggression, Maltreatment & Trauma, 14*, 19–42. doi:10.1300/J146v14n04_02

Kumpfer, K. L. (1998). Links between prevention and treatment of drug-abusing women and their children. In C. L. Wetherington & A. B. Roman (Eds.), *Drug addiction research and the health of women* (NIH Publication No. 98-4289). Washington, DC: National Institute on Drug Abuse.

Liebson, I., Tommasello, A., & Bigelow, G. (1978). A behavioral treatment of alcoholic methadone patients. *Annals of Internal Medicine, 89*, 342–344.

Lipovsky, J. A., Swenson, C. C., Ralston, M. E., & Saunders, B. E. (1998). The abuse clarification process in the treatment of intrafamilial child abuse. *Child Abuse & Neglect, 22*, 729–741. doi:10.1016/S0145-2134(98)00051-9

Marlatt, G. A., Baer, J. S., Kivlahan, D. R., Dimeff, L. A., Larimer, M. E., Quigley, L. A., . . . Williams, E. (1998). Screening and brief intervention for high-risk college student drinkers: Results from a 2-year follow-up assessment. *Journal of Consulting and Clinical Psychology, 66*, 604–615. doi:10.1037/0022-006X.66.4.604

Marlatt, G. A., & Gordon, J. R. (1985). *Relapse prevention: Maintenance strategies in the treatment of addictive behaviors*. New York, NY: Guilford Press.

Martin, G., & Pear, J. (Eds.). (1998). *Behavior modification: What it is and how to do it* (6th ed.). Upper Saddle River, NJ: Prentice Hall.

McConnaughy, E. A., Prochaska, J. O., & Velicer, W. F. (1983). Stages of change in psychotherapy: Measurement and sample profiles. *Psychotherapy: Theory, Research, and Practice, 20,* 368–375. doi:10.1037/h0090198

McLellan, A. T., Carise, D., & Kleber, H. D. (2003). Can the national addiction treatment infrastructure support the public's demand for quality care? *Journal of Substance Abuse Treatment, 25,* 117–121. doi:10.1016/S0740-5472(03)00156-9

McLellan, A. T., Kushner, H., Metzger, D., Peters, R., Smith, I., Grissom, G., . . . Argerious, M. (1992). The fifth edition of the Addiction Severity Index. *Journal of Substance Abuse Treatment, 9,* 199–213. doi:10.1016/0740-5472(92)90062-S

McMurray-Avila, M. (2001). *Organizing health services for homeless people: A practical guide* (2nd ed.). Nashville, TN: National Health Care for the Homeless Council.

Mertens, J. R., Lu, Y. W., Parthasarathy, S., Moore, C., & Weisner, C. M. (2003). Medical and psychiatric conditions of alcohol and drug treatment patients in an HMO. *Archives of Internal Medicine, 163,* 2511–2517. doi:10.1001/archinte.163.20.2511

Metsch, L. R., Crandall, L., Wohler-Torres, B., Miles, C., Chitwood, D. D., & McCoy, C. B. (2002). Met and unmet need for dental services among active drug users in Miami, Florida. *The Journal of Behavioral Health Services & Research, 29,* 176–188. doi:10.1007/BF02287704

Metzger, D., Woody, G. E., Navaline, H., McLellan, A. T., Meyers, K., Boney, T., . . . O'Brien, C. P. (1993, October–November). *The Risk Assessment Battery (RAB): Validity and reliability.* Paper presented at the meeting of National Cooperative Vaccine Development Group for AIDS, Alexandria, VA.

Milby, J. B., Schumaker, J. E., Raczynski, J. M., Caldwell, E., Engle, M., Michael, M., & Carr, J. (1996). Sufficient conditions for effective treatment of substance abusing homeless persons. *Drug and Alcohol Dependence, 43,* 39–47. doi:10.1016/S0376-8716(96)01286-0

Miller, W. R. (1992). *The Stages of Change Readiness and Treatment Eagerness Scale (SOCRATES).* Albuquerque, NM: Center on Alcoholism, Substance Abuse, and Addictions.

Miller, W. R., Benefield, R. G., & Tonigan, J. S. (1993). Enhancing motivation for change in problem drinking: A controlled comparison of two therapist styles. *Journal of Consulting and Clinical Psychology, 61,* 455–461. doi:10.1037/0022-006X.61.3.455

Miller, W. R., & Rollnick, S. (2002). *Motivational interviewing: Preparing people for change* (2nd ed.). New York, NY: Guilford Press.

Miller, W. R., & Rollnick, S. (2009). Ten things that motivational interviewing is not. *Behavioural and Cognitive Psychotherapy, 37,* 129–140.

Miller, W. R., Taylor, C. A., & West, J. C. (1980). Focused versus broad spectrum behavior therapy for problem drinkers. *Journal of Consulting and Clinical Psychology, 48,* 590–601. doi:10.1037/0022-006X.48.5.590

Miller, W. R., Tonigan, J.S., & Longabaugh, R. (1995). The Drinker Inventory of Consequences (DrIncC): An instrument for assessing adverse consequences of alcohol abuse. *Project Match Monograph Series,4.* (NIH Publication No. 95-3911). Retrieved from http://lib.adai.washington.edu/pubs/matchmonograph4.htm

Miltenberger, J. (2001). *Behavior modification: Principles and procedures* (4th ed.). Belmont, CA: Wadsworth Thomas Learning.

Mokdad, A .H., Marks, J. S., Stroup, D. F., & Gerberding, J. L. (2004). Actual causes of death in the United States, 2000. *JAMA, 291,* 1238–1245.

Moos, R. H. (2005). Iatrogenic effects of psychosocial interventions for substance use disorders: Prevalence, predictors, prevention. *Addiction, 100,* 595–604. doi:10.1111/j.1360-0443.2005.01073.x

Moos, R. H. (2007). Theory-based processes that promote the remission of substance use disorders. *Clinical Psychology Review, 27,* 537–551. doi:10.1016/j.cpr.2006.12.006

Moos, R. H., & Moos, B. S. (2003) Long-term influence of duration and intensity of treatment on previously untreated individual with alcohol use disorders. *Addiction, 98,* 325–337.

Moos, R. H., & Timko, C. (2008). Outcome research on 12-step and other self-help programs. In M. Galanter & H. D. Kleber (Eds.), *The American Psychiatric Publishing textbook of substance abuse treatment* (4th ed., pp. 511–521). Arlington, VA: American Psychiatric Publishing.

Muhuri, P. K., & Gfroerer, J. C. (2009). Substance use among women: associations with pregnancy, parenting, and race/ethnicity. *Maternal and Child Health Journal, 13,* 376–385. doi:10.1007/s10995-008-0375-8

Najavits, L. M., & Weiss, R. D. (1994). Variations in therapist effectiveness in the treatment of patients with substance use disorders: An empirical review. *Addiction, 89,* 679–688. doi:10.1111/j.1360-0443.1994.tb00954.x

National Abandoned Infants Assistance Resource Center. (2003). *AIA best practices: Lessons learned from a decade of service to children and families affected by HIV and substance abuse.* Retrieved from http://aia.berkeley.edu/media/pdf/best_practices_monograph.pdf

National Association of Alcoholism and Drug Abuse Counselors. (1986). *Certification commission oral exam guidelines.* Arlington, VA: Author.

National Association of Social Workers. (1992). Case management's cost, benefits eyed. *National Association of Social Workers News.* Washington, DC: Author.

National Center on Addiction and Substance Abuse at Columbia University. (1998). *No safe haven: Children of substance abusing parents.* New York, NY: Author.

Novaco, R. W. (1994). Clinical problems of anger and its assessment and regulation through a stress coping skills approach. In W. O'Donohue & L. Krasner (Eds.), *Handbook of psychological skills training: Clinical techniques and applications* (pp. 320–338). Boston, MA: Allyn & Bacon.

O'Farrell, T. J., & Fals-Stewart, W. (2003). Alcohol abuse. *Journal of Marital and Family Therapy, 29*, 121–146. doi:10.1111/j.1752-0606.2003.tb00387.x

O'Farrell, T. J., & Fals-Stewart, W. (2006). *Behavioral couples therapy for alcoholism and drug abuse*. New York, NY: Guilford Press.

Ohio Department of Alcohol and Drug Addiction Services. (2006). *Relapse rates lower when treatment follows detox*. Retrieved from http://www.odadas.ohio.gov/public/

Ondersma, S. J. (2007). Introduction to the first of two special sections on substance abuse and child maltreatment. *Child Maltreatment, 12*, 3–6.

Osterling, K. L., & Austin, M. J. (2008). Substance abuse interventions for parents involved in the child welfare system: Evidence and implications. *Journal of Evidence-Based Social Work, 5*, 157–189. doi:10.1300/J394v05n01_07

Otiashvili, D., Kirtadze I., O'Grady, K. E., & Jones, H. E. (in press). *Exploratory study comparing naltrexone + behavioral interventions compared to usual care: Drug use and HIV risk outcomes in methadone with drug free female partners* [Abstract]. College on the Problem of Drug Dependence.

Petry, N. M. (2000). A comprehensive guide to the application of contingency management procedures in clinical settings. *Drug and Alcohol Dependence, 58*, 9–25. doi:10.1016/S0376-8716(99)00071-X

Petry, N. M., Martin, B., Cooney, J., & Kranzler, H. (2000). Give them prizes, and they will come: Contingency management for treatment of alcohol dependence. *Journal of Consulting and Clinical Psychology, 68*, 250–257. doi:10.1037/0022-006X.68.2.250

Petry, N. M., Peirce, J. M., Stitzer, M. L., Blaine, J., Roll, J. M., Cohen, A., & Obert, J. (2005). Effect of prize-based incentives on outcomes in stimulant abusers in outpatient psychosocial treatment programs. *Archives of General Psychiatry, 62*, 1148–1156. doi:10.1001/archpsyc.62.10.1148

Powers, M. B., Vedel, E., & Emmelkamp, P. M. (2008). Behavioral couples therapy (BCT) for alcohol and drug use disorders: A meta-analysis. *Clinical Psychology Review, 28*, 952–962. doi:10.1016/j.cpr.2008.02.002

Preston, K. L., Umbricht, A., & Epstein, D. H. (2002). Methadone dose increase and abstinence reinforcement maintenance contingency and one-year follow-up. *Drug and Alcohol Dependence, 67*, 125–137. doi:10.1016/S0376-8716(02)00023-6

Prochaska, J. O., & DiClemente, C. C. (1983). Stages and processes of self-change of smoking: Toward an integrative model of change. *Journal of Consulting and Clinical Psychology, 51*, 390–395. doi:10.1037/0022-006X.51.3.390

Prochaska, J. O., DiClemente, C. C., & Norcross, J. C. (1992). In search of how people change: Applications to addictive behavior. *American Psychologist, 47*, 1102–1114. doi:10.1037/0003-066X.47.9.1102

Prochaska, J. O., & Velicer, W. F. (1997). The transtheoretical model of health behavior change. *American Journal of Health Promotion, 12*, 38–48.

Project MATCH Research Group. (1997). Project MATCH secondary a priori hypotheses. *Addiction, 92*, 1671–1698. doi:10.1111/j.1360-0443.1997.tb02889.x

Puigdollers, E., Domingo-Salvany, A. N., Brugal, M. T., Torrens, M., Alvarós, J., Castillo, C., . . . Vázquez, J. M. (2004). Characteristics of heroin addicts entering methadone maintenance treatment: Quality of life and gender. *Substance Use & Misuse, 39,* 1353–1368.

Ritsher, J. B., Moos, R. H., & Finney, J. W. (2002). Relationship of treatment orientation and continuing care to remission among substance abuse patients. *Psychiatric Services, 53,* 595–601. doi:10.1176/appi.ps.53.5.595

Ritter, A., Bowden, S. Murray, T., Ross, P., Greeley, J., & Pead, J. (2002). The influence of the therapeutic relationship in treatment for alcohol dependency. *Drug and Alcohol Review, 21,* 261–268.

Robin, A. L., Bedway, M., & Gilroy, M. (1994). Problem-solving communication training. In C. W. LeCroy (Ed.), *Handbook of child and adolescent treatment manuals* (pp. 92–125). New York, NY: Free Press.

Roll, J. M., Higgins, S. T., & Badger, G. J. (1996). An experimental comparison of three different schedules of reinforcement of drug abstinence using cigarette smoking as an exemplar. *Journal of Applied Behavior Analysis, 29,* 495–504. doi:10.1901/jaba.1996.29-495

Rosado, J., Sigmon, S. C., Jones, H. E., & Stitzer, M. L. (2005). Cash value of voucher reinforcers in pregnant drug-dependent women. *Experimental and Clinical Psychopharmacology, 13,* 41–47. doi:10.1037/1064-1297.13.1.41

Rosario, M., Salzinger, S., Feldman, R., & Hammer, M. (1987, April). *Home environments of physically abused and control school-aged children.* Paper presented at the meeting of the Society for Research in Child Development, Baltimore, MD.

Saunders, J. B., Aasland, O. G., Babor, T. F., de la Fuente, J. R., & Grant, M. (1993). Development of the Alcohol Use Disorders Identification Test (AUDIT): WHO collaborative project on early detection of persons with harmful alcohol consumption—II. *Addiction, 88,* 791–804. doi:10.1111/j.1360-0443.1993.tb02093.x

Saldana, L., Tuten, M., & Jones, H. (2007, April). *Adherence rating of therapists to Reinforcement-Based Treatment: Validation of the ART of RBT.* Paper presented at the Joint Meeting on Adolescent Treatment Effectiveness, Washington, DC.

Saxon, A. J., Calsyn, D. A., & Haver, V. M. L. E. (1990). A nationwide survey of urinalysis practices of methadone maintenance clinics. Utilization of laboratory services. *Archives of Pathology & Laboratory Medicine, 114,* 94–100.

Schaeffer, C. M., Swenson, C. C., Tuerk, E. H., & Henggeler, S. W. (2010). *Treating families with co-occurring child maltreatment and parent substance abuse: Outcomes from a 24-month pilot study of the Building Stronger Families program.* Manuscript in preparation.

Scherbaum, N., & Specka, M. (2008). Factors influencing the course of opiate addiction. *International Journal of Methods in Psychiatric Research, 17*(Suppl. 1), S39–S44. doi:10.1002/mpr.244

Schroeder, V., Kelley, M. L., & Fals-Stewart, W. (2006). Effects of parental substance abuse on youth in their homes. *Prevention Researcher, 13,* 10–13.

Shields, A., & Cicchetti, D. (1998). Reactive aggression among maltreated children: The contributions of attention and emotional dysregulation. *Journal of Clinical Child Psychology, 27*, 381–395. doi:10.1207/s15374424jccp2704_2

Silverman K, Chutuape, M. A., Bigelow, G. E., & Stitzer, M. L. (1999). Voucher-based reinforcement of cocaine abstinence in treatment-resistant methadone patients: Effects of reinforcement magnitude. *Psychopharmacology, 146*, 128–138.

Silverman, K., Higgins, S. T., Brooner, R. K., Montoya, I. D., Cone, E. J., Schuster, C. R., & Preston, K. L. (1996). Sustained cocaine abstinence in methadone maintenance patients through voucher-based reinforcement therapy. *Archives of General Psychiatry, 53*, 409–415.

Silverman, K., Wong, C. J., Umbricht-Schneiter, A., Montoya, I. D., Schuster, C. R., & Preston, K. L. (1998). Broad beneficial effects of cocaine abstinence reinforcement among methadone patients. *Journal of Consulting and Clinical Psychology, 66*, 811–824. doi:10.1037/0022-006X.66.5.811

Simpson, D. D., Joe, G. W., & Rowan-Szal, G. A. (1997). Drug abuse treatment retention and process effects on follow-up outcomes. *Drug and Alcohol Dependence, 47*, 227–235. doi:10.1016/S0376-8716(97)00099-9.

Simpson, D. D., Savage, L. J., & Lloyd, M. R. (1979). Follow-up evaluation of treatment of drug abuse during 1969 to 1972. *Archives of General Psychiatry, 36*, 772–780.

Slep, A. M., & O'Leary, S. G. (2001). Examining partner and child abuse: Are we ready for a more integrated approach to family violence? *Clinical Child and Family Psychology Review, 4*, 87–107. doi:10.1023/A:1011319213874

Slotkin, T. A. (1998). Fetal nicotine or cocaine exposure: which one is worse? *The Journal of Pharmacology and Experimental Therapeutics, 285*, 931–945.

Stevens-Simon, C., Dolgan, J. I., Kelly, L., & Singer, D. (1997). The effects of monetary incentives and peer support groups on repeat adolescent pregnancies. A randomized trial of the dollar-a-day program. *JAMA, 277*, 977–982. doi:10.1001/jama.277.12.977

Stitzer, M. L., Bigelow, G. E., & Liebson, I. A. (1980). Reducing drug use among methadone maintenance clients: contingent reinforcement for morphine-free urines. *Addictive Behaviors, 5*, 333–340. doi:10.1016/0306-4603(80)90007-6

Stitzer, M. L., Bigelow, G. E., Liebson, I. A., & Hawthorne, J. W. (1982). Contingent reinforcement for benzodiazepine-free urines: Evaluation of a drug abuse treatment intervention. *Journal of Applied Behavior Analysis, 15*, 493–503. doi:10.1901/jaba.1982.15-493

Stitzer, M. L., Bigelow, G. E., Liebson, I. A., & McCaul, M. E. (1984). Contingency management of supplemental drug use during methadone maintenance treatment. In J. Grabowski, M. L. Stitzer, & J. E. Henningfield (Eds.), *Behavioral intervention techniques in drug abuse treatment* (pp. 84–103). Rockville, MD: U.S. Department of Health and Human Services.

Stitzer, M. L., Iguchi, M. Y., & Felch, L. J. (1992). Contingent take-home incentive: Effects on drug use of methadone maintenance patients. *Journal of Consulting and Clinical Psychology, 60*, 927–934. doi:10.1037/0022-006X.60.6.927

Stitzer, M. L., & Petry, N. (2006). Contingency management for treatment of substance abuse. *Annual Review of Clinical Psychology, 2*, 411–434. doi:10.1146/annurev.clinpsy.2.022305.095219

Stone, S. (2007). Child maltreatment, out-of-home placement, and academic vulnerability: A fifteen-year review of evidence and future directions. *Children and Youth Services Review, 29*, 139–161. doi:10.1016/j.childyouth.2006.05.001

Swenson, C. C., Schaeffer, C. M., Henggeler, S. W., Faldowski, R., & Mayhew, A. M. (2010). Multisystemic therapy for child abuse and neglect: A randomized effectiveness trial. *Journal of Family Psychology, 24*, 497–507.

Swenson, C. C., Schaeffer, C. M., Tuerk, E. H., Henggeler, S. W., Tuten, M., Panzarella, P., . . . Guillorn, A. (2009). Adapting multisystemic therapy for co-occurring child maltreatment and parental substance abuse: The Building Stronger Families project. *Emotional & Behavioral Disorders in Youth, 9*, 3–8.

The TOPPS-II Interstate Study Group. (2003). Drug treatment completion and post-discharge employment in the TOPPS-II Interstate Cooperative Study. *Journal of Substance Abuse Treatment, 25*, 9–18. doi:10.1016/S0740-5472(03)00050-3

Timko, C., DeBenedetti, A., & Billow, R. (2006). Intensive referral to 12-step self-help groups and 6-month substance use disorder outcomes. *Addiction, 101*, 678–688.

Tuten, M., Defulio, A., Jones, H., & Stitzer, M. (2011). *A randomized trial of Reinforcement-Based Treatment and Recovery Housing*. Manuscript submitted for publication.

U.S. Department of Health and Human Services. (1999). *Blending perspectives and building common ground: A report to Congress on substance abuse and child protection*. Washington, DC: U.S. Government Printing Office.

U.S. Department of Health and Human Services, Administration for Children and Families. (1997). *National study of protective, preventive, and reunification services delivered to children and their families*. Washington, DC: U.S. Government Printing Office.

U.S. Department of Health and Human Services, Administration for Children and Families (2009, September). *Connecticut Child and Family Services Review Exit Conference*. Presentation at the Connecticut Department of Children and Families, Hartford, CT.

U.S. Department of Health and Human Services, National Institute on Drug Abuse. (2009). *Principles of drug addiction treatment: A research-based guide* (2nd ed.). Retrieved from http://www.nida.nih.gov/podat/PODATIndex.html

U.S. Department of Health and Human Services, Office of Public Health and Science. (2001). *Youth violence: A report of the Surgeon General*. Retrieved from http://www.surgeongeneral.gov/library/youthviolence/youvioreport.htm

U.S. Department of Health and Human Services, Substance Abuse and Mental Health Services Administration, Center for Substance Abuse Treatment.

(1997). *Substance abuse treatment and domestic violence: Treatment improvement protocol (TIP), Series 25.* Retrieved from http://www.ncbi.nlm.nih.gov/books/NBK14419/

U.S. Department of Health and Human Services, Substance Abuse and Mental Health Services Administration, Center for Substance Abuse Treatment. (1998). *Comprehensive case management for substance abuse treatment: Treatment improvement protocol(TIP), Series 27.* Retrieved from http://www.ncbi.nlm.nih.gov/books/NBK14516/#top

U.S. Department of Health and Human Services, Substance Abuse and Mental Health Services Administration, Office of Applied Studies. (2004–2005). *Young alcohol users often get alcohol from family or home.* Retrieved from http://www.oas.samhsa.gov

U.S. Department of Health and Human Services, Substance Abuse and Mental Health Services Administration, Office of Applied Studies. (2006). *Treatment episode data set (TEDS).* Retrieved from http://wwwdasis.samhsa.gov/teds05/TEDSD2k5Tbl2.5.htm

U.S. Department of Health and Human Services, Substance Abuse and Mental Health Services Administration, Office of Applied Studies. (2007). *Fetal alcohol spectrum disorders.* Retrieved from http://www.fasdcenter.samhsa.gov/educationTraining/FASDBASICS/FASDTheBasics.pdf

U.S. Department of Health and Human Services, Substance Abuse and Mental Health Services Administration, Office of Applied Studies. (2008). *The DASIS report: Employment status and substance abuse treatment admissions, 2006.* Retrieved from http://www.oas.samhsa.gov/2k8/employTX/employTX.htm

U.S. Department of Health and Human Services, Substance Abuse and Mental Health Services Administration, Office of Applied Studies. (2009). *Results from the 2008 National Survey on Drug Use & Health: National Findings.* Retrieved from http://www.oas.samhsa.gov/nsduh/2k8nsduh/2k8results.cfm

U.S. Department of Health and Human Services, Substance Abuse and Mental Health Services Administration, Office of Applied Studies. (2010). *The N-SSATS report: Clinical or therapeutic approaches used by substance abuse treatment facilities.* Retrieved from http://www.oas.samhsa.gov/2k10/238/238ClinicalAp2k10.htm

Vanderplasschen, W., Wolf, J., Rapp, R. C., & Broekaert, E. (2007). Effectiveness of different models of case management for substance-abusing populations. *Journal of Psychoactive Drugs, 39,* 81–95.

Young, N. K., Boles, S. M., & Otero, C. (2007). Parental substance use disorders and child maltreatment: Overlap, gaps, and opportunities. *Child Maltreatment, 12,* 137–149. doi:10.1177/1077559507300322

Zhang, Z., Gerstein, D. R., & Friedmann, P. D. (2008). Patient satisfaction and sustained Outcomes of drug abuse treatment. *Journal of Health Psychology, 13,* 388–400. doi:10.1177/1359105307088142

INDEX

Awards, 32, 82, 109–110. *See also* Incentives

Badger, G. J., 112
BCT (behavioral couples therapy), 146, 147
Beck Depression Inventory, 197
Behavior, social ecological models of, 217
Behavioral avoidance, 129
Behavioral contracts, 220
Behavioral couples therapy (BCT), 146, 147
Behavioral monitoring, 171
Behavioral substance abuse treatment, 4–6
Behavior change
    ambivalence as part of, 29
    behavior graphs as tool for tracking, 93
    client's responsibility for, 130
    motivation for, 60, 61
Behavior graphs, 93–107
    of behavior with significant others, 150
    in Building Stronger Families model, 223
    construction of, 95–97
    copies of, 220
    direct vs. indirect assessment, 94–95
    and financial barriers, 140
    graphing psychological symptoms, 183
    guidelines for, 99–103
    introducing clients to, 103–105
    logistics of, 97–98
    ongoing use of, 105–106
    purposes of, 22, 94
    sharing with team members, 176–177
    therapist training for, 172, 173
    types of, 98–99
Behaviorism, 165, 231
Benzodiazepine abuse, 15, 111, 203
Bigelow, G. E., 113
Bills, payment of, 111
Blum, Ralph, 3
Boredom, 135
Breath alcohol tests, 60, 221, 223
Brokerage model (case management), 124
Budney, A. J., 44

Building Stronger Families (BSF)
    model, 215–227
    case example, 225–227
    clinical bases of, 216–220
    components of, 220–223
    fidelity and quality of interventions in, 232
    history and development of, 215–216
    as home-based version of RBT, 234–235
    preliminary outcomes for, 223–224
    as real-world application of RBT, 229
Buprenorphine, 5
Burke, B. L., 58
Buy-in, 77–78

Cannabinoids, 166. *See also* Marijuana abuse
Caring, 149
Carr, E. G., 43
Caseload, 172–173, 230
Case management, 121–144
    addressing financial barriers, 140
    addressing legal/medical/mental health needs, 141
    challenges of integrating, 127–130
    and detoxification later in treatment, 141–142
    effectiveness of, 121–125
    facilitating safe and abstinent housing, 137–140
    interventions during first one to two sessions, 133–136
    ongoing client outreach in, 136–137
    and pretreatment detoxification, 131–133
    providing job assistance, 140
    in Reinforcement-Based Treatment, 7, 125–126
    resource libraries for, 143
    task analysis, 142–143
    therapist willingness to deliver, 163
Cash, as incentive, 111
Census, in RBT supervision, 175–176
Center for Substance Abuse Treatment, 125
Central East Addiction Technology Transfer Center, 180
Central nervous system depressants, 169

ABOUT THE AUTHORS

L. Michelle Tuten, MSW, LCSW-C, is an assistant professor in the Department of Psychiatry at Johns Hopkins University School of Medicine, program director of the Cornerstone Drug and Alcohol Treatment Program, and deputy research director of the Center for Addiction and Pregnancy in Baltimore, Maryland. She is a coinvestigator on several grants funded by the National Institute on Drug Abuse that examine the efficacy of motivational incentives and other behavioral interventions, including Reinforcement-Based Treatment, and she regularly conducts trainings on evidence-based models for treating substance use disorders. Ms. Tuten is codeveloper of an intervention, Family-Based Recovery, designed to treat families referred to child protective ser-vices for abuse or neglect associated with substance use. She has 12 years of experience in the study and implementation of evidence-based practices.

Hendree E. Jones, PhD, is a licensed psychologist in the state of Maryland and a professor in both the Department of Psychiatry and Behavioral Sciences and the Department of Obstetrics and Gynecology at Johns Hopkins University School of Medicine. Dr. Jones is the director of research for the Center for Addiction and Pregnancy and the executive program director of the Cornerstone Drug and Alcohol Treatment Program. She also has an appointment as a senior research psychologist at Research Triangle Institute International. Since 1994, Dr. Jones has been continuously funded by the National Institute on Drug Abuse (NIDA) as a principal investigator designing and leading studies that focus on in utero exposure to abused substances. She has published over 90 peer-reviewed publications, several book chapters, editorial letters, and non-peer-reviewed articles for clinicians. Dr. Jones has served on numerous review panels for NIDA, the National Institute on Alcohol Abuse and Alcoholism, the Substance Abuse and Mental Health Services Administration, and the Institute of Medicine. She has held multiple leadership positions within Division 28 (Psychopharmacology and Substance Abuse) of the American Psychological Association (APA) and is currently president-elect. She is a member of the Women's Health Research Coalition, the College on the Problems of Drug Dependence, and a fellow of both the Maryland Psychological Association and the APA. She currently serves on several editorial boards for peer-reviewed journals in the field of addiction.

Cindy M. Schaeffer, PhD, received her doctorate in child clinical psychology from the University of Missouri–Columbia and completed a postdoctoral fellowship in prevention science at the Johns Hopkins Bloomberg School of Public Health. The focus of her training and research has been on understanding the developmental trajectories that lead to juvenile offending and adolescent substance abuse and developing multisystemic (i.e., family, peer, school, community) interventions to address these problems. Dr. Schaeffer is now an associate professor in the Department of Psychiatry and Behavioral Sciences at the Medical University of South Carolina and a member of the Family Services Research Center faculty. Currently, her research involves developing and evaluating an ecologically based intervention aimed at improving the relationships of youth at risk for serious antisocial behavior with prosocial peers and adapting multisystemic therapy for families in which there is substantiated child abuse or neglect and caregiver substance abuse by incorporating Reinforcement-Based Treatment.

Maxine L. Stitzer, PhD, is a research psychologist and professor in the Department of Psychiatry and Behavioral Sciences at Johns Hopkins University School of Medicine. At Johns Hopkins University, she conducts clinical research at the Behavioral Pharmacology Research Unit, a nationally recognized drug abuse research laboratory. Her extensive grant-supported research program has focused on pharmacological and behavioral approaches to the treatment of substance abuse and reflects active research interests in illicit drug abuse and tobacco dependence. She has published over 200 scientific papers, coedited a book on methadone treatment, and founded the Cornerstone Treatment Research Clinic at Johns Hopkins University, where Reinforcement-

Based Treatment has been developed and researched. She is well-known for her work on contingent incentive approaches in substance abuse treatment, which are designed to enhance motivation for positive behavior change, including abstinence from drug use. She has been the recipient of numerous federal research grants and several awards for outstanding contributions to behavioral science research. She currently heads the Mid-Atlantic Node of the National Institute on Drug Abuse Clinical Trials Network, a project in which researchers and clinicians work together to test validated treatment methods in community clinics and disseminate these methods into service delivery.